Internal Difference and Meanings in the *Roman de la rose*

Internal Difference and Meanings in the *Roman de la rose*

Douglas Kelly

The University of Wisconsin Press

The University of Wisconsin Press
114 North Murray Street
Madison, Wisconsin 53715

3 Henrietta Street
London WC2E 8LU, England

2 4 6 8 10 9 7 5 3 1

Printed in the United States of America

Library of Congress Cataloging-in-Publication Data
Kelly, Douglas.
Internal difference and meanings in the Roman de la rose /
Douglas Kelly.
238 p. cm.
Includes bibliographical references and index.
ISBN 0-299-14780-0. ISBN 0-299-14784-3 (pbk.)
1. Guillaume, de Lorris, fl. 1230. Roman de la Rose.
2. Morality in literature. I. Title.
PQ1529.K45 1995
841'.1—dc20 95-6474

We can find no scar,
But internal difference,
Where the Meanings, are—
—Emily Dickinson

Contents

Acknowledgments

I am grateful to SunHee Gertz for taking the time and making the effort to correct numerous errors and infelicities in the penultimate version of my manuscript. The Press copy editor, Owen Hurd, removed or corrected numerous surviving infelicities, inconsistencies, and errors. I am also indebted to the Press's readers, William Kibler and a second anonymous, but very forthright, reader. The surviving faults are entirely my own. And, last but not least, I should like to thank Meredith McMunn and Lori Walters for their assistance in finding a manuscript illustration for the *Rose*.

Internal Difference and Meanings in the *Roman de la rose*

Introduction

> . . . œuvre insigne, l'une des plus retentissantes que le moyen âge ait jamais connues et qu'il faudra bien un jour réapprendre à lire.
>
> —Roger Dragonetti, "*La musique et les lettres*"

> It may be said of the *Roman* as a whole that it is a poem so foreign to us that we understand its easiest ideas only with great labor. Its real difficulties we may never even identify.
>
> —John V. Fleming, "Carthaginian Love"

The *Roman de la rose* is still the once and future problem it has always been in critical scholarship, a perpetual conundrum in the interpretation of medieval literature. It is not so much the diversity of interpretations that is at issue here. Scholars always diverge in interpretations, a fact no doubt fundamental to scholarship and criticism as we practice them today. But some texts not only divide scholars, they invite divisiveness. Such works go to the heart of personal convictions and tastes, posing moral and aesthetic problems that seem insoluble; they force issues that compel debate, yet are not susceptible of definitive solution. The *Roman de la rose* is one of those works.

It is therefore high time to take such disagreement seriously, seeing it as an effect the *Rose* demands of its readers. Where so many meanings are perceived, as the epigraph borrowed from one of Emily Dickinson's best-known poems suggests, then internal difference looms large. Difference exists internal to the *Rose* text itself, to be sure, in which diverse voices speak out on the authority of incompatible models while charting or evaluating Amant's pursuit of his rose. Textual differences appear as well, as we strive to recover Jean's *Rose* through the shimmering, often distorted prisms of surviving manuscripts. There is internal difference too among readers medieval and modern—medieval readers who read variant manuscripts and modern readers who rely on modern editions reconstructed from one or more of those manuscripts on the basis of modern theories of editing. And last, but not least—indeed, most important—internal difference among us readers, medieval or modern, who respond to the romance in sharp disagreement, which confirms Rosemond Tuve's astute observation that "Amor [the God of Love] is too interesting and complicated to turn him into steps in a drama in some single mind."[1]

Yet there is no scar—or, I should say, we find none. In the *Rose* Amant awakens to discover that the rose was only the subject of an erotic dream. The reader too reads and interprets his dream, then sets it aside, as if he or she were not directly concerned with an odd medieval poem about a lover's wish fulfillment dream—like Amant listening to Reason, Ami, or Faux Semblant. However, both scholarship and classroom discussion show that serious readers of the *Roman de la rose* do not set it aside with indifference, for Amant's dream contains both promises of reward and threats of emotional and physical violence. The dream story on how to pluck roses—for that is the literal lesson of the poem according to no better authority than Jean de Meun's own prologue to his translation of Boethius's *Consolation of Philosophy*—confronts us all with the implications of that dream and their consequences in the waking world of deceit and seduction. Amant's dream reminds us of this relationship by adumbrating its consequences in the waking world, especially through the exemplary stories that punctuate his progress, counterpointing the dream with alarming scenarios for continuations beyond the poem's climax and Amant's awakening.

Such contrasts have almost always pointed readers to Amant's fatuous adaptation of the principle of *contraires choses* to distinguish between seducing young and old women (*Rose* v. 21370–552). I shall return to this dubious application of a philosophical principle below. The reminder of the principle would certainly be perplexing to Jean's ordinary readers had he not provided a brief definition of it which, in fact, underscores the fortunate and unfortunate denouements to Amant's dream, points to the Boethian contrast between true and false goods, which looms large in the *Rose*, and uncovers the poem's allegorical mode to teach at one and the same time how to pluck roses and how foolish and, more often than not, devastating this violent act usually is for all concerned.

The thesis of this book is that we can understand Jean's *Rose* best if we accept its diverse meanings while reflecting on our—that is, each individual reader's—willingness, on moral, aesthetic, or hedonistic grounds, to accept or reject those meanings as guidelines for a love life or, indeed, for any moral life. Jean de Meun raises numerous issues in the *Rose*, issues on matters of love, the moral, social, and personal evaluation of love, be it in lust or friendship, charity or venality. The poem's definitive meaning dissolves therefore into diverse morals and definitive, but local glosses set forth by different textual voices as well as more intimate voices in the reader's own mind and conscience. We respond variously to those moral lessons by identifying with them, or by making distinctions that distance ourselves from them, perhaps finally rejecting outright the lessons offered and even the entire poem. Accordingly, the modern, late-twentieth-century reader, like our medieval counterpart, may choose his or her definitive reading, then go on to debate it with colleagues, friends, and students (as happens inevitably to anyone who conducts a seminar on the *Rose*). Hence, my thesis on the multiple meanings of the *Rose* is not a subterfuge to circumvent controversy and divergent interpretations. Rather, it meets these head on, not to propose a definitive, authoritative reading, but to set the reader squarely before the issues the poem raises. The *Rose* is not a discursive treatise, it is the heuristic investigation of a seduction.

Let us then move on to matters of critical scholarship. This book will consider both medieval and modern readings and interpretations of Jean's *Rose*. In doing so, it will locate the poem in the French tradition of reflection on morally and socially ambiguous or problematic topics like love as mirrored in Amant's dream (see Conclusion). This entails an exploration of the composition and transmission of the *Rose* in the Middle Ages, with special attention to the poem and medieval responses to it that have come down to us, for medieval readers evince the same sense of diverse meanings and internal difference that we do. Indeed, the *Rose* anticipates, elicits, and illustrates such diversity. Once again, Rosemond Tuve has shown the way: "Proper allegorical ambiguity is superbly illustrated in Jean de Meun's Rose, which is played upon by the shifting lights of first one character's conception of her, then another."[2]

The text of the *Rose* itself requires some additional introductory commentary here, although I shall return to the problem again in chapter 1. Of late, medievalists have become sensationally aware of *mouvance*, that is, variance in medieval manuscripts, subject as each manuscript was to error, correction, and adaptation in copying. Jean's own autograph is irremediably lost. The *Rose* itself survives in nearly three hundred more or less faithful copies still extant. Recent studies have made much of these manuscripts, especially of those in which scribes have deliberately altered the traditional readings. Still, while showing the undeniable interest and originality of such *mouvance* in *Rose* manuscripts, these studies consistently found their analyses on the standard editions of Langlois and Lecoy as representative of Jean's lost autograph. Therefore, those editions seem reliable enough for critical scholarship. Nonetheless, I have, whenever possible, used variant manuscript evidence based on direct examination or on important studies of the manuscripts to support, clarify, or nuance my own interpretation.

Manuscript *mouvance* does not seem to invalidate the critical position taken above regarding the *Rose*'s meanings and represented by the title of this book. In reading Jean's *Roman de la rose* in any of its manuscripts not contaminated by scribal errors alone, the reader is confronted with readings which anticipate and illustrate a given scribe's or scribal patron's internal difference. This commonplace is as true for the *Rose* as for any medieval work surviving in multiple manuscripts subject to scribal rewriting. They are further evidence of audience response to various features of Jean's *Rose*, as revealing for different audiences as for the first author's own version.

I propose to use medieval theoretical models to get at the *Rose*'s art and meanings and the moral and social issues it raises. Non-medieval models are certainly possible as interpretive prisms, but they do not fall within the purview of this book. This is not to say, however, that they lie outside the *Rose* reader's mind and that they will not return, sometimes with a vengeance, as the modern reader's internal difference emerges. I shall rely more specifically on the *accessus ad auctores* tradition—the "introductions" to canonical works like those Jean cites so often: Ovid and Boethius. Such introductions taught medieval students how to read and construe writing. Transferred to the realm of author or scribal interventions in rewriting—and we must remember that Jean de Meun rewrote Guillaume de Lorris by continuing him—the *accessus* pointed vernacular readers in the directions prescribed by authoritative sources and auctorial intention.[3] As far as the specific case of the *Rose* is concerned, I shall rely almost exclusively on the so-called Aristotelian *accessus* and its formal modes of treating matter to show how Jean treated the subject matter of his poem and the intentions that treatment served.

Beyond the parameters prescribed by the *accessus* tradition is the fact that the *Rose* is an allegory. More specifically, it uses the ironic mode to develop its allegory, such that the reader is continually confronted not only with the poem's literal story on plucking a rose, but also by its other, allegorical meanings, often stated in an ironic mode. For allegory makes at least two statements at one and the same time. Each such statement must, by definition of allegory, be "other," that is, different from the literal sense of its surface meaning. In terms of the *Rose*, Amant's story illustrates the plucking of a rose and something else—something necessarily "other" than that literal or surface story. That "other" statement is, of course, part of the controversy about the poem's meanings. I hope to show that the "otherness" lies both in the realm of multiple meanings and of internal difference on moral and social issues.

Several critical presuppositions emerge from the medieval *accessus* tradition and medieval use of allegory, presuppositions which one discovers in Jean's *Rose* as well. I shall set them forth briefly here, leaving fuller discussion and illustration for the ensuing analysis. A fundamental notion is that of poet as writer of allegory. Jean de Meun calls himself a poet and sees himself as carrying out the office of the poet by writing the *Rose* as an allegory. What is a poet in Jean's sense of the word? How does the poet's office conform to the medieval *accessus* tradition?

According to a traditional medieval sense of the designation common in the thirteenth century, the best poets rewrite source material, while adding little to it; Jean calls himself such a poet (*Rose* v. 15204–9). The initial primacy of the source is everywhere in evidence in medieval prologues, epilogues, and other auctorial interventions. Pedagogical tradition represented by the medieval arts of poetry and prose and by commentaries goes back to Horace's conviction that it is better to treat well-known subject matter than to invent something entirely new. However, this injunction does not require poets to reproduce faithfully their sources while rewriting them.

That brings me to my second point: poets study their sources in order to identify in them strategies of composition which they will deploy or adapt in rewriting. Such treatment results in the writing of a "treatise." According to the tradition of the Aristotelian *accessus* Jean used, poets use two modes of treatment: the *modus tractatus*, or "mode of the treatise," and the *modus tractandi*, or "mode of treating." Both modes subsume strategies of rewriting which the new author may use and which Jean for one actually drew on to continue and to reconstrue Guillaume de Lorris's incomplete beginning of the poem. The modes of treating antecedent matter are probably the most important feature of Jean's art in the *Rose*, both because they reveal his conception of composition and recomposition as rewriting, and because they suggest more clearly his auctorial intention in the poem.

Third, in addition to the aforementioned modes, poets also find in their antecedents rhetorical techniques like material style, natural and artificial order, amplifications like description and digression, and other stylistic embellishments that are fundamental to poetic rewriting in the Middle Ages. These techniques may function independently or in counterpoint on all allegorical levels of a poetic text. Such common means of rewriting are not artificial in the usual sense in which the word is applied to them. Properly used, they serve to articulate source material so as to achieve originality in rewriting. To be sure, such techniques may be and were used artificially, especially in classroom exercises. The same is true for classroom study of grammatical schemes like declension and conjugation. Still, the poet who learned how to conjugate *amare* may eventually use the word appropriately and with originality while conjugating it in conformity with grammatical norms. Given all these factors, the poet rewriting his or her source may change its meaning, scope, sequence of parts, emphases, or style. Hence, fidelity to sources is not a measure of artistic success; on the contrary, simple paraphrase or other kinds of literal repetition are deemed inappropriate. Restatement in different language, change of context, and correction illustrate the range of interventions the poet may make in source material. The *Rose* bears witness to these kinds of rewriting. In terms of medieval composition theory, the poet's art of rewriting is as fundamental as it is elementary. On the elementary level, the tropes and figures of rhetoric are the principal means to rewrite with originality. On the level of the skilled poet like Jean de Meun, these devices will have become as habitual as the rules of grammar. They are in fact storehouses of possibilities from which the mind may draw forms and modes of articulation appropriate to the effective expression of auctorial intention.

This brings me to my last point. Intention is a major factor in medieval writing. It may be explicit or implicit in any given work, and even become problematic in allegorical and ironic texts. In the *Rose*, intention is the crux of controversy. Nonetheless, in the *accessus* tradition, intention (*intentio*) was an important topic in introducing a new work. Throughout the *Rose*'s plot, authoritative voices also express various intentions with the plot. Intentional fallacy, albeit a modern critical control, cannot be ignored when we envision medieval versions of intention in general and the *Rose*'s expression of intentions in particular. When, for example, does a personification like Reason or Nature express the author's intention? I shall return to this issue in chapter 1.

Despite the controversy Jean's *Rose* has provoked literally through the centuries, there has been general agreement, in both medieval and modern times, on two points: Jean de Meun writes well, regardless of what the *Rose* teaches, and Amant appears in the work as a *fol amoureux*, or foolish lover. Moreover, the burden of medieval and modern critical investigation has sought to identify and evaluate the *Rose*'s "definitive meaning" (see v. 19474)—to little avail, as I have already suggested. Opinions on the definitive meaning, and definitive achievement, of Jean's poem diverge abruptly and continually in scholarly criticism. Today the divergences are as deep as ever, cutting as they do across national, political, disciplinary, moral, and gender lines. Jean first evoked them himself in his central auctorial intervention on language, women, and the religious in the *Rose* (v. 15105–272), and they surfaced anew in corrective rewritings and adaptations in the manuscript traditions and in the "Querelle de la *Rose*," which Christine de Pizan instigated at the turn of the fifteenth century.

Modern readings have done little to clear the air. For some, Jean's *Rose* is an encyclopedia prefiguring the Enlightenment. To others, it is a hodgepodge, proof that Jean was woefully inadequate when it came to organizing and synthesizing his material in conformity with a coherent intention. More recently, the *Rose*, when read through the prisms of Augustine of Hippo, is seen to reenact the Fall in Amant's sinful, ridiculous posturing and language. Others would correct the Augustinian context, viewing the work as a reflection of the Neoplatonic universe in which a foolish Amant achieves nature's purposes by willy-nilly inseminating the rose. To others, Amant's stumbling progress seems to point to a growing wisdom and experience, as in a medieval bildungsroman. Still others are content to read the *Rose* as a frankly carnivalistic, Rabelaisian hymn to hedonism. Most recently, the romance has been read principally as a misogynist treatise written to glorify rape.[4]

These salient global interpretations of the *Rose*'s definitive meaning illustrate the diversity and divergence in scholarly criticism I referred to above, as well as in the medieval reactions to the poem such criticism often reflects. This is not the place to assess them and other, more specialized interpretations. Fortunately, Heather Arden has published a thorough annotated bibliography of *Rose* scholarship. There is also a good assessment of work up to about 1980 in Karl-August Ott's *Der Rosenroman*, which supersedes while completing earlier such *états présents*. In this book I shall refer to earlier studies where my argument calls for it or when it seems otherwise appropriate.

But I must express one caveat. Any or all of these interpretations are *possible* readings of the *Rose* as long as the critic believes that he or she is correct. That is the realm of internal difference. However, none of them is an absolute, definitive reading. Moreover, the *Rose* itself imposes certain limits and constraints on possible readings which it will bear short of rewriting. Christine de Pizan knew as much when she both condemned the poem as she read it and corrected certain perceived deficiencies by rewriting some aspects of the poem positively in her *Epistre au dieu d'Amours* and *Dit de la Rose*. In these works she represents a different God of Love from Jean's, one who speaks out against both Ovid and Jean. Furthermore, she proposes a chivalric or courtly order devoted to a rose quite different as allegory from the one Amant pursues in Jean de Meun. Christine de Pizan will provide useful comparisons and contrasts to Jean de Meun in this book.

Let me here return to "Jean's rape of the rose."[5] The ambiguity of this statement focuses nicely on and reflects the very ambiguity of Jean's exemplary plot and its meaning, or, better yet, its meanings and concomitant auctorial intentions. It also points to and reflects diverse audience responses to the *Rose*—the internal difference that makes the poem so compelling and exasperating. As the reader follows Amant, analogous audiences arise within the text. These include the woman represented by the rose as well as the diverse personifications that constellate about her and Amant, regrouping and interacting while aggressively asserting their views or vigorously responding to the arguments or actions of others. Moreover, as the narrative proceeds, other potential audiences of readers suggest themselves: young and old, men and women in general and on different social levels, learned and illiterate, married and single, rich and poor, beautiful and ugly, and those of various sexual orientations.[6] Perhaps other such pairings or groupings will suggest themselves to the discerning reader. Beyond the late-thirteenth-century spectrum emerge in this way audiences Jean may or may not have intended but which have a place in the context of the *Rose*'s issues and the internal difference Jean himself acknowledged as implicit in the notion of multiple audience response over time.

The meanings of the story of a foolish lover are implicit in such audience response. Moreover, they are all essentially moral responses, a distinction which keeps the *Rose* within the ethical context assigned to most poetry in the *accessus* tradition. But the *Rose* does not impose a single absolute ethical view. Rather, it reveals through its readers how each of them responds to or interprets certain actions exemplified in the dream. In doing so, each reveals his or her own moral stance as well as the implied standards of orientation, evaluation, and moral finesse which that stance bespeaks. In the last analysis, the *Rose* will show us and others who we are—"Que nous et vous de nous meïsmes / Poïssons connoissance avoir"[7] [so that we might know ourselves better]—know ourselves in the full topical range of human attributes the *Rose* addresses. This book attempts, therefore, to show that this reading from a variant branch of *Rose* manuscripts actually expresses best the work's auctorial intention in the sense of *accessus* introductions. But it does so by raising issues, not by offering a definitive reading or interpretation.

Therefore, this book applies the medieval art of literary composition to one of the most important and controversial works of the Middle Ages: the *Roman de la rose* as Jean de Meun left signals for it to be read and reread. My purpose is to test the implications of the medieval art of composition in this specimen text—a masterpiece by many medieval and some modern standards, a failure by others. Specifically, this means weighing and testing the implications of a number of statements made by medieval theorists and authors, including Jean de Meun himself, on rewriting.

Historical criticism of medieval texts attempts to determine how those texts were written and how they were meant to be read in their own time and afterward. In such criticism, the scholar not only identifies the use of certain compositional techniques, he or she also attempts to interpret their function and significance for the art and meaning of the work. It points, moreover, toward readings that are, cumulatively, more nearly contemporary to the texts. Perhaps more important, in a specimen text like the *Roman de la rose*, which is of great importance both for its intrinsic qualities and for its influence, such readings can illustrate how medieval works themselves reveal the art by which they were written and in terms of which they were meant to be read, while pointing to ways we might interpret and appreciate them today on and in their own terms.

The *Roman de la rose* is an especially interesting case because of its demonstrated prominence and influence in the Middle Ages and because of the controversy that has swirled about it since it was written regarding its meaning or meanings, its artistry, and its misogyny. That Jean de Meun anticipated such divergent appreciations is as remarkable as it is perplexing. But the problem of the work's definitive meaning, and the corollary issues of its artistry and misogyny, by their very provocative character, is an indication that the *Rose* actually contains no one definitive meaning. Rather, like the medieval *jeu-parti*, which offers several minor, yet significant parallels with issues raised in the *Rose*, Jean's version of Guillaume de Lorris's dream poem forces the reader to review his or her own life and values by analogy with Jean's "mirror for lovers." Surely, no medieval work has retained its currency so much as this one, which no doubt explains why critical scholarship has not achieved a definitive reading of it, and probably never will.

1

Sources and Implied Audiences

Je ne say a quoy tant nous debatons ces questions, car je croy ne toy ne moy n'avons talent de mouvoir nos oppinions: tu dis qu'il est bon; je dis qu'il est mauvais.

—Christine de Pizan, *Le Débat sur le Roman de la rose*

[I don't know why we argue these issues so much, for I don't believe either one of us wishes to change our mind. You say it's good, I say it's bad.]

Jean de Meun enunciates an art of poetry in his auctorial interventions. I propose to set forth briefly in this chapter, then treat more thoroughly in succeeding chapters, the letter, modes of treatment or elaboration, and allegory of the poem in light of that art and of its multiple contributions to the composition of the work. Moreover, I shall follow the advice Jean de Meun himself gives to his readers on how the *Rose* should be read. Jean's voice is, after all, "auctorial"—it is that of an authority figure who assumes the voice of the person who wrote the work, a person whom the God of Love identifies and names as Jean Chopinel from Meung-sur-Loire (v. 10535–37).

AUTHOR AND INTENTION

Central to the problem of interpreting the *Rose* is the complex issue of authorial intent. What purposes did its authors have when writing the *Rose*? Is their intention, or intentions, readily perceptible to its readers? Hard questions, these. For whenever the issue of the "correct" reading of the *Rose* arises, diverse, incompatible solutions come forth. This is as true today as it was in the "Querelle de la Rose"—the debate as to the moral value of the *Rose* that broke out at the beginning of the fifteenth century. Indeed, the student of today may be inclined to conclude with Christine de Pizan that readers will never agree on the meaning, or the value, of this work.

To be sure, as both John Fleming and Pierre-Yves Badel agree, there was relatively little expressed discord among *Rose* readers prior to the "Querelle." Even in the "Querelle" itself there was agreement on both sides regarding two important features of the poem: both Guillaume de Lorris and Jean de Meun write well, and Jean's part of the work deals with a *fol amoureux*, a foolish lover.[1] So, perhaps, these areas of agreement among opponents can in fact serve as a point of departure for a new reading of the *Roman de la rose* in that, together, they orient the implied audience's reading. In the following study issues of intention loom large. I must therefore go beyond the statement in my introduction that intention was a common medieval desideratum in the interpretation of literature to say something about the problems of affective and intentional fallacies. Rather than analyze these fallacies and their varieties in detail, I shall put them in the contexts of medieval poetry like the *Rose*.

Poetry as a rhetorical mode seeks to sway emotion and thereby convince audiences of a line of argument. It uses affective means to achieve, directly or indirectly, a certain intention: to convince by logic, received opinion or authority, and emotion. Whether the poetic work is artistically and ethically successful depends, in this scheme of things, on how well it influences the audience. The *Rose*, therefore, presents a very real problem of interpretation, as the "Querelle" makes clear. It pleases some while displeasing others. Its lessons regarding the *fol amoureux* are well made for many, while many others find them so defective and unconvincing that its line of argument fails as rhetoric. Such readers tend to turn away from the text with scorn, or, in some instances, they wax eloquent about the work's encyclopedic, if rather chaotic, marvels. I hope to show that these diverse responses to the *Rose* are to be expected, and that they were even anticipated by Jean de Meun in his major intervention on language, misogyny, and false mendicants. The critic's problem is to find whether such diverse responses betray a coherent auctorial rationale and, therefore, are the result of auctorial intention. It seems to me that the solution to this problem is the litmus test of the *Rose* as medieval poetry.

The problem of intention is further complicated by the *Rose*'s dual authorship. As I have elsewhere proposed a reading of Guillaume de Lorris's part of the romance as it existed before Jean's continuation,[2] which I see no reason to revise, I shall return to it only occasionally in this book, where comparison and contrast seem useful. (This too fits the two sides in the "Querelle," both having perceived Guillaume's torso to be special and rather different from Jean de Meun's version.[3]) Here, I am principally interested in Guillaume's *Rose* insofar as Jean incorporated its some four thousand lines into his continuation.[4] This means, however, that we must ask ourselves whether Jean intended merely to complete the romance along much the same lines his predecessor started, or whether he sought to modify the first author's work to accommodate his own, different version of the plot.

The existence of two authors adumbrates a second problem for readers of our time as well. That is, the uncertainty as to which manuscript medieval readers had before them has complicated the issue of auctorial intention and medieval reader response to the *Rose*.[5] The problem is compounded for the works of authors like Gui de Mori or Guillaume de Digulleville, who rewrite the first two authors.[6] Does such adaptation imply fidelity or infidelity to the original? To which original?

The question of reception has dominated recent interpretations of the *Rose*. To be sure, medieval evidence as to how a work was read helps us to avoid "presentism," or the conscious or unconscious imposition of modern perceptions and preconceptions onto earlier writing.[7] But, by the same token, we must be careful not to commit the same error within the medieval period. That is, we must no more impose fourteenth- or fifteenth-century readings or illustrations on thirteenth-century works than we would impose twentieth-century readings on eighteenth-century texts.[8] Thus, my goal here is to attempt to read the *Rose* as Jean de Meun wrote it, insofar as the manuscript tradition reveals it in standard editions. My justification for relying on the standard modern editions is that scholars still use them to identify significant divergence in variant manuscripts.

I shall do so by examining Jean's artistry as "poet"—the artistry implicit in the notion of poet during his time and explicit in his own romance. Jean likens his art and intention to those typical of the poet in what is the earliest recorded reference to "poet" as a vernacular author.[9]

> Je n'i faz riens fors reciter,
> Se par mon geu, qui po vos coute,
> Quelque parole n'i ajoute,
> Si con font antr'eus li poete,
> Quant chascuns la matire trete
> Don il li plest a antremetre;
> Car si con tesmoigne la letre,
> Profiz et delectacion,
> C'est toute leur entencion.
> (V. 15204–12)

[I merely repeat what others have related, albeit in my game I add a word here and there—which costs you little. This is as poets are wont to do when each treats the matter he or she sees fit to take up. For, as literature shows, profitable instruction and pleasure is their sole intent.]

Profiz, or the Horatian *prodesse*, is "profitable instruction." Jean claims a few lines earlier that his own "escriture" is "toute . . . por anseignement" (v. 15172–73) [entirely for instruction]. Thus, according to Jean de Meun's own stated intention, the poet seeks to offer pleasing instruction.

Poets in this sense also write allegories. Reason makes this point in her use of the pleasure and profit commonplace to explain *integumenta* to Amant. She says that the integument has two levels, as does allegory which covers a valuable truth with a pleasing surface. Her fable on the castration of Saturn is such an integument. It is one of the "integumenz aus poetes" (v. 7138) that embellish Jean's *Rose*. Reading the *Rose* as integumental allegory requires attention to three aspects of its composition: its letter, its mode of treatment or elaboration, and its allegorical meanings.

The God of Love introduces Jean as the last in a line of poet lovers, the catalogue extending back through Guillaume de Lorris to Ovid, Catullus, Cornelius Gallus,[10] and Tibullus. All but Jean are dead. We are told that Jean, like Guillaume and Amant, will not heed Reason but will enjoy a long life blithely singing of love; moreover, so much does he cherish the *Rose* that he will complete the incomplete romance before dying (v. 10554–55). Although clearly laid out, the God of Love's words are nonetheless ambiguous in this passage. For Jean, Guillaume, and Amant lose their clearly distinctive roles and blend into a kind of triune persona through pronominal play.[11]

Quant Guillaumes cessera,
Jehans le continuera,
Enprés sa mort, que je ne mante,
Anz trespassez plus de .XL.,
Et dira por la mescheance,
Par poor de desesperance
Qu'il n'ait de Bel Acueill perdue
La bienvoillance avant eüe:
"Et si l'ai je perdue, espoir,
A poi que ne m'en desespoir",
Et toutes les autres paroles,
Quex qu'els soient, sages ou foles,
Jusqu'a tant qu'il avra coillie
Seur la branche vert et foillie
La tres bele rose vermeille.
(V. 10557–71)

[When Guillaume stops Jean will continue the work more than forty years after his death, so help me God; he will say, because of his misfortune and out of fear that he may have lost the earlier favor of Bel Acueil: "And I have perhaps lost it in fact, because of which I am on the verge of despair," and all the other words, be they wise or foolish, until he will have plucked the very beautiful rose from its green and leafy stem.]

The pronominal obfuscation necessarily raises the issue of "Jean's rape of the rose." Who plucked the rose—Guillaume, Jean, or Amant? Whatever the answer, the God of Love's account fits the intention expressed in the prologue to Jean's translation of Boethius: the poem will teach how to pluck roses.

The ambiguity of the pronominal referents also mirrors the very problem of the meaning of the *Rose*. The God of Love himself says the story requires an explanation, an explanation Jean will provide: "Puis vodra si la chose espondre / Que riens ne s'i porra repondre" (v. 10573–74) [Then he will explain the matter so well that nothing will be hidden]. Jean himself confirms this intent in his self-defense:

Et se vos i trovez riens trouble,
G'esclarcirai ce qui vos trouble
Quant le songe m'orrez espondre.
Bien savrez lors d'amors respondre,
S'il est qui an sache opposer,
Quant le texte m'orrez gloser;
Et savrez lors par cel escrit
Quant que j'avrai devant escrit
Et quant que je bé a escrire.
(V. 15115–23)

[And if anything in it perplexes you, I will clarify whatever troubles you when you hear me explain the dream. You will be well qualified to answer any questions about love, if someone raises objections, when you hear me gloss the text. By this work you will know all that I have written and all I intend to write.]

What the two foregoing passages accomplish is to move readers from the allegedly pleasurable letter—the plucking of the rose—to the stated intent—the profitable instruction to be acquired by reading the *Rose*. In the God of Love's words, Jean's continuation of the poem will save lovers from disasters like those suffered by his predecessors by teaching them about themselves and their actions. The *Rose* will be a "mirror for lovers" (v. 10621)—a *Miroër aus Amoreus*: "Tant i verront de bien por eus, / Mes que Reson n'i sait creüe, / La chetive, la recreüe" (v. 10622–24) [they will find in it so much profit, provided they don't listen to that wretched slaggard Reason]. In other words, lovers who ignore Reason will learn how to seize Jealousy's castle and pluck its roses.

These are the God of Love's words. Yet, the God of Love also says Jean shares Amant's rejection of Reason (v. 10542). Moreover, Amant himself is interested only in the letter of his story, not in the poetic elucidation of its integuments. To the extent that these statements are correct, then, Jean himself is no poet; like Amant, "Des poetes les sentances, / Les fables et les methaphores / Ne bé je pas a gloser ores" (v. 7160–62) [I am not now interested in glossing the meanings of poets, their fables, nor their allegories]. To the God of Love, Amant and Jean as lovers are mirror images of one another, just as the reader who follows the God of Love's lead will mirror them.

IMPLIED AUDIENCES

"Mirror" as image is variously applied in *speculum* literature. To be sure, it can show the reader as he or she is. But it can also show him or her as he or she ought or ought not to be,[12] through accurate, diverse, or even distorted images—a lesson widely conveyed through various rewritings of the Narcissus myth.[13] In doing so, choosing the term "mirror" raises the fundamental issue of reading the *Rose* as mirror: who is its implied audience, or better, audiences? What audiences does the text in fact address? Does the text communicate meaning to audiences in such a way as to be readily grasped? These questions are raised as early as the "Querelle." In response to them, both Christine de Pizan and Jean Gerson argue that Jean's rhetoric was so slanted toward immoral behavior that no audience, least of all one composed of foolish lovers, could perceive it as a moral indictment of their folly, whereas Pierre Col insisted that the *Rose*'s rhetoric had moved one lover to turn away from his foolishness.[14]

Actually, medieval works often postulate audiences—implied audiences—of greater or lesser accomplishment. For example, in the prose prologue to *Anticlaudianus*, Alain de Lille envisions three kinds of reading and, thus, three kinds of audiences. Young readers (*puerilem auditum*) will take pleasure in the literal sense, the better educated reader (*perficientem sensum*) will grasp its instructive but deeper moral sense, and the truly learned (*proficientem intellectum*) will penetrate to the profound allegories written for the intellect, the human faculty capable of knowing divine truths.[15] A real progression is articulated here; the reader should not stop at the aesthetic level, but, progressing from stage to stage, strive to read more deeply into the work's moral and theological allegories. Alain's structure of graded readers implies rereading of allegory, a topic to which I shall return in the next chapter.

Similarly, the *Rose* postulates a variety of readers; here, however, they constitute a dichotomy.[16] One group, uninterested in poetic allegories, will read the poem to find out what it literally teaches on how to pluck roses;[17] the letter of the text will please such readers. Another audience will go beyond the letter to get at the moral meanings or lessons set forth through various voices and modes of discourse. Ultimately, such readers will want to know how to sort out the different authorities in the text and discover the definitive meaning and overarching signification Jean promises to all who finish his romance.

These levels of readership exist in spite of the fact that the *Rose* is a vernacular work. Its implied audiences are not necessarily inept, although, as references in the text indicate, they may be unlettered—especially in the sense of being "ignorant of Latin." Various indicators suggest this. Citations of authority, for example, may merely refer to an authority, but they may also contain quotes or paraphrases of the source. Thus, a work as fundamental to the *Rose* as Boethius's *Consolation of Philosophy*, as seen from the point of view of Jean's Reason, was a closed book to many in the *Rose*'s audiences.[18] This is why, perhaps, Reason recommends its translation into French (v. 5007–10), since the implied audience will not always be skilled in reading such authorities in Latin, nor will it be able to rely on them in order to get at the *Rose*'s meaning. Nature is also speaking of just such audiences when limiting herself to "rough examples" that do not require subtle glossing.[19]

> Et por tenir la droite voie,
> Qui bien voudroit la chose amprandre,
> Qui n'est pas legiere a antandre,
> Un gros example an porroit metre
> Aus genz lais qui n'antandent letre;
> Car tex genz veulent grosse chose,
> Sanz grant soutiveté de glose.
> (V. 17360–66)

[In order to stay on track, whoever wished to take up the matter, which is not easy to understand, could use a rough example for lay folk who cannot read. For such persons want something roughly sketched out and plainly understandable without very subtle glossing.]

Although Amant seems capable of such glossing (albeit unwilling to practice his skill), he is not the only kind of reader or listener Jean evokes for the *Rose*. Rather, it is Amant's problem that audiences uninterested in subtle glossing must understand in terms of "rough examples" that do *not* require "very subtle glossing." Such persons will not be familiar enough with Boethius or with Augustine to recognize their voices in the *Rose*.[20]

This is not to say that an alert, educated Amant or a cleric proficient in Latin might not recognize echoes of both Boethius and Augustine in the *Rose*. Nonetheless, the essential lesson of the *Rose*—its *sentence*—must be accessible in this text which offers "grosse chose, / Sanz grant soutiveté de glose." This point is crucial to any interpretation of the *Rose*. Unlike the *Anticlaudianus*'s scholarly audiences, the unlettered lay reader of the *Rose* must be able to perceive the poem's intent and meanings even if he or she cannot read or does not already know its Latin sources and authorities. Otherwise, the unlettered audience is likely to see the *Rose*, as Jean de Meun puts it in the prologue to his translation of Boethius, only as a work on how to pluck roses. In short, whatever the subtlety of Jean's text and its allegorical gloss, the broad lines of its letter and allegory must be perceptible to that part of its audiences which the narrator and others describe as lay and as uncomfortable or unwilling to cope with anything more than "rough examples." The *Rose* certainly contains more than that, just as Alain's *Anticlaudianus* contains more than meets the eyes of its elementary readers. Nonetheless, the *Rose* must, like the *Anticlaudianus*, serve as "rough example" of its allegorical lessons or it fails by the very standards it enunciates. I hope to show that it does not fail its unlettered listeners anymore than it does its more accomplished readers. By unlettered audiences, I am not implying stupid audiences. Stupid audiences are foolish like Amant, who could read *integumenta* if he wanted to.

CONTEXTS, ALLEGORIES, AND MEANINGS

Now, the *Rose* is not a simple moral treatise. If it were, we should have little trouble reading or understanding it. We should all agree that it merely tells how a dreamer plucked a dream rose after several marvelous adventures. This is the sustained, obvious literal reading proposed by the text. It is also the one that permitted Pierre Col and Christine de Pizan to agree that Amant is a *fol amoureux*. But their disagreement as to the quality, intent, and meaning of the work demonstrates that more sophistication is required to appreciate the *Rose* as integumental allegory. Here the difficulties begin.

At the other extreme from the simple, literal response to the *Rose* as the story of a *fol amoureux* is the detailed allegorical gloss like that proposed by John Fleming for verse 5348. Fleming suggests that "Qui cercheroit jusqu'an Quartage" [were one to seek as far away as Carthage] is a reference to Augustine's sins as a young man living in that city.[21] To me, this reading sounds far-fetched. Nonetheless, impossible as it may seem, it is in fact a possible gloss to the text within the Augustinian context Fleming proposes for the *Rose*.[22] That is, Fleming's gloss is a useful suggestion regarding the reading of medieval allegory, both as to its constraints and open-endedness. A medieval glossator who knew the *Confessions* might very well have added Fleming's allegorical reading of the line, provided it fit the general intent of the text as he or she was glossing it.[23] Since to Fleming the *Rose* has an essentially Augustinian context, it is open to his reading. The issue, of course, is whether Fleming's Augustinian context is the context of Jean's *Rose*. More importantly, could an unlettered audience have perceived it without knowing Augustine? For example, when Reason offers the fable on Saturn's castration, she also expresses her willingness to explain its hidden meaning. Amant declines to hear her out and, thus, does not get beyond the fable and its literal sense. The uninformed reader could, unwillingly, be in precisely the same quandary that Amant willingly places himself in if the text does not offer clear glossing. Likewise, unless the Augustinian reading is perceptible without reference to Augustine's texts, then—supreme historical irony!—the literal reading will lure the uninformed reader or audience of the *Rose* into an interpretation diametrically opposite to the Augustinian allegory of the Fall.

An allegory usually provides both its own context and representative readings of the letter according to that context. These representative readings serve as a reminder that keeps our understanding on track. If context and representative readings are either absent or incoherent, the text does not provide a sustained reading, either because it is poorly written or because it seeks deliberate ambiguity in order to elicit irony, debate, or even a double or multiple truth. The latter is the apparent presupposition of most *Rose* scholarship.[24] But, especially in these cases, "sub-sets" of readings may also obtain. In other words, such texts will include explicit representative readings that support coherent, derivative, implicit readings the reader may add by drawing on his or her own knowledge and wit.

The thirteenth-century *Queste del saint graal* is an especially useful illustration of explicit and implicit allegorical readings, since it shares these features with the *Rose*. It is from the same century as the *Rose*, it is less controversial, and it has a double context embracing a part, the *Queste* itself, which has been added to a larger whole, the *Prose Lancelot* and, beyond that, the subsequent branches added to the beginning that produce the entire *Lancelot-Grail* cycle.

The *Queste* explicitly contrasts human love, or lust, with chastity and virginity, or unconstrained sexual abstinence. The antithesis between such love on the one hand and chastity and virginity on the other is textually defined and evaluated. Interpretations of the life and adventures of the principal knights reiterate and illustrate the distinction, in the light of explicit biblical models and analogues. Furthermore, within the context explicitly elaborated in the text, one may gloss inexplicit parts much as Fleming does to the Carthage allusion in the *Rose*. Many have done so, none more thoroughly than Pauline Matarasso.[25] Some of her readings may seem at first glance as far-fetched as Fleming's did to me. Nonetheless they remain possible and coherent interpretations that might have been made by a medieval glossator, especially one as informed about the Bible and its medieval readings as the *Queste* hermits and Matarasso herself are. The important factor is that these added glosses are not essential to a sustained, elementary reading of the *Queste* and its explicit glosses. They simply suggest themselves to the informed reader once an explicit context has been identified.

Matters become more complicated when readers attempt to situate the *Queste* in the context of the *Prose Lancelot* and the larger *Lancelot-Grail*. Here modern interpretations diverge. Is the cycle in fact incoherent, or is it meant to show irony, to elicit debate, or to manifest a double truth, the one valid in the context of terrestrial chivalry, the other in that of celestial chivalry?

My point is not to resolve that issue here. I wish merely to recall the potential in allegory for multiple readings, some even imposed on the other (as I think Jean's is on Guillaume's), while recognizing constraints that control the number of possible readings—constraints like irony, overriding context, explicit statement in the text, narrative stance, superposition or hierarchy of different contexts, the actual circumstances of *manuscriture*, or manuscript contents, including continuations, incomplete texts, scribal interventions, and the audience's role in evaluating and further interpreting the different contexts. None of this precludes a hierarchical progression in reading like that suggested for readers of Alain's *Anticlaudianus*, a hierarchy that includes movement toward better or worse.

POETS AND SOURCES

In the case of the *Rose*, allegorical strategies are founded on the medieval notion of the poet as one who provides pleasure and instruction in the allegorical mode. Jean de Meun identifies himself as such a poet, as we have observed. The poet, he goes on to say, "recites": "Je n'i faz riens fors reciter" (v. 15204)—literally, "I do nothing more than relate, that is, cite or quote again," with a minimum number of additions, in order to please and instruct. Jean does indeed repeat what others have written, drawing so extensively on his sources that early scholarship read the *Rose* principally as an encyclopedia.[26]

However, Jean's words must be read in context, as mere verbatim quoting was not perceived in his time as desirable. Let us then put his words into their twelfth- and thirteenth-century context. Matthew of Vendôme, in his twelfth-century *Ars versificatoria*, warns his pupils against faithful reproduction, even paraphrase, of the sources they nevertheless are bound to use.[27] A more elementary treatise, Gervase of Melkley's *Ars versificaria*,[28] states that the author may rewrite the source in the same way while polishing the source (*idemptitas*), in a similar way while deflecting the source through analogy (*similitudo*), or in the opposite way by distorting the source material into something different from or contrary to its original sense (*contrarietas*). All these procedures are commonplace modes of medieval rewriting. In using them, the writer will reproduce the first author's conception of the work in a new version that goes beyond the original, in a way that conjures up dwarves who see farther because they observe from the shoulders of giants. And, indeed, the romance tradition from which the *Rose* emerges adopts these principles of composition.[29] In this manner, the poet, as Jean understands the office, collects matter from antecedent sources and combines it so as to—in "reciting" and rewriting—tell a new version with a newly delineated shape or meaning that both pleases and instructs.

This perspective on using earlier material underscores the fact that aspiring poets learned their "skill"[30] by study of the authors. There is frequent reference to what they may in this way learn about composition, with any number of works designated specifically by their authors or medieval commentators as representative of the poetic art: Vergil, Ovid, Jean de Hauville, Alain de Lille, Bernardus Silvestris, and others.[31] By implication, then, an author using a source could draw from it not only "quotable" material, but also strategies for rewriting a new work based on that material as model.[32]

In identifying sources, we must remember that their validity for interpreting the *Rose* obtains only if the audience knew them and could readily recognize their use. As we have observed, such intertextual use of Latin sources virtually excludes that unlettered audience which Jean seems to project and which required signals other than authoritative allusions to get beneath the literal surface of the rose quest. If the sense of the source is neither textually explicit nor easily perceived, the work cannot achieve its purpose of profitable instruction. In this sense, the *Rose* would truly need an appended commentary or marginal glosses. Otherwise the ignorant would be duped because they could understand only the literal sense or perhaps nothing at all. Although this may in some cases be inevitable, auctorial statements in the *Rose* suggest that its audiences were supposed to be able to understand its messages. If they still failed to do so after a good faith effort, the work was, as I said above, a failure by its own standards.

Two other problems emerge in evaluating the use of actual sources, problems that go beyond implied audience and auctorial rewriting of antecedent material. First, the author's version of the source may differ from our own; we may even require a lost manuscript reading in order to be complete or accurate. In the light of Matthew of Vendôme's sense of invention, it is more likely, however, that the new author actually revised the source to fit his or her own understanding of it or to fit a different model for the new work.[33] In the final analysis, both critic and audience must rely on the sense proposed by the text before him or her, not on that of actual or presumed sources.

The next and final problem we must face in evaluating actual sources is equally troublesome. If a model of interpretation fits a work, this does not mean that it has to or was supposed to. There are enough archetypes available to make almost anything mean almost anything else. This is obvious if one uses modern models unknown to the Middle Ages to interpret the text, such as models from Freudian or Jungian psychoanalysis or form sociological theory. By the same token, a contemporary medieval model may seem to fit. This does not mean that the model was intended. Once again, we need explicit textual signals that define the model. Furthermore, the model must be credibly available to the author in his or her time.

JEAN DE MEUN AND HIS SOURCES

In our case, Guillaume de Lorris was Jean's first author and primary source, as we know, since Jean incorporated Guillaume's beginning into his continuation.[34] Generally speaking, the first author was a major figure in the medieval approach to rewriting. For example, the author of one minor version of the Trojan War refused to divulge his own name, ascribing the work to Dares because the latter was the first author.[35] Similarly, Joseph of Exeter's *Ylias*, another version of the Trojan War, is often the work meant by the designation to Dares,[36] even though Joseph made extensive changes on and additions to this source. Benoît de Sainte-

Maure also thoroughly reworked Dares with the *Roman de Troie*, although he insisted that he added very little to his source.[37] The incomplete Dares was for Benoît what Guillaume was to Jean: a work in need of other sources and developments to complete its plot and realize its new author's intent.

Such closure can be horizontal or vertical. Horizontal closure brings a given plot to conclusion, as in Jean's *Rose*. But closure can also, as poetic integument, elicit potential meaning from a source, a meaning which the new author construes, but which the first author did not intend. This also occurs, I believe, in Jean's continuation. Indeed, it has generally been recognized that, by continuing and rewriting Guillaume, Jean also paraphrases in part his first author, beginning his continuation with lamentations analogous not only to those with which Guillaume's version concludes, but also those which precede Reason's appearance in this first version (v. 2935–54). But, as we have noted, simple paraphrase is considered inept in the medieval art of poetry. As poet, Jean needed to endow Guillaume's *Rose* with new meaning. Like Benoît de Sainte-Maure, Jean in fact changed a lot, adding extensively from other sources and from his own invention. Yet, unlike Benoît, he appended these changes to the end of his predecessor, whose text he left otherwise intact.

Two major sources whose importance we shall evaluate are Ovid and Boethius. Both served as models as well as sources *stricto sensu* for Jean de Meun's rewriting of Guillaume de Lorris. They are to Jean de Meun what Dictys and the *Homerus latinus* were to Benoît de Sainte-Maure: supplementary sources.

As to Ovid, the medieval authority on love, he is ranked by the God of Love in his pantheon together with Guillaume and Jean himself—all of whom "bien sorent d'amors trestier" (v. 10493) [knew how to discourse on love well]. For Jean, Ovid's major treatises are the *Art of Love* and the *Remedia*. They are cited at length, albeit in new combinations, by Ami and the Vieille. Moreover, virtually all speakers cull examples from the *Metamorphoses*. Similarly, Boethius's *Consolation of Philosophy* is cited as authority by both Reason and the Jealous Husband. In addition to Ovid and Boethius, other authorities are evoked by Jean in the same passage in which he casts himself in the role of poet. Jean bases their authority on their experience with women—experience, the narrator insists, which was not fabricated. "Mes por ç'an escrit les meïsmes / Que nous et vos de vos meïsmes / Poïssons connoissance avoir" (v. 15181–83) [They put them into writing so that we and you might know you yourselves].

As may be surmised by discussion thus far, this passage and Jean's actual use of sources raise many problems, but solve none. Four major problems relevant here are: the integrity of the edited text vis-à-vis manuscript variants; the authority of the figure in the text citing the source to authorize his or her argument; audience knowledge of the sources cited; and Jean's actual choice, deployment, and adaptation of sources in his text. I shall conclude this chapter by reviewing these four general points that bear on Jean's *Rose.*

First, the multiplicity of manuscripts raises issues of textual integrity and variant versions used by intended and perceived audiences. Sylvia Huot's recent investigations into the manuscript tradition for the *Rose* as well as the reception of later readers and authors reviewed by Pierre-Yves Badel make it incumbent upon the scholar to take into account, when dealing with reception, what manuscript version of the *Rose* a given reader may have known. Nonetheless, the manuscripts which are most likely close to Jean de Meun's own version have been identified and edited. These manuscripts and the modern editions based on them are close enough to what Jean de Meun wrote to make the editions based on them reliable, especially those by Lecoy and Langlois. Even those who have studied major manuscript adaptations rely on these editions to identify major variants and other interventions. These editions form the basis of comparison for studies of variant manuscript traditions.

To be sure, it is never possible to be absolutely certain about modern editions of medieval works. And, indeed, the validity of reception as an indicator of medieval reading of an original text declines in proportion to the uncertainty regarding the actual version read, which is not to say that the variant manuscripts do not have their own claim to our attention as indicators of later, local *Rose* reception. For example, in the very lines just cited from Jean's intervention addressed to women readers, there is a significant discrepancy among some manuscripts. Women are urged to read Jean's authorities in order to know themselves better: "Que nous e vos de vos meïsmes / Poïssons connoissance avoir"[38] [so that we and you might know you yourselves]. But among the variants to these lines, we find the following: "que nous et vous de *nous* meïsmes"[39]—that we, both men and women might know ourselves! What are we to learn from the authorities on women—what women have in common, what men and women have in common with one another, or what men are like? The preponderant manuscript tradition supports the first reading; yet, some readers knew only the second version wherein two different possible meanings emerge. The distinction is important, even if it is only the result of a common confusion in manuscripts between *n* and *u*, since inclusion and exclusion of genders is an important feature of Jean's *Rose*, as we shall see. When manuscript variants present problems like this, I shall devote special discussion to them.

The second problem is the identity and authority of the voice citing the authoritative source. Whereas Reason does not jar expectations by citing Boethius in Jean's first explicit reference to him (v. 5007), the Jealous Husband does so when he cites the same author in the second (v. 8919). Each citation raises the issue of the validity not only of the authority but also of the agent's use of the authority. Jean himself alerts us to this problem in two passages. In one he suggests that, if his authorities are wrong (v. 15193–94)—and he does not believe they are (v. 15197–202)—the reader should correct them. This is precisely what Christine de Pizan did with another of the Jealous Husband's authorities, Matheolus, when she wrote the *Cité des dames*. One reader's tastes are not another's. Although the misogynist narrator of Matheolus appears, like Amant, as the perfect fool and as such made readers like Pierre Col laugh at them, neither provoked Christine de Pizan's laughter.

However, the Jealous Husband is also unable to see how foolish his misogyny is. Does Jean as author, in putting Boethius into the Husband's mouth, mean to authorize such misogyny? What must we think of Reason's wish to see Boethius translated if the likes of the Husband misread him so badly? To be sure, Jean cautions his audience against taking each speaker as an authority merely because he or she speaks. The mere citation of authority may therefore distort the first author's meaning to fit the character of the speaker: "li diz doit le fet resambler" (v. 15160) [words ought to fit the deed]. If the speaker's language does not fit the source cited, his or her language is inaccurate and unauthoritative even when it cites canonical authority. Still, the audience must in some way be made aware of such differences in order for it to comprehend their import in the *Rose*'s allegory.

We have observed that in a new work of art an author was expected to rewrite sources and may even reshape old material in order to instill new meaning into the new work. Such adaptation conforms to poetic practice and authorizes allegory as a useful mode for adaptation. It is the foundation for the image of medieval dwarves perched on the shoulders of ancient giants. Yet, as Marie de France puts it so well, rewriting as recreation is not unfaithful to ancient authority; rather, it elicits that authority's veiled or hidden meaning and sets it forth more clearly for medieval moderns. I shall not quote again the oft-quoted lines from the prologue to her *Lais*, but merely recall her main point in them: that rather than correction, subtlety and revelation are the standards for rewriting received sources.

However, by rewriting, what if the medieval author fails to achieve his or her expressed intention? Jean's whole intervention in defense of his *Rose* is a response to actual or anticipated criticism—criticism that brands his continuation as objectionable because of its foul language, misogyny, and representation of religious corruption. Jean's defense of the last charge is typical. He claims that his representation of Faux Semblant as a religious strikes only those who fit the description—that is, those who put themselves in his aim by mirroring the character illustrating, in this case, religious hypocrisy. Faux Semblant includes some religious among his followers, but not all religious exemplify Faux Semblant. This explanation indeed fits the new title Jean gives to his continuation of Guillaume: *Miroër aus Amoreus*. He intends to ridicule only those who see themselves reflected in the romance. But, to return to the question, how reliable is the textual mirror? I address that issue in chapter 5.

The third problem referred to above asks how well informed the *Rose*'s audiences were about the sources Jean cites. For example, how many women knew Latin well enough to consult the authorities Jean recommends to them or detect the irony in the Jealous Husband's reference to Boethius?[40] Reason puts her finger on this issue when she states that it would be well if someone were to translate Boethius so that lay people might profit from reading him. This certainly indicates that at the time Jean wrote the *Rose* he knew of no French-language translation of the *Philosophiae consolatio*.[41] His intention again meets that expressed some one hundred years earlier by Benoît de Sainte-Maure, who wrote the *Troie* for the benefit of those without Latin.[42] This brings us back to the crucial issue of the lay audience. Unless Jean's implied public knew Latin well and had read the works he cited or was in a position to verify his explicit or hidden quotes and references by consulting a clerical authority (cf. v. 18254–56), these statements mean that a vast intertextuality is foreclosed to them. In fact, Jean's interventions elsewhere suggest that his implied audience would not be interested in such scholarship. For example, in reviewing the problem of divine foreknowledge and free will, Nature says she does not intend to elaborate on a subject so difficult to understand, since lay audiences want rough examples requiring no extensive glossing. Since Nature's explanation is based on Boethius's argument for free will her words are tantamount to saying that her audience would not desire to know Boethius. Later, she evokes the same audience—"genz lais" (v. 18247)—to justify cutting short the discussion of optics. Lay folk want a general, easily understood explanation. Clearly, reading Boethius would require an effort and a will the lay audiences did not possess, and which they were in any case not inclined in indulge in, even in translation. Surely this would be true for works by Augustine and Alain de Lille too.

The issue here intersects with the second problem raised above. If Reason thinks that the laity should have access to a good translation of the *Consolation*, yet Nature implies that its members would not be interested in it—which seems to be true of Amant as well—where should the reader as audience locate him- or herself? Certainly, knowledge of sources may interest scholars because intertextual subtleties or details may enrich our reading of the *Rose*. But we scholars are not the only audience Jean envisaged. If the *Rose* is intended for a wider audience, then it must be readily comprehensible without recourse to sources readers cannot easily comprehend, and might not wish to read or even have access to.

The implied audience was probably not presumed capable of the intertextual reflection scholars undertake at this distance in time from the thirteenth century. But our examination of that intertextuality can show how Jean came to write the *Rose* and what he wanted an unlearned yet perceptive and apparently critical audience to learn from hearing it read. That the audience could be critical is vouched for by the intervention in which Jean responds to criticism of his language, misogyny, and antifraternalism. That his answers were not satisfying or convincing to all is apparent from the history of *Rose* reception until as late as the "Querelle" at the turn of the fifteenth century.

The fourth problem mentioned above is that we must take account of Jean's originality, his new array of material in the *Rose*. If the Jealous Husband cites Boethius, Nature cites Aristotle, and Reason cites Ovid, what artistry explains these rather astonishing choices of authorities by such diverse, unlikely voices? Medieval conceptions of rewriting suggest that we must assume and identify the rhetorical strategies the new version adopts and adapts from the sources by rewriting and rearranging them with new material and in new contexts.

I shall begin with the letter—the literal *Roman de la rose*. Fundamental to any reading of the *Rose* that aspires to recover its *sentence* is the obvious meaning of its literal text for a lay public unskilled in subtle glossing. This requires examination of the voice relating the dream—the narrative's Jean de Meun. The ensuing chapters follow the guidelines set down in the introduction. Chapter 2 will identify the literal levels—the interlaced and juxtaposed narratives and narrative segments that make up the dream plot of the *Rose*. It will consider the content and arrangement of the literal matter subject to allegorical rereading and elucidation. But before discussing that allegory, chapters 3 and 4 analyze Jean's treatment of the plot—his *modus tractandi*, that is, the modes of treatment of his poetic material that produce coherent, sustained readings of the text. Those readings are the subject of chapter 5.

I have deliberately cast the topics of each chapter in the plural. As I hope to show, the *Rose* has more than one literal level, mode of elaboration, and allegorical reading. Indeed, that plurality is a fundamental feature of the romance. It ultimately allows us to escape the confusion of earlier efforts to reconcile differences and reduce the *Rose* to a single, unified plot and meaning; we may hope thereby to achieve a deeper appreciation of the network of materials, treatments, and meanings that make up the work's montage—its combination of literal and allegorical materials.[43] In doing so, we may also discover something about ourselves.

2

The Literal Texts: Language and Letter

Amors ont fet de moi grant miröer:
Qui sages est, grant essample i puet prendre.
—Oede de la Couroierie

[Love has made a great mirror of me. The wise can find in it a powerful example.]

READING ALLEGORIES

In the *Prison amoureuse*, Jean Froissart, alias Flos, receives a letter from his friend and correspondent, Rose. The letter reports a dream Rose had which he wants Flos to interpret. In order to understand better the intent of the dream, Flos says he first read some six folios before returning to the beginning.

Des foelles lisi jusqu'a sis
Et puis recommenchai mon tour
A la premiere page, pour
Mieuls concevoir et cler entendre
A quoi la matere poet tendre,
Qui me sambla belle et jolie.[1]

[I read up to six leaves, then began again at the beginning in order better to comprehend and clearly understand what the intent was of the matter that seemed to me beautiful and pleasant.]

The dream is an allegory. Flos's reading of it suggests that to understand an allegorical work, whether a dream like that contained in Rose's letter, or the *Roman de la rose* itself, the reader must first construe the literal narrative. This includes a first reading of at least a significant part of the work in order to identify the context and intent of its subject matter. The first reading focuses on the matter until the intent is clear; the second reading is informed by that intent. Jacqueline Cerquiglini has likened such reading to the deciphering of anagrams: one must learn how to take the constituent elements of the anagram apart and put them back together again in the second reading.[2]

The anagram provides an excellent analogy for this chapter. The anagram is made up of letters that may, in enigmas, signify no more than the letters of the alphabet they represent; or they may form a word or sentence with its own obvious literal meaning. But the reader must determine what other meaning or meanings the letters have, often by rearranging them so as to show a second sense. Similarly in allegory one must begin with the letter. *Littera gesta docet*, according to a medieval commonplace—the letter is the story. In the *Rose* this is the dreamer's story of how he tried to pluck the rose and, in Jean's continuation, succeeded in doing so. In this chapter I shall therefore focus on the *Rose*'s letter—its language and plot in the light of the major sources Jean de Meun rewrites, Ovid and Boethius—in order, in subsequent chapters, to facilitate the kind of allegorical rereadings Froissart's passage exemplifies.

Froissart is reading allegory as a medieval reader might. I propose to apply Froissart's paradigm for rereading to the *Roman de la rose*, beginning, as he did, with the literal level—the "matere . . . belle et jolie" in Froissart's words, which recalls Guillaume de Lorris's recommendation of his own "matire . . . bone et nueve" (v. 39)[3] [good, new matter]. In doing so, we shall be alert to contexts and intentions that prepare for rereading one or more times. And since allegory is clearly an organizing device of the *Rose*, and since readings of allegory must begin with the letter, that is where I shall begin discussion in this chapter. But first a few words about allegory itself.

By definition allegory traditionally has at least two levels of meaning: the literal and the allegorical. Each level is "other," that is, different in meaning from the other level (*aliud . . . aliud*). Yet, each level is a necessary complement to the other and is, indeed, essential to full understanding of the work. As an extended metaphor, allegory is a trope which effectively transforms a word or thought from its proper meaning into another meaning.[4] This is what Reason does, for example, when she uses the word *coilles*—roughly, "testicles" (v. 5507)—in its proper sense, then endows it with another sense as part of an *integumentum*. Reason argues that *coilles* is the proper word for the referent and that the word literally designates what it refers to, Saturn's testicles. But once we have understood that much, Reason continues, we must also realize that the word has in her mind a second meaning different from its literal sense, but equally important. That is the integumental explanation of how good love is replaced by harsh justice in her account of the decline of humanity from the Golden Age to the Iron Age that began when Jupiter castrated his father Saturn.

Imbedded in Reason's justification of her language is a second allegory, one which Amant will adopt later in order to speak improperly on the literal level. Reason argues that had she named "coilles reliques" and "reliques coilles" (v. 7081–82), Amant would have faulted her for using the word *reliques*. Yet, he himself improperly uses *reliques* and similar religious language to describe the sex act by which the rose is plucked, thereby covering up rather than unfolding a literal meaning. Here, allegory has replaced the literal in order to embellish, but also to veil what is literally being referred to. In both cases, we have allegory, which can be understood and appreciated only after we grasp the letter of the text and its literal context.

As in the *Prison amoureuse*, neither the literal nor the allegorical level offers a single reading. There is more than one *matière* just as there is more than one allegorical reading in the composite *Roman de la rose*. This is certainly due in part to dual authorship. But it also derives from the multiple interlacing narratives of the dream and from the different voices—the narrator and other speakers whose commentary punctuates and complicates the reading and interpretation of the work in its totality. Since allegory elaborates upon the literal and the second sense or senses, the literal sense must be understood first, and authorities in the Middle Ages traditionally viewed the letter as the *sine qua non* of any allegory.[5]

We are familiar with the multiplication of levels in allegory's second level, like the allegorical, tropological, and anagogical levels of biblical exegesis, or the even greater number of levels in texts like the moralizations of Ovid (including, for example, "historical" and "astrological" readings[6]). But the *Rose* also contains more than one literal plot, and thus more than one literal level. The plots include Amant's waking experience; his dream as such; the personal experiences recounted by some personifications, especially Ami and the Vieille; numerous mythological examples like Venus's loves; historical examples like Nero, Manfred, and Heloise and Abelard; and, finally, brief exemplary tales that support various points, like Phanie and Croesus. The strategies Jean uses to deploy these literal but diverse plots are imitated and adapted principally from Guillaume de Lorris, Ovid's *Ars amatoria*, and Boethius.[7]

THE *ROSE*'S PLOT

Most of the literal narratives are amplifications of the main plot, Amant's dream experience. Alan Gunn and Daniel Poirion have distinguished the narrative in Jean's poem from its amplificatory departures in orations, sermons, dialogues, debates, and digressions.[8] Yet, both show how difficult it often is to disentangle and section off the main plot from its amplifications. Nonetheless, the primary plot in Jean's continuation—albeit truly overwhelmed by the amplifications—is more extensive than in Guillaume. By primary plot I mean the story of Amant's progress toward his goal, not the separate narratives that punctuate and amplify his story. Since Amant's dream narrative is the source of and the frame for the orations, sermons, dialogues, debates, and digressions that make up its amplifications, and since the plot is the foundation for the *Rose*'s allegory, the reader must grasp that plot well before proceeding to an appreciation of the amalgam of topical and allegorical glosses on it.[9]

Jean's "first author" is Guillaume de Lorris.[10] Guillaume's romance is also the first part of Jean's. Moreover, the plot summaries show that in Jean's part "On reconnaît, dans un ordre différent, l'intrigue suivie par Guillaume de Lorris: tentative de détournement par Raison, conseils d'Ami, fidélité confirmée à Amour, essai de se concilier Bel Acueil pour s'approcher de la rose, obstacle représenté par Danger, Honte et Peur, secours de Vénus armée d'un brandon enflammé."[11] Guillaume de Lorris is not only the *Rose*'s first author. He is also Jean's primary source and narrative model.

The episodes identified in both authors by Gunn, Poirion, Lecoy, and others may be roughly schematized as follows (GL = Guillaume de Lorris, JM = Jean de Meun). Amant asks for Rose, that is, the rose (GL 2771–903 = JM 14723–86),[12] but she rebuffs him (GL 2904–34, 3493–542 = JM 14787–5045). Amant bemoans his bad luck (GL 2935–54, 3920–4028 = JM 4029–190). Reason intervenes (GL 2955–3082 = JM 4191–7200), followed by Ami (GL 3083–134 = JM 7201–9984). Just as Jealousy mobilizes her forces (GL 3510–742), so too the God of Love does his (JM 10409–1984). Jealousy raises the castle (GL 3779–919), which the God of Love lays siege to (JM 11985–5104, 15273–860). The Vieille is brought in to guide Bel Acueil (GL 3902–8j = JM 12355–4689). Finally, Amant takes the castle (GL 3486 = JM 20673–1749).

Jean's originality emerges in the last episodes, which include the first attack on the castle and its capture in the second attack. Guillaume promises to relate these events, but does not do so in his surviving torso.

> Des or est droiz que je vos conte
> Coment je fui melez a Honte,
> Par qui je fui puis mout grevez,
> Et coment li murs fu levez

Et li chastiaus riches e forz,
Qu'Amors prist puis par ses esforz.
(V. 3481–86; emphasis mine)[13]

[Now it is right for me to tell you how I got into trouble with Shame, who caused me a lot of grief, and how the castle walls were raised which Love afterwards captured by his armed attack.]

Into these episodes of siege and assault Jean introduces Faux Semblant; the Vieille's discourse; the first, unsuccessful penetration into Jealousy's castle, which falls short of its goal because of Peur's firm resistance and Amant's decision not to resort to rape (v. 15563–601, 15623–28); Nature's complaint to Genius; Genius's sermon; and the intervention of Venus. The major change, noted as early as Gui de Mori's second adaptation of the *Rose*,[14] is the reintroduction of Venus and a conclusion different from that in Guillaume's announcement of his own projected conclusion: Venus, not Love, takes the castle.[15] Thus Jean's major source is in fact "unfaithfully" reproduced in order to rewrite Guillaume's projected conclusion. Venus and Genius cooperate to effect the final "consummation," while the God of Love stands by.

There is additional evidence of Jean's infidelity to his source. Three major events distinguish Jean's plot from Guillaume's: Venus's and Genius's intervention, Amant's attempt to enlist Richesse's aid in order to buy the rose, and, last but hardly least, his decision to accept deceit and betrayal—and thus seduction—following, thereby, Ami's counsel and preparing for the introduction of Faux Semblant and Abstinence Contrainte among his attributes just after the romance's mathematical midpoint (v. 10875; v. 10890 in Langlois's edition). This is by far the most important change because it alters fundamentally the notion of love inherited from the God of Love's instructions in Guillaume's poem and prepares the way for Venus's triumph after the God of Love's failure.

Traïson me covint tracier
Por ma besoigne porchacier;
Onc traïstres n'avoie esté,
N'oncor ne m'en a nus resté.
(V. 10273–76)[16]

[I was obliged to practice deception in order to reach my goal. I had never betrayed anyone nor has anyone yet accused me of doing so.]

Betrayal with impunity is Faux Semblant's talent. Moreover, in adapting Ami's counsel to give as little as possible despite profligate promises, Amant will abandon generosity as well after having failed to achieve his goal on the road of Trop Doner (v. 10038–239) and will assume the greediness of Faux Semblant (v. 11203–30, 11523–36).[17] Payen has noted that Largess plays only a token role in the attack on Jealousy's castle, giving a shield to Franchise colored with promises and entreaties (v. 15303–11).[18] Indeed, Amant's self-serving largess breaks a tenet not only of the God of Love, but also of Reason who in Jean approves of the exchange of small gifts between lovers who fit her definition of *amitié*, or friendship (v. 4549–56). His intention to deceive and betray survives the conclusion, where Amant refers to his subsequent infidelities after the rose has been plucked, justifying sexual sampling as analogous to culinary sampling (v. 21521–31).

The place of deceit in seduction is a commonplace issue in medieval poetry. Several *jeux-partis* catch the moment of decision between deceit and honesty in love.

> Le quel ariés vous plus chier,
> Ou vo dame a gaaingnier
> Outre son gré, par droite traïson,
> Ou li servir loiaument en pardon
> Trestoute vo vie,
> Et si s'en tiengne a païe?[19]

> [Which would you prefer: to win your lady against her will, by outright deceit, or to serve her faithfully all your life, but without recompense, and leave it at that?]

This poem seems to ask us to choose between Jean's version of Amant's love and Guillaume's. In another *jeu-parti*, one speaker argues that a woman's refusal admits any kind of violence to bring her in line, much as the Jealous Husband does (LXXX); still another contrasts such violence with complacency analogous to that recommended by Ami (XXXV, LXXVII, CXXXIII). The scenarios Jean adapts are thus commonplace. They would be easily recognized by audiences familiar with issues raised in the tradition of "courtly deceit."

Also stemming from Amant's adoption of treachery and deceit, Jean adapts Guillaume's *Rose* in other ways. He introduces, for example, new elements while deleting others from Guillaume's version of love as set forth by the God of Love in his commandments to Amant. First, Ami's advice to feign indifference to the rose in Guillaume is personified in Jean as Faux Semblant and Abstinence Contrainte. These agents of deceit overcome Male Bouche, the agent who earlier betrayed the cooperation of the God of Love and Bel Acueil following the kiss in Guillaume's poem. The Vieille also deletes generosity and fidelity from the God of

Love's commandments (v. 12981–13030). Bel Acueil should show no generosity, even in small things. The woman should also abjure fidelity in order to profit from a multiplicity of lovers. The Vieille's advice shows her no longer to be the effective enemy of love envisaged by Guillaume, but rather a go-between who profits not only from encouraging lovers and bringing them together, but also from promoting the woman's deception of her lovers.

These statements place both Amant and Bel Acueil squarely among the seducers. Theirs is the "art de baraz" (v. 21442), the art of deceit personified by Faux Semblant's father, Barat. Faux Semblant may well be an attribute of Amant in the *Rose*, but the notion he personifies is very much part of the Vieille's lesson to Bel Acueil. The model for both men and women is, of course, Ovid's art of love—the art Jean mined for both Ami and the Vieille: "Ausinc doit fame par tout tendre / Ses raiz por touz les homes prendre" (v. 13559–60) [that is how a woman must set her snares everywhere to catch all men]. These adaptations capture in large measure Jean's extensive use of material drawn from Ovid's *Ars amatoria*.[20]

Ovid's three books treat both the man and the woman in the game of love, thereby allowing Jean license to reveal the mind of the woman in the *Rose*, which was largely neglected by Guillaume de Lorris. Still, Guillaume does name a woman, Rose, whom he says he loves (v. 40–44). She is analogous to the rose who becomes the object of Amant's dream quest. Let us therefore follow the *Renart* paradigm as allegory.[21] The *Renart* cycle conflated the irascible human named Renart with the fox, or *goupil* in Old French, so that the proper noun became synonymous with the deceitful fox. Similarly, we may refer to Amant and Rose, each with his and her attributes, attendant personifications, and plot.

Doing so reveals that Jean draws from Ovid an art of seduction which he incorporates liberally into Ami's advice; for Rose he puts into the Vieille's mouth material drawn from the third book of the *Ars amatoria* on how women may manipulate seduction to their own advantage. The personification of Faux Semblant and the cooperation between him and the Vieille after he introduces Amant into the castle develop the plot in the direction of mutual seduction involving both pleasure and deception. In fact, Ovid provides a context and ambience that allows Guillaume's plot not only a horizontal progression from sight to consummation, but also a vertical curve downward, a descent from a quest for love to a quest for multiple sexual conquests. Both Jean and Ovid address a coeducational student body.

Jean's *Rose* contains no postcoital continuation. Amant merely returns to the waking world in the last line. But we can easily surmise what would have happened afterward, as in Ovid, from the numerous examples that punctuate the discourses of the *Rose*'s speakers. Branching out from Jean's literal adaptation of Ovid, other literal amplifications are compared to and thereby integrated into the plot as well. This reversal of the normal order of events—relating what takes place in a topical scheme like the postcoital preservation of love (*conservatio amoris*) or decline of love (*deminutio amoris*) ahead of time—is referred to in rhetorical and poetic handbooks as artificial order.[22] Amant and Rose can see in these narratives sequels to their own story in diverse, but analogous scenarios. Here, artificial order serves, subliminally as it were, to caution Amant and Rose as to the consequences of their acts. The denouement of these plots stands in stark contrast to the projected joys of orgasm that initiate them, as we shall see (pp. 37–38, 75).

Jean's continuation is told in artificial order in this sense by various speakers: Reason, Ami, and Richesse for Amant, the Vieille for Rose. Such a strategy permits illustration of the nefarious effects of *amour maladie*, as Reason defines it at the same time Amant imagines future bliss and Rose looks to future conquests and plunder. It also spreads out before the mind's eye the diverse fates of lovers—not much different from those foreseen by Reason—as related by those knowledgeable and experienced voices who participate in the seduction. An array of possibilities emerges as the literal narrative progresses through the experiences of the speakers, notably Ami and the Vieille, and the numerous mythographic and historical examples: love as friendship and as malady in conjugal, extra- or premarital, and adulterous relationships.

Prospects are gloomy on the path of friendless love in Jean's *Rose*. Both men and women mutually use, abuse, and deceive one another, as both Ami and the Vieille attest. To assert one's own authority, like the Jealous Husband in marriage, is no way to happiness either. Whether the Husband's complaint about his wife's activities is correct or not, whether she is the unjustly abused wife or the profligate adulteress, life and love for him and her are wretched. The Vieille herself, when young, loved without benefit of marriage, yet her experiences are not unlike those of the Jealous Husband's wife. Her love was a failure. As she admits with the benefit of hindsight: to have stayed with her gambling, abusive, useless *ribaut* was stupid. *Caveat Rosa*!

These examples are warnings, practical warnings which support Jean's integration of Boethius on the rewards of false goods. Reason forewarns, Ami and the Vieille forewarn. Yet Amant, like Ami and the Vieille before him, perseveres in his descent into the transitory joys and inevitable calamities of *amour maladie*. The conclusion of the *Rose* suggests a like fate for the woman. Like Andreas Capellanus, another source for the *Rose*, Jean displays an array of exemplary situations; but unlike those in the *De amore*, all the examples point to calamity and misfortune. A glance at the *Rose*'s mythological examples tells the same story: Paris and Oenone, Juno and Jupiter, Hercules and Dianira, Jason and Medea. . . . The exemplary loves that illustrate Ami's and the Vieille's instruction end in infidelity, abuse, and disaster. As the Vieille advises Bel Acueil, one gives nothing, but grabs everything—including more and more lovers. Paradoxically, one finds no love. "Jean fully intended as one of his points the one great and shocking omission from his book: any character who loves anyone."[23] In other words, Jean's *Rose* is a negative *exemplum* that raises moral issues.

Let us then turn to Jean's third major source, Boethius. Here too minor verbal alterations reveal major adaptations of Guillaume's version. Issues in Boethius are moral, as based on authoritative precept or on individual moral sense. Jean combines them by making Boethius both source and model. It is indeed astonishing how many aspects of Boethius's *Consolation* are mirrored in Jean's *Rose*.[24] This is especially evident from Jean's translation, where verbal echoes alert the reader to analogous passages in the *Rose*. To be sure, Jean does not merely copy or paraphrase Boethius. For example, as Patricia Eberle notes, Jean's Nature modifies Boethius on predestination.[25] On the authority of the Bible, that is, Nature rewrites the mirror Boethius says God gazes on as God's own mind.[26]

Perhaps more obviously, Jean's continuation begins with lamentations just as Boethius's *Consolation* does. Thus, Philosophy's condemnation of the songs of secular muses mirrors Reason's critique of Amant's love, thereby transforming Guillaume's part of the poem into Boethius's hopelessly secular, elegiac songs. The *chansonettes* of Boethius's youth recall the lyric *chansons* which Guillaume transformed into an allegorical dream.[27] It follows that Reason's appearance rehearses that of Philosophy. Similarly, Jean's adoption of dialogue and debate as the principal mode of amplification is adumbrated not only in the dialogue of Philosophy and Boethius, but more specifically in projected dialogues between Boethius and Reason herself, like that in Book V of Jean's translation of the *Consolation*: "Se *R*aison voloit a ces chosez encontre respondre et deist . . . "[28] [If Reason wished to respond to these matters, saying . . .].

But there are noteworthy cautionary notes to heed. To begin with, nothing in Jean's translation of Boethius explicitly draws these parallels between the *Rose* and the *Consolation*. In the preface to the translation, as we have observed, Jean refers only to its literal intent: "Je Jehan de Meun qui jadis ou Rommant de la Rose, puis que Jalousie ot mis en prison Bel Acueil, enseignai la maniere du chastel prendre et de la rose cueillir" (p. 168. 2–4) [In the *Roman de la rose*, beginning with Jealousy's imprisonment of Bel Acueil, I Jean de Meun once taught how to take the castle and pluck the rose].

Another difference is that Boethius is older than Amant. Although Reason and others warn him, Rose, and the reader about the advent of old age, Amant is still young and *cupidus*, in Matthew of Vendôme's sense. That is, among the "extrinsic topoi," Matthew identifies age (*aetas*) with an example from Ovid: "A iuvene et cupido credatur reddita virgo?" (*Ars versificatoria* §§1.82 and 1.115) [Could a woman be returned a virgin by a passionate young man?] The Ovidian quote aptly foreshadows Amant. By contrast, Boethius's age and stage in life befits a man on in years, one who has known sorrow and loss and is disposed to heed the voice of Reason. Amant is only starting out in life and, in context, is himself a virgin. His prurient lust fits Matthew's description and his own nature as *fol amoureux* when he refuses to heed Reason's counsel.

These differences mark Book II of the *Consolation* as a break between the two works. Boethius is prepared to heed Philosophy, whereas Amant is unwilling to listen to Reason. In other words, Jean's narrative deflects from Boethius's path to consolation, digressing into the seige of Jealousy's castle and the plucking of the rose (v. 9973–76, 10223–24, 10317–38, 21730–31). By this digression, Jean's mirror image of the *Consolation* refracts, even distorts, the source. The question naturally arises whether Jean is correcting Boethius or rewriting him, using antithesis to teach the same lesson, much as, in the *Anticlaudianus*, Alain de Lille rewrote Claudian's *In Rufinum* by inventing a *homo novus* to replace the evil Rufinus.

In the context of the *Consolation*, the *Rose* functions as a special instance. That is, among the exemplary kinds of false goods Philosophy enumerates—wealth, honor, power, fame, and bodily pleasures—the *Rose* focuses on the last. To be sure, other false goods, in Boethius's sense, are introduced at various places in the text, but they serve principally as digressions that establish analogies with the goal of plucking the rose or further Amant's progress toward that goal. For example, if Richesse were cooperative, Amant might more quickly achieve his ends, just as honor or fame might enhance his chances of winning favor in Rose's eyes, making her more pliant. Similarly, lust for power is at issue in the near rape with which the tournament involving Amant and Rose ends. Thus, Jean has condensed an array of Boethius's false goods into a compact collection that focuses on carnal delight as the supreme good in Amant's eyes (cf. Boethius, Book III Prose ii.1–47/2.1–12).

Reason's evaluation of false goods is indeed modeled on Philosophy's.[29] At the beginning of the *Consolation*, Boethius suffers from a "maladie de pensees" (Book I Prose ii.11/2.5.10–11)[30] (mental illness); in the *Rose*, Amant suffers from the same malady. Reason's translation of Andreas Capellanus's definition of *passio* includes this expression: "C'est maladie de pensee" (v. 4348). That is why, she says, Amant is a *fol amoureux* (v. 4212, 4643, 5457; cf. v. 6564–66), and, as stated earlier, both sides in the fifteenth-century "Querelle" agree with her. In the context of Jean's *Rose*, then, folly is the rejection of reason in favor of carnal rewards. When Amant rejects Reason at the end of his debate with her, it is because the rose, or carnal delight, is more important to him than is reason. To Boethius's Philosophy, this overturns the divinely established hierarchy. The Latin text reads: "Iam uero qui bona prae se corporis ferunt, quam exigua, quam fragili possessione nituntur!" (Book III Prose viii.7.13–14) [Indeed, those who prefer carnal goods—how weak and uncertain are the possessions they rely on!]. Jean's translation makes the link to the *Rose* even more specific than Boethius's text by adding to it a contrast with those goods Reason provides: "Or apert donques ja comme cil s'apuient a petite et a foible possession qui metent les biens du corps *au dessus de leur raison*" (Book III Prose viii.12–14)[31] [Now it is apparent how those who value carnal goods *more than those of reason* are relying on weak and uncertain possessions]. When Amant places his conquest of Rose above Reason's friendship, he rests his happiness on weak and uncertain foundations.

Thus Jean's *Rose* is indeed an "anti-Boethius" in the sense that Alain de Lille's rewriting of Claudian is an *Anticlaudianus*. Just as the *homo novus*, or New Man, is the opposite of the anti-hero in Claudian's *In Rufinum*, so Amant is the opposite of Boethius in the *Consolation*. Moreover, Jean also re-creates some of the forces in Allecto's army gathered to fight the New Man in the *Anticlaudianus* in his own *Rose*. It is remarkable to what extant the following lines on Lust and Folly provide material for the *fol amoureux*:

> Assiduus fomes scelerum carnisque tiranus,
> Peccati stimulus, delicti flamma, reatus
> Principium, predo nostre racionis et hostis,
> In tantam pugne rabiem bellique furores
> Currit, in auxilium cuius mouet arma Reatus,
> Velle malum, Calor illicitus, damnosa Voluptas.
> Stulticiam non turba minor, non rarior armat
> Conuentus procerum; comes est Ignauia, Ludi,
> Segnicies, Nuge, Garritus, Occia, Sompni.[32]

["The ever-present tinder-box of evil deeds, the tyrant of the flesh, the goad to sin, the flame of transgression, the source of guilt, the enemy and

> plunderer of our reason flies into a great rage for battle and a fury for war: Guilt, Malevolence, unlawful Passion, ruinous Pleasure take up arms to help him. No smaller host, no less packed assembly of chiefs equip Foolishness with arms: her companions are Laziness, Frivolity, Indolence, trifling Talk, Chatter, Leisure, Sleep."]

Jean's *Rose*, then, is also an "anti-*Anticlaudianus*." We understand the one by comparing it to its opposite, and both point to the same moral lesson.

In other words, Jean has expanded the *Rose* into a masterful instance of *contrarietas* in Gervase of Melkley's sense: "Contrarietas est a rebus vel dictionibus contrariis ornata sententia, cuius species sunt allegoria et entimema" (*Ars versificaria*, p. 155.1–2) [*Contrarietas* is an ornate sentence made up of opposing things or words; its species are allegory and the enthymeme]. Importantly, allegory can be shaped by various forms of irony. This, in the end, is what distinguishes the *Rose* in its relations to Boethius as source from the *Anticlaudianus* and its source. For by writing the contrary of what Boethius does, it does not appear on the surface to correct the source. Amant sees his love throughout as a supreme good. Readers correct the perspective, because of the subsidiary material persisting in the allegory, thereby producing irony, that is, a trope that "confiteri videbitur quod negare intendit" (*Ars versificaria*, p. 155.8–9) [acknowledges what it appears to deny]. The *Rose* furthermore illustrates the enthymeme through the *contrarium*, which occurs "quando duobus repugnantibus positis alterum probatur vel improbatur per reliquum" (*Ars versificaria*, p. 158.1–2) [when two contradictory statements are posited, the one is proved or denied by the other]. Thus, two readings exist at the same time, intending to privilege one by inference. Allegory as a species of *contrarietas* disproves its letter as a self-sufficient meaning and condemns seduction by both men and women. It does so by teaching that one should not pluck or offer roses because the action is foolish and morally wrong.

The *Rose*'s two readings are reflected in the reception of the *Rose* from the Middle Ages to this day. Either the work teaches us in worldly fashion how to pluck roses, as Jean's preface to his translation of Boethius states; or it shows us the moral degeneration such activity represents, a picture with which Boethius would surely agree in principle. These readings fit the two possible titles Patricia Eberle has proposed for Jean's *Miroër*: "Lovers' Glass" in which the Amants and Roses of the world may view themselves, and Love's "optical instrument" that offers "a multiplicity of perspectives on the subject of love and in the dream-vision itself."[33]

In this sense, Ovid and Boethius are two distinct mirrors through which Jean refracts Guillaume's dream into new forms and meanings. The literal text is analogous to Ovid's art of seduction; as such, it undercuts the "courtly" intent of Guillaume's beginning by recourse to deceit. By the Boethian refraction, the *Rose* reads as a counterexample of the *Consolation*, anticipating the definitive conclusion in the fifteenth-century "Querelle": Amant is a *fol amoureux*. This refraction also undermines the "courtly" intent of Guillaume, contrasting Guillaume's elevation of sentiment from lust to love with the degeneration of Amant from Reason's "reasonable loves" to a deceitful, carnal love dominated by Faux Semblant. This descent is specifically marked by Amant's appeal to Richesse for quick gratification and, when this option is denied him, by the reception of Faux Semblant and Abstinence Contrainte among Love's barons. In the feminine complex[34] of Rose, a similar decline is marked by the Vieille's and, apparently, by Bel Acueil's rejection of Love's commandments to be faithful and generous within one's means, commandments that distinguish love as friendship between man and woman in Reason's analysis.

To be sure, the major Boethian counterpoint begins to be obvious even before Reason departs. But once deprived of reason, the one faculty by which Amant can know himself and his actions, he is left with only bits and pieces of truth, like Boethius when he was unable to answer all the questions Philosophy put to him about himself (Book I Prose vi). Like the various specialized schools of ancient philosophy, Boethius as prisoner believes he possesses the whole truth when he has only its shreds (Book I Prose iii). The same holds for Amant. Thus, it is not surprising to hear Genius mix literally true images of Paradise with a deficient morality based on carnality. The corrupt imagination (Book III Prose i.17–22/5, Prose ix.91–94/31.82–85),[35] uninformed by reason, knows, yet does not know the truth about itself (Book V Meter iii.19–26/25–31). Like the first-person narrator in Svevo's novel, *La coscienza di Zeno*, Amant might say of himself: "Posso ritenermi un buon osservatore ma un buon osservatore alquanto cieco."[36] [I may consider myself a good observer, but one with rather poor sight.]

This particular dynamic is important for interpreting Amant's satisfaction at the end of the *Rose*.

> Quant an si haut degré me vi,
> Que j'oi si noblemant chevi
> Que mes procés n'iert mes doutables,
> Por ce que fins et agreables

> Fusse ver touz mes biensfeteurs,
> Si con doit fere bons deteurs,
> Car mout estoie a eus tenuz
> Quant par eus iere devenuz
> Si riche.
>
> (V. 21713–21)

[When I saw myself so advanced that I had nobly succeeded and my goal was no longer in doubt, so that I would be fair and pleasant toward all my benefactors, as a good debtor ought to be—for I was very beholden to them when by their intercession I had become so prosperous.]

These words apparently contradict Philosophy's assertion that those like Amant are never truly satisfied (Book II Meter ii). The words deceive, as Jean's addition to Boethius's assertion, shown below in italics, points in the direction of Amant's true dissatisfaction beyond the end of the *Rose*: "Si leur semblera il que il n'ont encores riens aquis, mais leur cruele rapine devoranz les chosez aquises euvre encores sa gueule *et ses girons*[37] *et bee a plus avoir d'autre part*" (Book II Meter ii.8–10/12–14) [and they will think they have gained nothing; rather rapaciously consuming everything they acquire they open their maul *and their lap and seek to have even more*]. Before Faux Semblant joins Love's ranks, Amant is prepared to die in possessing the rose; nonetheless, after that possession, he details other conquests: the wayside furrows and holes, young and old, he has opened his breeches or tunic for (v. 21367–404; cf. 21509–31). The rose-(bush) itself has no doubt been returned to by others, despite Amant's fatuous trust in Rose's fidelity (cf. v. 21630–37 with v. 12963–70).

Paralleling the dramatic irony informing the Boethius figure's delusion that he has knowledge of the complete truth, Amant's blissful ignorance cannot, after all, be satisfactory: "Car quant il regardent non mie l'ordre des chosez, mais leur *tenebreus* entalentement [= Boethius's affectus], il cuident ou que li laisirs des maus fere ou que li eschapemens sans paine soit beneureuz" (Book IV Prose iv.96–98/27.86–87) [For they do not consider the order of things, but instead their *dark* desire, presuming either that the ease to do evil or escaping from it without difficulty is happiness]. Amant reduces the Boethian contrast between age and youth (Book I Prose i), rehearsed as well by Reason (v. 4400–514), to a comparison between old and young *cons* (v. 21405–552). Even carnal pleasure seems to elude Amant. He expresses only pride and nervous, chattering relief after an objective, virtually clinical description of the spilling and mixing of seed.[38] Amant's moral blindness is perfectly evident here, and would be so even to those who cannot read Boethius, because Jean has patterned the entire seduction on moral blindness. Hearing Genius's sermon and Amant's enactment of its lesson would make that obvious to any alert medieval reader prepared to reflect on what he or she has heard about how one merits salvation.

THE NAMES OF THINGS

The metaphorical clinical description is critical, for names change in the corrupt imagination, and with them our perception of things. Philosophy warns Boethius of this: "Vous vous esjoissiés en nomer les chosez par faulz noms qui sont d'autre nature que vous ne leur mettéz assuz, si comme il est legierement prouvé par le fait de ces chosez meismez" (Book II Prose vi.62–64/19.55–57) [you delight in incorrectly naming things which have a nature different from those which you assign to them, as can be easily demonstrated on the evidence of the things themselves]. Her words raise the issue of the proper use of language, which is critical to working with the literal level of the *Rose* allegory. The fault against nature to which Boethius refers is as egregious as those grammatical faults against Nature castigated in the opening poem of Alain's *De planctu Naturae*.[39] Indeed, Amant's own abuse of language is patent in the description of his sex act, where he substitutes religious language for the proper names of genitals. As we have seen, the effect, at once ironic and ludicrous, is anticipated and enhanced to underscore improper language. Reason asserts:

> Se je, quant mis les nons aus choses
> Que si reprendre et blasmer oses,
> Coilles reliques apelasse
> Et reliques coilles clamasse,
> Tu, qui si m'en morz et depiques,
> Me redeïsses de reliques
> Que ce fust lez moz et vilains.
> (V. 7079–85)

> [if I, when I assigned to things the names which you correct and blame me for in this way, had called balls[40] relics and relics balls, you, who carp at me scornfully, would tell me that relics was an ugly, vile word.]

Reason is appealing to a source and authority that everyone in Jean's implied audience knew and could understand: the French language. That is, everyone could understand it literally. But literal understanding is not sufficient in the *Rose*. The language used must be proper, and, as Jean himself later reiterates, it must be suitable to the subject and audience.

Amant's shock at Reason's language raises the issue of decorum. Although he gets over his shock quickly enough, the issue does not go away for all that. It is simply more important than a *fol amoureux* like Amant can fathom.

Let us begin with the text. Reason makes four assertions regarding *coilles*. First, in the account of the castration of Saturn, she uses the word not only literally, but—like Amant later—as a simile too: "Cui Jupiter coupa les coilles/Ses filz, con se fussent andoilles" (v. 5507–8) [Whose balls his son Jupiter cut off, as if they were wieners[41]]. Second, the objects can be named more courteously, or at least more metaphorically, as most women do, whether they be "preude fame" (V. 6906)[42] or French women in general (v. 7101); neither Reason nor Amant objects to their language (v. 6906, 7101–22, 7169–74). This, ironically, raises the possibility that Amant's later use of religious words for sexual members is permissible. Third, to name them outright is to use the proper name Reason bestowed on them by the authority vested in her by God to name things and parts of things which He created. Fourth, the *coilles* are part of an *integumentum* and thus have a second meaning, just as Amant's *reliques*,[43] *bourdon*, and *escharpe* do at the end of the *Rose*, that is, the religious objects by which he designates metaphorically his and Rose's genitalia.

Reason insists that her choice of the word *coilles* is proper in usage and therefore proper in choice; in addition, as a necessary part of the castration fable, the word has a second signification. We do not learn from her what the specific integumental sense of the word is because such glosses do not interest Amant at the moment. If they had, we might have realized how faithfully he lives out the Saturn fable at the end of the *Rose*. I shall return to this below (pp. 85–87) when discussing the exemplary reading of the fable. For the moment I should like to examine Reason's language in the light of what Boethius and some others say about proper language.

Philosophy explains in Book II of the *Consolation* that the improper use of words falsifies them and our image of nature in general (Book II Prose vi.61–66/19.55–59). In Book III, she returns to the subject of proper usage, invoking the authority of Plato: "Comme tu aies apris par la sentence de Platon qu'il couvient que les paroles soient cousinez aus chosez dont il parlent" (Book III Prose xii.102–3/38.95–96) [As you learned from Plato, words should properly be related to the topics under discussion]. Reason too cites Plato's *Timaeus* on the correct use of language to underscore her authority (v. 7069–75). Jean justifies his own choice of words in an obvious paraphrase of Boethius as he would translate him:[44] "Les voiz aus choses voisines/Doivent estre a leur fez cousines" (v. 15161–62) [Words must be related to their referents]. This is proper usage.

However, as Jean himself admits, even proper usage may not please everyone. Indeed, Poirion has noted that "l'impertinence de la parole fait douter du message."[45] Jean's own defense of his language suggests that it displeased many among his contemporaries. He mentions those who objected to his "paroles/Semblanz trop baudes ou trop foles" (v. 15131–32) [words that seem very bawdy or foolish], an echo of Amant's own reference to Reason's "parole / Si esbaulevree et si fole" (v. 5671–72) [so shameless and foolish a word]. Words that offended Christine de Pizan and Jean Gerson, it seems, were just as likely to seem offensive in the thirteenth century.[46]

Nor did decorum in *integumenta* first become an issue with Jean de Meun. Macrobius rejected a version of the castration fable because such matters are inappropriate in philosophical or moral discourse, as well as in allegories regarding the divinity.[47] Indeed, his language—"Saturnus pudenda Coeli patris abscidens" [Saturn cutting off his father Coelus's shameful members]—is certainly less racy than Reason's language. Macrobius's circumlocution forces the question of Reason's—and thus her author Jean's—shamelessness. Is her use of the specific word *coilles* and the accompanying comparison with *andoilles* decorous or indecorous? Gustav Ineichen has reminded us that poetic qualification of words gives them a different meaning from their plain or literal sense.[48] But does this justify the choice? Would it be appropriate in Boethius, Macrobius, or the Bible? Or, as Christine de Pizan pointedly asks Pierre Col: "Pour quoy ne les nonmes plainnement en ton escripture sans aler entour le pot?"[49] [Why don't you name them outright in your writing instead of beating around the bush?]

There is no simple solution to issues like these. There was none in the thirteenth century. The Fall initiated the decline and corruption of all things human, including proper language. Decorum is a means to correct language, making it fit context and audience alike. At issue is the medieval notion of Material Style. Briefly put, Material Style requires that persons appear, speak, and act such that appearances, speech, and actions conform to the type they represent.[50] According to John of Garland, Charlemagne may be described as a lover of peace ("pacis amator"), but not of his wife ("blandus amator / Vxoris").[51]

To determine the propriety of Reason's language for medieval audiences, it is instructive to regard both how other writers treat the castration of Saturn in Old French, and, more generally, in what contexts the words *coilles* and *andoilles* commonly appear together. In the *Rose* manuscript tradition, some scribes excised the specific words from Reason's summary of the fable (see p. 168 n. 46). Moreover, the *Ovide moralisé* related the castration of Saturn as part of an integument. If its anonymous author was less puritanical than Macrobius, his choice of words nonetheless differs from Reason's in the *Rose.* "Les genitaires li trencha, / Et dedens la mer les lança" (1:651–52)[52] [He cut off his genitals and threw them into the sea]. Note that the *Ovide moralisé*'s Material Style seems decorous in the Boethian context. Indeed, "genitaires"—genitals—was proper enough for Christine de Pizan to use in her own version of the castration of Saturn in the *Epistre Othea.*[53] This quick survey alone suggests that Jean's use does not seem proper.

Still, John Fleming has argued that *coilles* is the proper name for "testicles," a claim which, he asserts, "would seem to be fully justified in the light of the etymological history of Latin *culleus* in the Romance languages."[54] If he means by "etymological history" the history of usage and semantic range, he should cite his sources; the phonological and morphological development alone of the word into the Romance languages will tell us nothing about its usage proper or improper. Joking about *coilles*, *andoilles*, or any other sexual member before a passionate young man like Amant is situationally and rhetorically improper. Even we scholars still tend, I think, to use the French word rather than any English equivalent when talking about the *Rose* passage with students.

But this example may be influenced by "presentism." So let us look at use of Reason's questionable language in other medieval texts. The French translation of Abelard's *Historia calamitatum*, attributed to Jean de Meun,[55] offers some help in its version of that scholar's own castration. The word "coillons" regularly translates the Latin's *genitalia* and *testiculi.*[56] Interestingly, Abelard uses the word to refer only to his servant's testicles which were removed as punishment for betraying his master; Abelard refers only to his own *plaga* or *plaie*. The actual castration is described in euphemistic paraphrase: "Ilz me tolirent icelles parties de mon corps par lesquelz je avoye forfait ce dont ilz se plaignoient"[57] [They removed those parts of my body with which I committed the crime they were complaining about]. At no time does Abelard or the French translator indulge in humorous comparisons like that which Reason makes with *andoilles*. Besides Abelard's personal reasons for the shame and outrage he felt, which others either lamented or pointed to with horror, he is particularly sensitive to God's awful judgment upon castrates, recalling biblical texts that clearly exclude from church victims of the abomination.[58] We are far removed from Reason's bantering joke or even Nature's and Genius's disapproval of castration.

Other evidence includes Jean Le Fèvre's *Respit de la mort*,[59] a serious, moralistic *memento mori*. As noted by Fleming, Jean Le Fèvre uses the word *coillons* in an amplification on the analogy between the microcosm and the macrocosm distantly reminiscent of that in Bernardus Silvestris's *Cosmographia*.

> Et les couillons sont par dehors
> Pour aidier a l'engendreüre;
> Ou par trot ou par anbleüre
> Se joingnent pres de l'orifice.
> (V. 894–97)

[The testicles are on the body's exterior to assist in reproduction; they join at a trot or amble near the opening.]

The equine metaphor does recall the jocular tone adopted by Reason, as does another metaphorical reference to the testicles further on in the *Respit*: "Venus regarde les couillons / Aussi comme ce fussent bouillons, / Et les vaissiaux a la semence" (v. 923–25) [Venus influences the testicles, as if they were bubbles, and the spermatic chords]. This is because she seeks reproduction (*Respit* v. 954) and desire (v. 966). I know of no other instance of the word apart from blatantly farcical texts that, by definition, do not speak with the voice of Reason.

These farcical instances surely inform Reason's speech. It is indeed remarkable that she does evince a certain erotic surface, especially when she attempts to seduce Amant into loving her.

> Met, s'il te plest, en moi t'entente.
> Sui je pas bele dame et gente,
> Digne de servir un preudome,
> Et fust empereres de Rome?
> Ci veill t'amie devenir
> . . . .
> Por Dieu, gar que ne me refuses.
> Trop sunt dolentes et confuses
> Puceles qui sunt refusees,
> Quant de prier ne sunt usees,
> Si con tu meïsmes le prueves
> Par Echo, sanz querre autres prueves.
> (V. 5767–71, 5803–8)

[But, please, turn your love to me. Am I not a beautiful, noble lady worthy of serving a courtly man, even the Roman emperor? I want to become your sweetheart. . . . For God's sake, be careful not to reject me. Maids who are rejected suffer grievously and are at a loss as to how to act, since they are unaccustomed to making advances; you yourself prove it with the example of Echo—no other proof is required.]

We know what Reason means: Amant should turn to reason. Otherwise she participates in no way in the deceit practiced or taught by Amant or the other voices in the *Rose*. Yet, she did use, in suspect fashion, the word *coilles* to describe the castration of Saturn. *Genitaires* and *coilles* seem to be the only proper nouns available about 1275 when Jean wrote the *Rose*.

If we consider the limited lexicography available to Reason in her narrative context, it appears that human language has become so corrupt in usage since the Golden Age ended with Saturn's castration that the proper noun for testicles has become improper. Like the decline of love and justice exemplified in Appius's court, human sexuality and the language used to describe it have degenerated to such an extent that most proper nouns for sexual members have become improper. Reason herself recognizes that words no longer have the pristine quality they possessed when God and then Adam first pronounced them—"espoir que non, / Au meins celui qu'eles ont ores" (v. 7056–57)[60] [perhaps not, at least that meaning which they have today]. Present connotations do not retain the uncorrupted meaning God gave things and the word with which he created them. If there is a weakness in Reason's argument, it is precisely her failure to take into account how much language has degenerated and with whom she is speaking. As Marc-René Jung has pointed out, "d'après le *De interpretatione* d'Aristote, les noms possèdent une signification conventionnelle, due à la tradition, à l'histoire. L'homme ne saurait sortir du contexte historique sans courir à sa perte. Ceci, Raison est incapable de le comprendre. Elle est une lectrice [et une enseigante!] imparfaite."[61] *Genitaires* was, after all, available to her and did not require a metaphor to complete the referent's image. Lexicographical evidence shows that it was still proper among those anxious about moral standards and the language used to talk about sexuality. *Nature* was also a permissible synonym for male and female genitalia, although it too had become lewd or scatalogical in some expressions by the thirteenth century.[62]

It is noteworthy that the metaphor *andoilles* has been improper from Old French until today. One of the most blatantly obscene bequests in Villon's *Testament*, for example, brings the two words *coilles* and *andoilles* together again with several others to make an especially salacious statement.[63] *Andoilles*—"penis" in the plural to fit the comparison with testicles—metaphorically completes the image of Saturn's genitalia, an image that seems intended by manuscript illustrations of the castration. Still, its use raises more questions, making jocularity an improbable response.[64]

The *Roman de Renart* offers some clues, including sexual violence among its examples.[65] Some antics in Branch I are reminiscent of Amant and Rose, the Vieille and her *ribaut*, and the Husband jealous or not and deceitful wives like those the Jealous Husband and Nature evoke. The

Renart's very language rehearses Reason's in describing and defending her explicit wording for the castration of Saturn. When Isengrin returns home castrated, his wife is most distressed.

> Dame Hersant sovant le hate
> Et cil se torne et ele tate
> Ileuc ou la coille soloit
> Estre par raison et par droit:
> Ne trova mie de la coille.
> "Lasse, fait ele, ou est m'andoille
> Que ci ileuc vos soloit pandre?"
> (V. 2711–17)[66]

(Lady Hersent won't leave him be. He turns away and she touches him there where his scrotum used to be by reason and by right. There was no scrotum. "Alas," she exclaims, "where is my wiener which you used to have hanging there?")

This passage exemplifies the context in which Reason's language is customary in medieval literary documents. It hardly suggests that her words satisfy the demands of thirteenth-century decorum.

But perhaps it was not meant to. Susan Stakel has stated that, "properly understood, the *Roman de la rose* . . . would make its audience squirm."[67] Reason's language has had just that effect on many readers. It resolutely moves Jean's *Rose* close to satire as cruel as that in Swift's *A Modest Proposal* or as ferocious as that in most of La Fontaine's fables, as, for example, in the ant's response to the the cicada's assurance that she sang for everyone all summer long: "Vous chantiez? J'en suis fort aise. / Eh bien! dansez maintenant." Reflection and second thought tell us that such cruelty hardly supports a work ethic. The issues such poems raise are important because, as many have pointed out, "right reading of allegory" anticipates ethical decision followed by action.[68] "Right reading" includes second thought when we try to grasp the allegory in the letter. In the allegory lies the satire.

Such satire may be variously glossed. For example, in another La Fontaine fable, "Le loup et l'agneau," we are told at the outset what the moral is: "La raison du plus fort est toujours la meilleure." The blatant immorality of this moral, which the ensuing fable illustrates, forces a second reading that corrects the fable such that we see how immoral the moral is, all the while we know that we can do little to change the way the world turns. Something similar is happening in Jean's *Rose*. We are told that it is an art of plucking roses, that is, of seduction. Yet the violence, cruelty, and stupidity that punctuate the telling stop readers short, inciting them, in Heather Arden's words, "to define their critical assumptions."[69] Ultimately, then, readers must subjectively resolve issues associated with gender, authority, and self within the totality of the *Roman de la rose*. Both a man and a woman confront one another in Jean's *Rose*, and its implied audience includes both men and women.

This does not mean that both (Amant and Rose, men and women) are not castigated by various voices in different parts of the *Rose*. As Peter L. Allen puts it: "The reader is forced to confront a series of conflicting representations of the meaning of love and of the place of man and woman in it. The tension of seeing illusions from both sides is very strong, and makes the experience of reading these texts a highly problematical one."[70] Yet, as Maureen Quilligan rightly observes, "After reading an allegory . . . , we only realize what kind of readers we are, and what kind we must become in order to interpret our significance in the cosmos."[71] Is this a desirable effect? In answering the question, readers of the *Rose* reveal the propriety of their own sexuality, its acts and its vocabulary, at the same time they mirror more or less accurately the work being read. The same holds for those who do not squirm while reading the poem, either because they nudge one another and snicker like Genius's congregation, or because they regard with deep disapproval near Rabelaisian excesses, or, finally, because they feel uninvolved in such issues. The *Rose* is indeed a mirror. It reveals the morality of whoever looks into it. With this perception we can go back to the beginning and read the *Rose* a second time.

But before concluding this chapter it should be noted that my use of Jean's major sources does not violate the principle laid down in the first chapter regarding the *Rose*'s implied lay audience. Although its members would have known Guillaume de Lorris's beginning, its knowledge of Ovid and Boethius is not necessary to understanding the *Rose*. Jean's rewriting is sufficient to communicate the sense of Ovid and Boethius when he uses them. My analysis of the sources merely corroborates the reading of the literal plot while pointing to Jean's artistry in construing that plot. It is to that artistry that we must now turn our attention.

3

The Scientific and Philosophical Modes of Treatment

Ma grant joie en dormant iere
Si granz que nel puis conter.
En veillant ne truis maniere
De ma dolor conforter.
—Thibaut de Champagne

[My joy while asleep was inexpressibly great. Upon awakening I find no way to assuage my grief.]

Jean retitled the *Rose* "*Miroër aus Amoreus*," a fact whose significance Patricia Eberle has demonstrated in regard to treatment of "mirrors" in the romance.[1] Literal lenses, prisms, and mirrors—all *miroërs* in Jean's French—could distort, deflect, or faithfully render their source of light (v. 18014–30, 18123–200). As Eberle goes on to point out, Jean uses the word "mirror" in five senses: mirror as such, optical glass, God and his "transmitters" (or the agents that transmit the divine will into action), the eye, and the *Rose* itself. The *Rose* reverberates with semantic changes on *miroër* that generate the multiple literal readings of the word, readings that illuminate variously the narrative, its speakers, and their words and reveal different kinds and levels of love in the process. Readers may in turn see themselves reflected in the diverse shapes of the *Rose*'s "polymodality."[2]

Significantly, Eberle goes on to show that the transmission of light is, as a process, analogous to the art of poetry, which itself transmits sources through the new work. The process she describes is poetic invention, "including *amplificatio*, *abbreviatio*, and the use of *colores*, as well as the invention of fictions."[3] These familiar features of medieval composition are among those Jean draws on to shape and color his version of the *Rose*, as Gunn's study has demonstrated. In terms of medieval composition theory, the art is fundamental and elementary. Invention relies on devices for restating, adapting, or entirely changing the meaning of source material. At its most elementary level—that of tropes and figures of rhetoric—the future writer learns to rewrite with originality. These diverse forms and modes of treating a given subject matter are devices for rewriting, providing the mirrors and lenses through which we read Jean's *Rose*, as Eberle has shown. They illustrate the poet rewriting his or her sources.

INTRODUCTIONS TO MEDIEVAL WRITINGS (I)

The commonplace features of medieval rewriting acquire special focus with the emergence of the so-called Aristotelian *accessus ad auctores* in the late twelfth and thirteenth centuries. The emergence of the Aristotelian *accessus* brought with it a special attention to the "treatment" of the work—its *modus* or *forma tractandi* in literary works.[4] The "mode" or "form of treatment" identifies the ways in which the author treats, that is, develops and amplifies his or her work. The plot of Jean's *Rose*—Amant's actual adventures—albeit comparable in length, is nonetheless far more "developed" and "amplified" than Guillaume's version. This is because Jean *treats* Guillaume's image of the quest differently.

The general features of Jean's *modi* were identified in the "Querelle" at the turn of the fifteenth century.[5] Badel has suggested that some decades after 1402 Laurent de Premierfait claimed that the *Divine Comedy* adapted major features of the *Rose* in order to respond to Christine de Pizan's unfavorable comparison of Dante and Jean de Meun. Laurent asserts that Dante knew Jean de Meun's poem so well that it inspired him to "contrefaire au vif le beau *Livre de la Rose*"[6] [reproduce closely the model of the beautiful *Book of the Rose*] in the *Divine Comedy*. Whether Laurent's statement is true or not,[7] it is clear that he thought that Dante derived the separation between heaven and hell from Genius's vision of the Park of the Lamb and the Garden of Deduit (a model also traced by Laurent to the *Aeneid*, Book VI). The fact that Laurent perceived common schemes in these works does tell us something about the *Rose* itself as well as how he himself may have read the French poem, especially given the fact that he could not have read the *Divine Comedy* because he did not know Italian.

First, however, I must make an important terminological distinction. The *Divine Comedy* deploys two *modi* or *formae*: the *modus* or *forma tractandi*, which I have been discussing, and the *modus* or *forma tractatus*, or "mode or form of the treatise." This *modus tractatus* refers to the artful division of a work into formal parts. It is a conventional and simple organizing principle. In the *Rose*, it consists of Guillaume de Lorris's two-part prologue, the first part being a disquisition on true and false dreams (v. 1–20), the second an *accessus*-like introduction to Guillaume's dream about Rose and to the *Roman de la rose* itself (v. 21–44). The next part of the *tractatus* is Guillaume's narrative, which Jean says is incomplete, and which he continues and concludes.[8] Within this scheme, certain uneven units are recognizable, centering for the most part on specific personifications who dominate large tracts of text, notably, Reason, Ami, Faux Semblant, the Vieille, Nature, and Genius.

However, the *Rose*'s rudimentary *modus tractatus* differs remarkably from its complex *modus tractandi*. The different modes and forms of the *modus tractandi* are not so fixed as the partitions in the *modus tractatus*. The *Rose*'s *modus tractandi* is therefore not susceptible of simple outline or identification of procedures, unlike its *modus tractatus*. I shall analyze it here by beginning with the *modus tractandi* as laid out in the Can Grande Letter on the *Divine Comedy*.

In the letter to Can Grande attributed to Dante, the Italian author defines the *modus tractandi* of the *Divine Comedy* as a whole and of the *Paradiso* in particular. "Forma sive modus tractandi est poeticus, fictivus, descriptivus, digressivus, transumptivus, et cum hoc diffinitivus, divisivus, probativus, improbativus, et exemplorum positivus."[9] [The form or mode of treatment is poetic, fictive, descriptive, digressive, metaphorical, and also defining, classificatory, affirming, denying, and exemplary.] In the light of Laurent de Premierfait's assertion that the *Divine Comedy* is modeled on the *Rose*, without paraphrasing it, it is indeed fascinating to discover that the *modus tractandi* attributed to Dante's epic essentially describes the same set of devices in the *Rose*. To be sure, the second set of *modi* in Dante's list was widespread, having been at least in part analogous to rhetoric's traditional five parts of an oration: prologue, narrative, division, proof and counterproof, and peroration.[10] This would have made them readily familiar to academically trained authors like Jean de Meun.

The modes are essentially argumentative. The second set of modes—the philosophical and scientific—are easier to explain. They define issues, separate them into their constituent parts, prove what they assert and invalidate alternative arguments, and support their case by appeal to exemplary material. Critically, Jean adumbrates some of these *modi* in the section on "destinees," which proves that he knew and used the principle of the *modi tractandi*. Here, Nature explains how she would have developed the topic and, implicitly, how Jean develops other topics that belong to his subject.

Des destinees plus parlasse,
Fortune et cas determinasse
Et bien vossisse tout espondre,
Plus opposer et plus respondre,
Et mainz examples an deïsse.
(V. 17697–701)

[I would say more about "destinies," defining fortune and chance, and would indeed explain everything, set up more oppositions and responses and propose many examples.]

Elaboration ("plus parlasse," "tout espondre") would therefore identify the different varieties of destiny, fortune, and chance by definition and division ("fortune et cas determinasse"[11]), with arguments for and against ("opposer" and "respondre"), and with supporting examples ("mainz examples").

To see how the *modi* are used in the *Rose* in more detail, I shall devote the rest of this chapter to the scientific and philosophical modes, the second set in the Can Grande letter as well as those intimated in Nature's words on how she would treat the "destinees." In chapter 4 I shall examine the first or poetico-rhetorical set of modes from the Can Grande letter. This will permit an investigation of the *Rose*'s allegories in chapter 5. The rearrangement of the two sets of *modi* permits me to move from the devices more appropriate to the literal sense to those that treat more of the allegorical level.

The first set we shall examine, the scientific and philosophical modes, reveals on the literal level of Jean's allegory both the literal intention of the poem—to show how Jealousy's castle is taken and the rose plucked—and an underlying irony which suggests to the reader that that simple, hedonistic reading is an inadequate expression of the full meaning of Amant's dream. First, the defining mode identifies key terms in the context of love while showing how, in Jean's continuation, a certain semantic slippage occurs in the use of commonplace words, a slippage paralleling Amant's own slide from Guillaume's ideal love toward deceit and seduction. The classificatory mode in turn arrays different kinds of love and evaluates them such that the third mode, the argumentative, can set forth arguments for and against different kinds of love. Finally, the exemplary mode puts the *Rose*'s array of loves, including Amant's own seduction of Rose, into a kind of universal history. By comparison with the various love stories and other exemplary material recounted in the poem, Amant's own story acquires new contexts which tend to turn his erotic dream into a potential nightmare for both him and, especially, Rose. For love, as history and literature show, leads almost inevitably and universally to disaster. The contrast between literal happiness and implicit disaster alerts the reader to the rich allegorical implications of the poetic and rhetorical modes, which I shall discuss in chapter 4.

To summarize, the *modus tractandi* permits soundings of different parts of the *Rose*. These turn out to be selective probings of its treatment of the literal sense that, I believe, point toward the allegorical context and intention of the poem. This is because the *modi* referred to by Dante are used extensively in Jean's *Rose*. Thus, they allow insightful and compelling soundings that reveal the poem's intention or intentions and its meaning or projected meanings taken as a whole. For convenience, Dante's two groups of five *modi* will be treated in separate chapters. The division fits what have been loosely termed, respectively, the poetical and rhetorical modes and the scientific and philosophical modes. That is, the two sets are drawn from *accessus* traditions that describe, in the first instance, poetic and rhetorical works, and, in the second, scientific and philosophical works.[12] The former describes the manner of expression, the latter the truth of expression.

THE DEFINING MODE *(Modus diffinitivus)*

Defining words and variations within their semantic range is a major feature of allegories like the *Rose*. Specific terms may have specific meanings in one context or for one speaker, yet change or be replaced in a different context or for different speakers. Similarly, a vocabulary may vary in affective range, and authors may play on the semantic possibilities of a word to accommodate new contexts and intentions. Native speakers will be familiar with semantic range of words, and carefully chosen definitions may well fix the meaning and assure common understanding. These lexicographical features of the defining mode are especially important and prominent in interpreting personifications who act out the semantic potential of the word they personify. A given personification may personify any one or several dictionary meanings of its given name. We have observed this in the case of Reason, who personifies both the mental faculty and human language.

First and foremost, the defining mode offers definitions. Definitions assure that words will be understood in the sense desired by author, narrator, or some other voice in the text. The best-known example in the *Rose* is Reason's translation of Andreas Capellanus's definition of *amor* as *passio*, or "maladie de pensee" (v. 4348), to define Amant's love as carnality. As it turns out, Reason's definition refers to only one species of love, as opposed to Andreas, for whom the definition includes all possible kinds of love. That is, Andreas defines only species of the general *amor passio*, whereas Jean broadens the scope of the word *amor* to include kinds of love that fall outside Andreas's definition, like friendship, charity, and love of reason. Reason also defines these kinds of love in order to distinguish them from Andreas's kind. The array of loves not discussed under Andreas's definition prepares for Reason's condemnation of love as "maladie de pensee" and the distinctions she makes between it and other kinds of good and bad love. Amant's love, she argues, does not aim at reproduction; it can—as the plot bears out in Amant's case—lead to seduction and betrayal. These distinctions set contexts wherein the commonplace attributes of good lovers illustrated in the carole of the Garden of Deduit slip semantically and affectively into surface qualities, thereby covering the deceit and seduction Susan Stakel has shown to be central to Amant's love in Jean's *Rose*. "Fins amanz se faignent, / Mes par amors amer ne daignent" (v. 4361–62) [They feign to be worthy lovers, but they do not deign to love in the true sense of the word]. It follows that false lovers are not really *fin amant* because they do not love *par amors*. There is, therefore, at least one kind of love between men and women—that which is *par amors*—which is different from Amant's as defined and delimited by Andreas's definition. Lovers who love *par amors* as Reason uses the expression do not pretend to love, they do love. They are truly *fin amant*. Their love is a kind of friendship, as we shall see.

According to Reason there is more than one kind of love available to Amant: friendship (*amitié*), charity as love for one's neighbors, the natural desire to have children, love of reason, prostitution, or lovemaking for profit, and homosexual attraction. Curiously, Reason does not mention love for God. Except for friendship, I shall return to this exemplary array under the classificatory mode.

Friendship, or *amitié*, can be treated here because Reason also provides a definition of it (cf. v. 4637): "C'est bone volanté conmune / Des genz antr'els, sanz descordance, / Selonc la Dieu benivolance" (v. 4656–58) [it is shared good will toward one another among persons, without strife and in harmony with God's benevolence]. For this definition, Reason names Cicero as source and authority, by which she means the *De amicitia*. Her reference, however, has obscured the fact that Reason's discussion of friendship responds to Amant's request for an explanation of the good love Reason accepts between men and women—making the French *amitié* a more accurate term than the English for her conception of friendship.

Si m'avez vos rementeüe
Une autre amor mesconneüe
Que je ne vos oi pas blasmer,
Donc genz se peuent entramer
(V. 4633–36)

[You mentioned another unappreciated kind of love which I don't hear you condemn and which is possible.]

Here, Amant is referring to Reason's words in verses 4549–69:[13]

Ne cuides pas que jes dessenble:
Je veill bien qu'il aillent ensanble
Et facent quant qu'il doivent fere
Conme courtais et debonere
. . . .
Bone amor doit de fin[14] queur nestre:
Don n'en doivent pas estre mestre
Ne quel font corporel soulaz.
(V. 4559–62, 4567–69)

[Don't presume that I would separate them. I want them to be together, to do everything they are supposed to do courteously and properly. . . . Good love must be born of a noble heart; gifts should not dominate it anymore than carnal pleasure.]

Definitions are therefore used not merely to define, but to discriminate among different senses and evaluations of the same word. In the case of love, definitions identify different kinds (*natures*, *manieres*) of love (cf. v. 4641, 4650).

In the *Rose*, love as friendship may also be between two persons of the same or opposite sex, as is evident in several parts of Reason's analysis of love. Single gender friendship is based on Cicero as first author, "intergender" friendship on a topical option in Jean's *matière* that seems to derive from the rewriting of Cicero's *De amicitia* in Aelred of Rievaulx's *De spiritali amicitia*.

According to Aelred, friendship began when God created Eve to be Adam's companion.

Postremo cum hominem condidisset, ut bonum societatis altius commendaret: *Non est bonum*, inquit, *esse hominem solum; faciamus ei adiutorium simile sibi*. Nec certe de simili, uel saltem de eadem materia hoc adiutorium diuina uirtus formauit; sed ad expressius caritatis et amicitiae incentiuum, de ipsius substantia masculi feminam procreauit. Pulchre autem de latere primi hominis secundus assumitur, ut natura doceret omnes aequales, quasi collaterales; nec esset in rebus humanis superior uel inferior, quod est amicitiae proprium.

(*De spiritali amicitia* I.57)[15]

[After He had made the first man, in the interest of fostering good human fellowship, He said: "It is not good for man to live alone; let us make him a companion who is like him." Nor indeed did the divinity make that companion out of merely similar nor even the same matter. Rather as a more explicit incitement to charity and friendship He created woman from the substance of the male himself. It was a most excellent thing that the second human was drawn from the side of the first one so that nature might teach that all men and women are equal, as it were standing side-by-side with one another, and that there is no one superior or inferior in human relations, which is the distinctive characteristic of friendship.]

Original sin brought about the decline of such friendship into self-indulgence, avarice, envy or jealousy, and inequality. In its train came the world of Ami and the Vieille, of the Jealous Husband, and of Amant and Rose—a world of contention and rivalry, hatred, mistrust, and deceit (cf. *De spiritali amicitia* 1.58). These are also the effects of the castration of Saturn, which ended the Golden Age of equality, love, and justice.

Aelred first identifies three kinds of love: spiritual love (*amor spiritalis*), carnal love (*amor carnalis*), and wordly love (*amor mundialis*) (*De spiritali amicitia* 1.38–49). However, since his emphasis is on love or friendship among monks, he devotes most of his attention to the first kind, which, although closest to the perfect, prelapsarian love of Adam and Eve, is not the immediate object of love as friendship which Reason extols in the *Rose*. Beneath spiritual love Aelred locates love for those living in "this world," or "saeculariter uiuentes" (1.33). It includes carnal love, which is unreasonable because its goal is carnal delight, and worldly love, which is based on avarice, seeks profit, and vacillates with fortune. In these we recognize Amant and Rose as, respectively, Ami and the Vieille would have them be.

However, human love has redeeming qualities. It may even rise above carnality and venality in the direction of spiritual love. This is the direction of human as distinguished from spiritual friendship.

Huius amicitiae uitiosae principium quosdam plerumque ad quamdam uerae amicitiae prouehit portionem; eos scilicet qui primum spe lucri communis foedus ineuntes dum sibi in iniquo mammona fidem seruant, in rebus dumtaxat humanis, ad maximum perueniunt gratumque consensum. Attamen uera amicitia nullo modo dicenda est, quae commodi temporalis causa suscipitur, et seruatur.

(1.44)

[The beginning of this kind of friendship often lifts some persons toward a certain portion of true friendship. Those namely who first enter into the bond of friendship in the hope of common gain remain faithful to one another in times of financial adversity, at least as far as human relations are concerned, and achieve the greatest and pleasing harmony. Nonetheless such friendship can in no way be termed true friendship, for it begins and endures for the sake of temporal goods.]

Rising still higher, humans attain the natural friendship (*amicitia naturalis*, 1.61)[16] instituted by God and nature between Adam and Eve so that humans might live together happily in mutual support.

Natural friendship seems to be a kind of love Reason recommends, defining and explaining it as follows:[17]

> Ainsinc leur queurs emsanble joingnent,
> Bien s'entraiment, bien s'entredoignent.
> Ne cuides pas que jes dessenble:
> Je veill bien qu'il aillent ensanble
> Et facent quant qu'il doivent fere
> Conme courtais et debonere;
> Mes de la fole amor se gardent
> Donc les queurs esprennent et ardent,
> Et soit l'amor sanz couvoitise,
> Qui les faus queurs de prendre atise.
> Bone amor doit de fin queur nestre:
> Don n'en doivent pas estre mestre [= *amor mundialis*]
> Ne quel font corporel soulaz. [= *amor carnalis*]
> (V. 4557–69)

[Thus do they join their hearts together—they love and give themselves to one another. Don't think that I wish to separate them. I want them to go through life together doing what they must do courteously and graciously. But let them avoid foolish love which causes hearts to flare up and burn, and let their love be free from greed which incites hearts to grab. Good love should be born of a discerning heart; gifts should no more be its master than carnal pleasure.]

The "fin queur" of verse 4567 do not love with the *amor mundialis* or *carnalis* evoked in the last two lines of the quote. Good love (*amor naturalis*) is not covetous; the partners share a common desire for mutual support and affection. Reason does not say much more about such *amitié* between men and women because Amant manifests no interest or faith in it. But such love is obviously part of Reason's conception of friendship. Mention of it leads to her adaptation of Cicero to a love Reason looks on with favor: "Tels meurs avoir doivent et seulent / Qui parfetemant amer veulent" (v. 4671–72) [That's how those must and usually do act who wish to love perfectly]. Amant's rejection of Reason is also a rejection of love as friendship. Ami's kind of love is an obvious consequence of that rejection, corresponding as it does to Aelred's *amor carnalis*.

Friendship involves Jean de Meun with another important source for his ideas on good love, Héloise of the Letters in Abelard's *Historia calamitatum.*[18] To be sure, Jean puts her views into the mouth of the Jealous Husband, who is more interested in Héloise's willingness to be Abelard's concubine than in her opinions on a love at once free, consensual, and equal. Nonetheless, as Emmanuèle Baumgartner has astutely recognized, something more noble shines through the Jealous Husband's words, if not through his mind. It is the good love Reason extols. The originality of the author of those Letters, as Herbert Silvestre has observed, "fut de placer dans la bouche d'une femme au-dessus de tout soupçon la défense diserte et circonstanciée d'une thèse qui, en réalité, n'a jamais vraiment été favorite qu'auprès de représentants du sexe masculin, du moins jusqu'à une époque très récente."[19] Perhaps, however, the notion of the "union libre"[20] is not the best to describe what Jean makes of Héloise's words. Supported by Aelred and authorized by Cicero, Reason and Héloise extol a kind of friendship which is neither platonic love nor the philogyny of the troubadour tradition. Christine de Pizan seems to have envisaged such friendship as well.[21] It is Aelred's natural friendship and Reason's *amitié.* But Amant is not interested in that kind of relationship with Rose either.

Lionel J. Friedman convincingly demonstrated that Reason's definition of friendship and her developments on it derive from Cicero as filtered through such lenses as biblical references to friendship used by Aelred of Rievaulx, Saint Anselm, and others who interpret and modify Cicero's words. Of these sources, Aelred speaks not only of male friendship, but also of friendship, or *amitié,* between man and woman. As discussed earlier, friendship began when God created Eve, who was created for the sake of friendship. Friendship became corrupt when *cupiditas* (Amant's kind of love) emerged. *Cupiditas* between two male friends is homosexuality; between male and female friends it is *amour maladie* as defined in Reason's translation of Andreas Capellanus's general definition of love.

Yet, for all this detail, Jean's translation of Andreas's definition of *passio* is incomplete, omitting, as it does, the phrase "et omnia de utriusque voluntate in ipsius amplexu amoris praecepta compleri"[22] [and they desire to satisfy all love's commandments by common consent in the embrace of love]. The notion does re-enter somewhat transformed, in the definition of friendship as "bone volanté conmune / Des genz antr'els, sanz descordance" (v. 4656–57) [shared good will between persons with no disharmony]. Clearly, Reason's *praecepta* are those of friendship, not of "sick love." Reason's informing notion of friendship includes fidelity, secrecy, and generosity—traits which Amant will reject under the guidance of false friendship, that is, Ami. The Vieille advises Rose to do the same.

Definitions help identify conduct that falls outside of the definitions. When Amant decides at the midpoint to become a "traitor" in love, we know that his subsequent *amour par amours* is not the kind Reason defines as friendship. We also know that he feigns to be a *fin amant*, which gives rise to the personification Faux Semblant. Yet, not all agents are as exacting as Reason, who is the agent established by God to say what words mean and thus, by naming things, to define them. Other agents are less concerned with definitions and more with choice within a word's semantic range or its lexicographical options, with meanings that express a specific worldview and conduct. Such play on meaning is common in allegory. Guillaume de Lorris uses it effectively for different personifications, notably those of Dangier and Jealousy.[23] A good example in both Guillaume's and Jean's *Rose* is the word *franchise*. Differences in semantic range account for the various meanings of *franchise*, as proposed by Reason, Ami, and the Vieille at different moments in their discourses, as well as for Amant's own personification, Franchise, during the seduction of Rose.[24]

To begin with, *franchise* in Guillaume de Lorris defines nobility. It connotes exemption from servitude and the open display of noble or aristocratic attributes; it also implies candid, forthright speech and conduct,[25] and characterizes both Amant and Rose. One of the arrows in Guillaume's *Rose* which emanates from Rose and strikes Amant is, indeed, named Franchise (v. 942).[26] As for Amant, although one of the personifications in the carole of Deduit's Garden is Franchise, by assimilation, all the participants are "Franches genz et bien enseignies / Et gent de bel afaitement / . . . tuit comunement" (v. 1280–82) [freeborn, well mannered persons, of noble, handsome comportment one and all]. The God of Love later includes Amant among those he distinguishes from those unworthy of serving him, as seen in the kiss of homage he grants Amant:

> Je n'i lesse mie touchier
> Chascun vilain, chascun porchier,
> Ainz doit estre cortois et frans
> Cui ge ensint a home prans.
> (V. 1935–38)

[I don't let just any villein or swineherd touch me there; rather those I allow to do me homage must be courteous and noble {*frans*}.]

The traits fit Franchise's later intervention in support of Amant, especially in overcoming the opposition of the villein, Dangier.[27] In Guillaume's *Rose*, *franchise* is consistently a positive attribute.

In Jean's continuation, the personification Franchise reappears as a baron in Love's army (v. 10422). She participates prominently in the attack on Jealousy's castle at Dangier's gate (v. 10707–8), which also conforms to Guillaume's role for her. In the tournament, or *mêlée*, she again attacks Dangier, but unsuccessfully (v. 15273–357). But other attributes undercut her positive role in Guillaume's version. Her lance from the forest of "Chuerie," or "cajolery," with its iron point of "douce priere," or "gentle entreaty," is of no avail against Dangier's club from the forest of "Refus," or "denial" (v. 15287).[28] Thus, Franchise's weapons suggest only a surface *franchise*, since open, candid speech has given way in Amant's quest to treason and betrayal, the domain of Barat and his son Faux Semblant. Franchise is also sent with Douz Regart to summon Venus to the siege (v. 15602), and she intervenes in the surrender of Jealousy's castle (v. 21251) to ask for the surrender of the rose (v. 21284). Her candor at this point underscores Franchise's semantic rewriting in Jean de Meun. She has become an ironic personification.

This is evident even earlier in Amant's less than candid attempt to cajole Dangier into imprisoning him with Bel Acueil.

> Dangiers, fis je, biau gentis hon,
> Frans de queur[29] et vaillanz de cors,
> Piteus plus que je ne recors,
> Et vos, Honte et Poor, les beles,
> Sages, franches, nobles puceles,
> En fez, en diz bien ordenees,
> Et dou lignage Reson nees,
> Soffrez que vostres sers deviegne.
> (V. 14926–33)

> [Dangier, I said, handsome nobleman of open, gentle heart {*frans*} and valiant person, more sensitive to mercy than words can express, and you, beautiful Shame and Fear, prudent, freeborn {*franches*} noble maids proper in deeds and words, born of Reason's lineage, allow me to become your slave.]

Jean thereby manipulates Guillaume's sense of *franchise* in Amant's appeal. As in Amant's surrender to the God of Love in Guillaume, to surrender can manifest *franchise*. But in Jean, Amant's candor is surface candor, as the lance from Chuerie suggests. In other words, Franchise offers to become not a vassal, but a serf. She is trying to dupe Rose's guardians. Although Amant is still practicing deceit, Dangier is not taken in: he refuses to lock the fox in the hen house (v. 14984).

In Jean, therefore, Franchise has become an ironic personification in league with Faux Semblant and Abstinence Contrainte. To read her only as Franchise, not as false Franchise, is to be victimized as Male Bouche was when he took Faux Semblant to be only Semblant and Abstinence Contrainte to be only Abstinence. Amant is not only a foolish lover, he is also a false lover. His duplicity attracts positive attributes to obscure the fact that they have no real meaning in his life.

Jean modifies Guillaume's sense of *franchise* in another aspect as well. Different personifications use the word to refer to free will (v. 17388–89, 17440, 17460–61, 17543, 17683, 17716) and, more generally, to the natural freedom granted to human beings by God and Nature (v. 8211, 9467, 18843). According to Nature, to use that freedom properly requires the assistance of Reason.

> Ainz font bien ou mal franchement
> Par leur vouloir tant seulement;
> N'il n'est riens for eus, au voir dire,
> Qui tel vouloir leur face eslire
> Que prandre ou lessier nou poïssent,
> Se de reson user vossissent.
> (V. 17231–36)[30]

[Rather they are free to do good or evil at will. To tell the truth, nothing external obliges them to choose to will in such a way that they cannot accept or reject doing so—provided they be willing to use reason.]

Jean here emphasizes *franchise* pejoratively as freedom without reason. Unlike in its aristocratic and moral sense, the excesses of *franchise* uninformed by reason mark the realignment of the personification as a surface appearance in configuration with Faux Semblant. *Franchise* needs reason to be honest and correct. Overbearing *franchise* in nobility is, after all, *orgueil* (v. 6735–46). It slides into *dangier*, or "sovereignty," in the overbearing Jealous Husband.

Guillaume's concept of *franchise* is corrupted because *franchise* excludes the assent of reason in various instances in Jean's version of the *Rose*. For example, religious who did not rationally choose their vocation came to regret their loss of freedom (v. 4414–32, 13937–48). Marriage may produce the same loss, according to the Vieille, especially for women (v. 13845–936).[31] But what she says is, in the final analysis, true for both men and women (v. 13929–36, 14057–73). This potential for loss applies in all conjugal relations in which, like the Jealous Husband, one spouse tries to impose the law of *seigneurie* or domination on the other. For one imposes *seigneurie* at the expense of one's own *franchise*. The husband in such marriages is unfree and bound like a tyrant (v. 5273–76), as the Jealous Husband shows.

This excursus on *franchise* could be extended to other words and personifications that pass from Guillaume to Jean, words like Courtesy,

Pitié, Ami, and the Vieille. But, in general, the advent of Faux Semblant reduces all the noble qualities of Amant and Rose to surface appearances that hide or mask deceit and cover vices or defects. These contrasts are, in fact, systems of opposites that distinguish between deceiving appearances and revealing truth. Faux Semblant is, of course, opposed to such revelations and therefore agrees to speak about himself only in the most general terms. He is willing to define himself, but not to reveal himself.

Faux Semblant's self-definition sets up a series of oppositions, as, for example, that between permissible and unauthorized mendacity (v. 11239–478). He is applying a fundamental principle of definition, that of *contraires choses* which Amant mentions toward the end of the *Rose*. This is in fact the logical operation of definition, proceeding by the clear delimitation of opposites or "contraries." "D'après Aristote, pour définir une chose, il est nécessaire d'avoir la connaissance de son *contraire*, du moins dans un genre accidentel, car les *contraires sont les seules différences vraiment spécifiques*. Par définition en effet, ils doivent appartenir à un même genre et réaliser la plus grande opposition qui se puisse concevoir dans un genre."[32] Faux Semblant distinguishes between good and bad mendacity while Reason opposes good and bad love; Amant, in his tirade on *contraires choses*, can distinguish only young and old *cons*. In doing so, each marks his or her own primary attribute by the general term being defined by contraries: mendacity, love, and genitalia.

Thus, Jean adapts a technique and strategy used by Guillaume de Lorris, play on semantic range and diversity, which includes not only the definition of terms but also play with lexicography and semantic range. Besides the technical definition that identifies terms, there is play on readily recognizable or explicable "dictionary" meanings of a word, as well as the abuse of them by wrong-headed or deceptive agents. These meanings would be either readily perceptible to native speakers, even in the lay audiences Jean envisages, or easily explained to them, as in the notion of *naturele franchise* as human freedom. *Jeux de mots* takes care of the rest. The technique, for better or worse, is analogous to Chrétien de Troyes's notion of *jeu de vérité*, or *double entendre*.[33]

THE CLASSIFICATORY MODE (*Modus divisivus*)

The discussion of the defining mode shows that Jean de Meun makes distinctions, notably in the array of meanings Reason assigns to different kinds of love and, therefore, to the different love lives Amant may choose among, from carnality through friendship to charity. In doing so, Reason also classifies each type as morally good, bad, or neutral. Although the specific evaluation of each kind may vary from speaker to speaker in the poem, the principle of classification is ever present. This principle is the classificatory mode, or *modus divisivus*.

The *modus divisivus* is not the same as the *modus tractatus* discussed above (p. 54). The latter is the artificial division of a text into formal parts, the former is the formal result of analysis of the subject matter into its constituent species. Thus, according to the Can Grande Letter, the *modus tractatus* of the *Divine Comedy* is the division into three books, in each of which are thirty-three cantos plus a prologue canto to Book I, and, finally, the verse and rhyme scheme are *terza rima*. The *modus divisivus* is different. It accounts for the reflection in the poem of a universal order extending from the center of Hell to the triune God.

An obvious division in the *Rose* is that between Amant and Rose themselves. They are the male and female foci, complexes, or configurations of images and attributes about the male and female centers. The juxtaposition of heterosexual lovers is apparent from the *gradus amoris*, *conservatio/deminutio amoris*, and *scala amorum* that order their relationship. Like most commonplaces, the *gradus amoris* is a supple scheme that admits of diverse evaluations and adaptations in context.[34] Conventionally, it begins with the first spark of love at sight or hearing and terminates with the first experience of intercourse; the scheme is a basic structuring and ordering device in the *Rose* narrative. However, both Ovid's *Ars amatoria* and Andreas Capellanus's *De amore*—authorities known and used by Jean, as we have seen—add two important corollary schemes to the *gradus amoris*. One is the postcoital continuation, which relates the preservation or decline of love, or *conservatio/deminutio amoris*. Although Jean makes some vague allusions to Amant's future experiences, there is no real continuation after the rose is plucked. Amant wakes up, the dream ends. However, Jean does adapt Book II of Ovid's *Ars amatoria*, which treats the *conservatio*, in the Ami and Vieille sections, thus foreshadowing a continuation had Amant's dream not ended. Furthermore, other alternative schemes are adumbrated in Reason's anatomy of love—notably her words on love as friendship.

The *Rose*'s *gradus amoris* begins in Guillaume's section and continues with adaptations and a conclusion in Jean's. In following the commonplace stages in love from first encounter to consummation, the *gradus amoris* provides a principle of division to both Guillaume's and Jean's *modus divisivus* and forms a link between them. It also serves a profounder function. The *modus* is divided not by analysis of an overarching idea, but rather by an image containing stages in progress toward a specific goal as love or sexual intercourse.[35] Since the goal of Amant's pilgrimage is the rose, and since the rose is an object of sexual desire defined by Reason as carnal love, then plucking the rose as sexual gratification is the context and intention that defines the stages in the *gradus amoris* leading to that goal. Thus the poem's use of *gradus amoris* effectively divides its narrative to reflect the principle of the *modus divisivus* and Amant's love as Reason defines it. Elsewhere Jean similarly associates definition with division such that oppositions serve to delimit and define parts of a whole. For example, in judging alchemy's transmutation of one species into another, Nature observes how the alchemist produces his transforming elixir

> Don la fourme devroit issir
> Qui devise antr'eus leur sustances
> Par especiaus differances,
> Si conme il pert au defenir.
> (V. 16048–51)

[from which should emerge the form that distinguishes substances from one another by specific differences, as one may observe in the procedure for defining.]

Now, although Guillaume de Lorris began the account of the *gradus amoris* and Jean de Meun continued and ended it, Jean introduced a fundamental change. He redefined love and adapted Amant's progress accordingly. That redefinition translates into action when Amant and Rose decide to delete the two tenets of fidelity and generosity from the God of Love's commandments as given by Guillaume de Lorris. This midpoint decision provides another basic division in the poem. Stakel has shown that, in a first concentric grouping, Ami and the Vieille, and, in a second, Reason and Nature,[36] relate to Faux Semblant or deceit. In fact, Amant's version of the *gradus amoris* is contextually not unlike the scheme for sin which Brunetto Latini derives from pride ("superbe," "orguil"[37]). Pride, as self-love and disdain of another's worth, opposes virtues which support human society and uphold good love rather than disrupt them, making Latini's *gradus peccatorum* analogous to Jean's *gradus amoris*:

> Car orgoils engendre envie, et envie[38] engendre mençoigne, et mençoigne engendre decevance, et decevance engendre ire, et ire engendre malevoeillance, et malevoellance engendre ennemistié, et ennemistiés engendre bataille, et bataille desront la loi et gaste la cité.[39]

[For pride engenders envy, envy engenders falsehood, falsehood deceit, deceit anger, anger ill will, ill will enmity, enmity strife, and strife undoes social order and lays waste the community.]

This too illustrates *modus divisivus* as stages in sin.

This brings us to the last corollary scheme mentioned above: what one might call a hierarchy of loves, or *scala amorum*. Andreas Capellanus envisages not only Ovid's two schemes before and after the first consummation, he also establishes a hierarchy of lovers based on the degree of nobility, whether by blood or by mind, and on the degree of abstinence. The levels manifest Material Style, a technique that identifies orders in the world on a scale from higher to lower.[40] Such orders are analogous to the kinds of distinctions Reason makes among loves.[41]

By adapting Andreas's definition of love to describe Amant's love, Jean is implicitly locating the array of loves the *De amore* describes on a scale to which Reason adds species of love that are reasonable but which Andreas does not mention; afterward Amant himself descends progressively below any reasonable love in his single-minded pursuit of the rose.

Andreas also admits topical variations on each rung of the scale. That is, he addresses a variety of sexual circumstances or orientations that he finds incompatible with love as he defines it: sodomy, prostitution, satyrism, nymphomania, impotence, and so on. Then he draws a social scale extending from peasants at the bottom to the religious at the top. Excluded from any kind of love are nuns (presumably because they are brides of Christ, although Andreas does not say so) and peasant men (their uninterrupted labor is necessary for the economy). Another distinction is that between *amor simplex*, or "simple love," based only on the physical attractiveness of the object of love (and thus akin to Amant's love in Jean's part of the *Rose*) and *amor sapiens* or *doctus*, which is inspired by the inner worth of the loved one. The latter is further divided into *amor mixtus*, which includes intercourse, and *amor purus*, which does not. In addition, Andreas, like Jean, distinguishes between blood nobility and nobility of mind. Further topical adjustments are made according to age, sex, chivalric or courtly accomplishments, degree of nobility, attractiveness, and other categories. If the scheme were taken seriously, it would engage rather actively the *finesse* of *fin'amor*.[42]

For his part, Jean's Reason divides love into two groups of good and bad love separated by natural love, which is morally neutral, since "amor naturel" (v. 5733) is the desire to have children, an urge that Reason says humans share with animals. The scale extends upward through friendship, including friendship between men—nothing is said about friendship between women—and friendship between men and women, love for humanity (v. 5413), and, finally, love of reason it- (or her-)self. All the bad loves reject or are indifferent to procreation, friendship, and reason. They are acquisitive; covetousness, avarice, purchase, force, or *seigneurie* are their most common by-products. If we were to propose an Aristotelian *accessus* to the *Rose*, it would thus, as a *modus tractandi*, include *con-*

trarietas under division in conformity with the logical principle of opposites misapplied by Amant at the end of the *Rose* (v. 21543–52)—Reason also bases her analysis on this principle (v. 4334, 4733–40, 4863–66[43])—and *gradatio*, which identifies an array of good and bad loves like friendship, prostitution, charity, and love of reason.

Let me return briefly to friendship since its heterosexual manifestation in the *Rose* has never been examined, but is obviously important. Reason distinguishes between good love that is generous and bad love based on covetousness (the kind the Vieille promotes) or carnality (Amant's kind) (v. 4568–69). Good love, Reason argues, arises in a "discriminating" (*fin*) heart. "Bone amor doit de fin queur nestre" [Good love must be born of a discriminating heart] (v. 4567), adding:

> Et soit entr'els conmunité
> De touz leur biens en charité,
> Si que par nule entencion
> N'i puisse avoir excepcion.
> (V. 4659–62)

[so that they might share in charitable community all their possessions without exception.]

Heterosexual friendship, whether or not it includes sexual consummation, is clearly a species of love as friendship in Reason's disquisition. Such love may indeed be as rare as male friendship was for Cicero (v. 5345–64, 5375–403), but it is nonetheless possible, according to Reason. Furthermore, the concern of lovers for the loved one, constancy, communality of possessions, mutual defense of honor, preservation of life, openness, the ability to keep a secret and to control one's tongue, readiness to please and act for the beloved—all these features of *bone amor* spring from a *fin queur* and constitute a *fin'amor*. They are obviously not found in either Amant or Rose, nor in most of the other exemplary lovers depicted in the *Rose*.

Love as friendship, then, is ineffectual in the *Rose*. This is true for virtually all the different kinds of good love, including the experiences of both of the protagonists and of the mythological, legendary, and historical figures that mirror the *gradus* and *conservatio/deminutio amoris* as well as the *scala amorum*. Nor do they ever intend such love. The sole exceptions are Reason herself and Héloise. Héloise's special relation to Abelard is so unusual that it can hardly be called happy, even as friendship. It is, rather, phoenix-like. Good loves themselves are undone by evil persons in cases like Lucrece, Phillis, and Oenone, who all die because love slides into deceit. Even Phanie's filial piety fails to save her father. Virtually none of Reason's good loves is positively exemplified in the *Rose*. All her examples fall under harsh Iron Age law.

The comparison by contraries and gradations underlies Reason's specialized definition of Amant's malady. Reason's procedure is consistent with definitions that postulate opposites within a scale of kinds of love. Furthermore, since any definition includes its varieties, the inclusion of prostitution and sodomy (like Orphée's, v. 19599–656) in the definition of the malady is apposite. No "bad love" uses the sex act for its original, "natural" purpose of procreation. It may, of course, be redeemed by it, as in Pygmalion's case (see pp. 76–78).

Amant's goal is certainly not procreation, even though the stages in *gradus amoris* for both good and bad sexual love are essentially the same. Furthermore, the *gradus amoris* distinguishes the two from other kinds of love insofar as a full *gradus* is necessary for each, whereas it is not essential to other kinds—whether "good," like friendship, charity, and love of reason, or "bad," like prostitution and rape. In addition, both kinds seem to assume the conservation of love, or, at least, of lovemaking; neither requires fidelity. The Vieille's "toutes por touz et touz por toutes" (v. 13856) [all women for all men, all men for all women] seems to correspond *grosso modo* to Amant's view of his sex life at the end of the romance. Both Ami's and the Vieille's instruction is predicated on a sexual relationship that extends for some time beyond first intercourse; this holds as well for "natural love" and for friendships that include a *gradus amoris*.

COLLECTIVE PROOF, OR THE PROBATIVE AND REFUTATIVE MODES

(*Modus collectivus*, or *probativus* and *improbativus*)

Disagreement as to the moral or social worth of different kinds of love, and their arrangement on a scale of good, bad, or neutral, leads to debate about their worth and meaning. This is the well-known disputational mode of the *Rose*, whereby different personifications present their views on love, and, indeed, wherein Amant makes his case, and Rose hers, during and about the seduction. Such debate may follow logical patterns, but more often than not in the *Rose* it is emotional, relying on the rhetorical strategies that move audiences and sway opinion. Sophistry can and does find a place, as one might expect from a love founded on deceit and aiming at seduction.

The scholastic veneer of the *Rose* has long been recognized, at times orienting modern readings of the romance. All scholastic discourse, which includes instruction, declamation, and disputation, relies on proof for and against propositions—the *modi probativus* and *improbativus*.

Taken together, as they are in the *Rose*, these constitute the *modus collectivus*.[44] Some studies have already established the use of logical demonstration in the *Rose* through syllogism, enthymeme, and sophism or false argument.[45]

Since the dividing mode points to ordered divisions established by the goal of the literal plot and its *gradus amoris*, we may ask by what reasoning Amant convinces Rose to say "Yes." To be sure, Venus is a powerful incentive and stimulant in support of Amant's argument.[46] Yet argument and consent are also verbal. Rose's consent comes in response to a syllogistic argument. The syllogism is arranged differently in the exchange, but may be summarized as follows: Courtesy quotes Vergil in her major premise: "Amors vaint tout" (v. 21302) [Love conquers all]. The minor premise refers to Amant: he has overcome all the defenses around Bel Acueil and the rose—Male Bouche, Jealousy, and the rest (cf. v. 21295–96). Ergo, "nous la devons recevoir" (v. 21303) [we should accept it], that is, accept any such love, including Amant's.

The syllogism is obviously defective. That love conquers all does not mean it or Amant must or should conquer all. The force of this "sneaky argument," to use SunHee Gertz's phrase, lies principally in the urging of Courtesy. "Biau tres douz filz," she exclaims to Bel Acueil, "por Dieu merci, / Ne vos lessiez pas bruler ci" (v. 21281–82) [Handsome, most sweet son, for God's sake, don't just stand there and burn!]. Courtesy is hypocritical, as the reader learns when Amant, who has accepted deceit as a means to his ends, is courteously said to be "leal" (v. 21285) [faithful]. Courtesy continues: "N'onques ne vos fist un faus tret / Li frans, qui onques ne guila" (v. 21288–89) [Nor did the honest, candid fellow ever cheat or deceive you]. Ironically, this statement comes just before Amant describes the different kinds of *cons* he has known since seducing Rose. The God of Love himself is violently forcing the issue—with emphasis on force—relying on the sexual drive by which Love and Venus cooperate and conquer: "Amors . . . s'an efforce, / Qui mout i a mise grant force" (v. 21295–96) [Love strives to do his very best, he who put such great effort and force into it].

The situation is eminently rhetorical. A combination of means has been deployed to make Rose *docilis*, *benivola*, and *adtenta*—receptive, well-disposed, and attentive.[47] As the foregoing appeal of Courtesy shows, one ploy that succeeds is self-praise: "Nostrum officium sine adrogantia laudabimus" (*Ad Herennium* I.v.8) [By praising our services without arrogance]. To convince Rose in this way, Amant must sway her emotions. Therefore the persuasion, such as it is, is supported by emotional appeal: sophistic courtesy, security, fire—Venus's own devices. Rose capitulates and surrenders her flower.

The exchange of the major arguments pro and con between Amant and Rose rests on emotional appeal. That is, Venus and Genius have aroused the sexual appetites of both Amant and Rose, coordinating them by urgent appeal and argument. Verbal seduction accompanies and incites arousal. Whether the seduction be viewed as good or bad, its success depends on rhetorical schemes. Thus, the invention and arrangement of a well-organized plan of action requires figurative amplifications that argue Amant's case; memory must keep all this in mind, and blandishing gestures must support his appeal. Even rhetoric used for illicit or deceptive purposes must rely on the five-part scheme of invention, arrangement, embellishment, memory, and gesture. It does so here.

Amant is practicing the kind of rhetoric Ami taught him. For example, Ami suggests that if a loved one discovers her lover's infidelity,

> Et s'el n'a pas prise provee
> D'eus .II. ensemble la covee,
> Mes bien en chiet en jalousie,
> Qu'el set, ou cuide, estre acoupie,
> Conment qu'il aut, ou sache ou croie,
> Gart soi cil que ja ne recroie
> De li nier tout pleinemant
> Ce qu'ele set certainemant,
> Et ne soit pas lenz de jurer.
> Tantost li reface endurer
> En la place le jeu d'amors,
> Lors iert quites de ses clamors.
> (V. 9777–88)

[And if she didn't catch both of them in the act of making love, but is jealous because she knows or thinks he's unfaithful to her, whether she knows or just thinks it, deny unstintingly what she knows for sure, and don't spare oaths of fidelity. Right away make her play the game of love on the spot, whereupon all her outcry will cease.]

This is Ami's kind of unsophisticated rhetoric, a rhetoric supported by Faux Semblant. In like vein, the Vieille informs Rose as to how she may counter in word and gesture, sometimes supporting Amant, sometimes denying, and ever keeping him emotionally unstable so as to secure control and gain her own advantage. "Sire," the woman should exclaim,

> "c'est la some,
> Foi que doi saint Pere de Rome,
> Par fine amor a vos me don,
> Car ce n'est pas por vostre don.

N'est hom nez por cui ce feïsse
Por nul don, tant grant le veïsse.
Maint vaillant home ai refusé,
Car mout ont maint a moi musé.
Si croi qu'ous m'avez anchantee,
Male chançon m'avez chantee."
Lors le doit estroit acoler
Et besier por mieuz affoler.
(V. 13653–64)

["to put it briefly, by the faith I owe Saint Peter of Rome: I give myself to you out of sincere love. It's not because of your gift. I wouldn't do this for any man's gift, no matter how big it was. I have refused many a worthy man, for a lot have pursued me in vain. I think you have cast a spell over me, beguiling me with magic incantation!" Then she must embrace and kiss him in order to drive him even wilder.]

Gestures remain major arguments for both the men and women, whether in debate or seduction, acting as both proof and counterproof, as the two preceding passages demonstrate. The tournament that precedes the taking of the rose exchanges arguments by words and gestures among combatants. Amant's appeal, as expressed by his personified attributes, is based on an ostensibly sincere love that, in his heart of hearts, he has abandoned for deceit and seduction. Suspecting this, Rose's personified defenses underscore her opposition based on her domination, or Dangier, over Amant as well as her sense of fear and shame (Peur and Honte) as to what is happening and will happen to her. The whole is colored, of course, by the rising insistence of Amant's and Rose's own bodies, inflamed by Genius and Venus, and ultimately moved to act through physical arousal.

Emotional appeal is a legitimate device in rhetoric. Reason herself uses certain blandishments on the literal level to "seduce" Amant. Reason is the faculty not only of logical demonstration, but also of persuasive speech. She too can appeal to the emotions and, indeed, imply seductive gestures (v. 5765–71). But, in her case, the argument in favor of herself and against rejection is of no avail. Amant prefers Rose. He will remain true to his first master, the God of Love, rather than let Reason serve him. These instances underscore the range of argumentative ploys used in the *Rose*, from logic to sophistry, from sound reasoning to emotional and physical arousal.

THE EXEMPLARY MODE (*Modus exemplorum positivus*)

Examples counterpoint the plot and arguments of the *Rose*. They are an effective rhetorical device, especially for lay audiences (as Jean points out), since they give the appearance of reality to the formal arguments and definitions they illustrate and tend to make credible. But they are also a slippery foundation for argument since an opponent may turn the example to his or her own ends, as often occurs in the *jeu-parti* and other allegorical works like Richard de Fournival's *Bestiaire d'amour* and the woman's response to it.[48] Indeed, Jean de Meun sees it as his office as poet to treat examples in his way. I have already suggested how they alert the reader to the continuation of Amant's and Rose's affair, a continuation which promises to be violent and deceitful, as treacherous and disastrous as most of the exemplary love stories we hear. Especially important in this discussion are the contradictory examples of Pygmalion, whose story conforms by and large to Reason's outline of a good, or at least neutral, love, and the Sleepwalker's dream and awakening, a *mise en abyme* that is remarkably analogous to Amant's own dream.

Examples are basic units in the romance aesthetic. As *fabulae*, they serve to illustrate a work's intention. Moreover, within a given work, they may express a specific speaker's more limited context or intention. Therefore, in interpreting them, one must evaluate the speaker's place within the total work's economy and stated intention. In allegory, these matters are further complicated by the two or more different readings, literal and allegorical, which allegory entails. The complexity of such reading is illustrated by two of Reason's examples treated above: the castration of Saturn and Croesus's dream, in the latter of which reliance on the literal rather than the allegorical interpretation of a dream leads to disaster and death.

Given the complexity of the exemplary mode in the *Rose*, with respect both to the art with which Jean deploys examples and their contribution to the interpretation of the total romance, I shall set forth the scope of the following discussion at the outset. The validity of this outline should emerge from the detailed analysis that follows it. Moreover, it will help orient the reader to my line of argument in this section.

First, Jean uses examples to counterpoint Amant's and Rose's *gradus amoris*, suggesting thereby its consequences while both are still at some remove from consummation. Applying the principle of *contraires choses*, we too, as readers, can see how the imagined bliss of consummation almost inevitably gives way to regret, despair, and disaster.

Second, Jean constructs a virtual catalogue of exemplary stories, especially in the context of love as *maladie*, by the temporal and social range of the examplary personages themselves. Not only do we go back in time to the Golden Age, we also move right up to the thirteenth-century present of Charles d'Anjou and Manfred, and of Ami and the Vieille. On a diachronic scale, these last examples also suggest social interrelations ranging from divinities and kings through urban marriages and adulteries to wastrels and prostitutes.

Third, each speaker in the *Rose* relates and interprets the examples from his or her own perspective, much as Croesus and Phanie variously interpret his dream as good or bad. When specific fables recur, as in the case of the Golden Age and of the Mars and Venus affair, the reader can mentally compare the different accounts and evaluate their cogency by his or her own standards. Of course, this implies rereading and reflection on meaning along the lines of the Froissart model.

Fourth and last, the commonplace closure of all the exemplary additions—with the astonishing exception of Pygmalion—is disaster. This is the case no matter how the examples are interpreted locally, and whether or not the speaker's interpretation takes the disaster into account. The paradigm for this reading is Phanie's interpretation of her father's dream. His literal reading of the dream is optimistic, but in the end it proves to be wrong. Although he rejects his daughter's interpretation, it is the right one. Had Croesus heeded her warnings, however, he could have escaped disaster. By the same token, the literal reading of the *Rose* favors Amant's opinion about love; and there is no disaster that turns the dream into a nightmare. Amant and the reader must awaken to reality in order to discover that the dream is a literal and allegorical *insomnium*, or wish fulfillment dream. In this equation, Jean de Meun represents Phanie and the reader is Croesus, Amant, Rose, or some variant or antithesis of one of them. The reader must decide to identify with the character or stand at a distance.

Thus, examples function as part of a rhetoric. They illustrate in order to elucidate topics and argue issues. They probably are the most constant, and slippery, mode of argumentation in medieval allegories. Yet, the mode is suitable for the lay audience Jean seems to address; it was considered especially effective for young learners like Amant.[49]

> Et por tenir la droite voie,
> Qui bien voudroit la chose amprandre,
> Qui n'est pas legiere a antandre,
> Un gros[50] example an porroit metre
> Aus genz lais qui n'antandent letre;
> Car tex genz veulent grosse chose,
> Sanz grant soutiveté de glose.
> (V. 17360–66)

[In order to hold course, whoever wished to take up the matter, which is not easy to understand, could introduce a rough example for lay folk who cannot read. For such persons want something roughly sketched out and plainly understandable without very subtle glossing.]

Such examples appeal to the imagination, making visible to the mind's eye the intended meaning, and thereby arguing convincingly by making the image appear real and true.

The *Rose* examples include several sets of interlocking and partially mirrored loves. All are *post factum* in the sense that they continue as well as terminate an affair after first consummation. All adumbrate in this way potential plots for both Amant and Rose beyond the end of the romance. In analyzing these scenarios, I propose to abstract the story told from the speaker. The use made of the story by the speaker will be discussed under the allegorical levels in chapter 5. What I am looking for here is the kind of example chosen and its formal relation to the *gradus amoris* and the *conservatio/deminutio amoris*.

A major example is Pygmalion. By mirror effect, he contrasts with Narcisse (as Jean incorporates Guillaume's figure into his adaptation) and Orphée. On the one hand, Pygmalion is linked to the gods through Venus, who brought to life the statue he falls in love with; furthermore, his grandson, Cynaeus, was seduced by—or rather tricked into having intercourse with—Pygmalion's great granddaughter, Mirra. Their son by incest, Adonis, became Venus's lover. Thus, Mirra joins Delilah as an exemplar of deceptive women who betray their men.

In the *Rose*, moreover, Pygmalion himself is the Ovidian exemplar of the final scenes. Generally, although not always, the scenes' comic features have been perceived as satirical.[51] Yet the immediate effect of the humanization of the statue does exemplify Reason's natural love (a mutual accord leading to delight and the birth of a child, Paphus,[52]) and thus serves to redeem Pygmalion's foolishness and the intervention of Venus. By Reason's standards, the birth of the child is neither good nor bad—it is, however, natural and thus correct. But Mirra's incest is not the result of Pygmalion's bad seed; rather, it comes about through the intervention of a "vielle" (v. 21162), who led Mirra to her father's bed. No sin except original sin is inherited.[53]

My valorization of the Pygmalion example may astonish some of Jean's readers. However, the text supports reading it as a love acceptable to Reason.[54] Jean as narrator says that one may as well liken the image in Jealousy's castle to Pygmalion's statue as one would a mouse to a lion, *contraires choses* in size, majesty, and nobility, a comparison the inflamed lover later restates in the opposite sense (v. 21191–97). Moreover, Pygmalion did not fashion the statue in his own image, to fit his own personal desires, or to gain a wife to dominate as the Jealous Husband did. Rather, he wanted to prove his artistic skill and acquire renown for the achievement (v. 20792–95). In this he resembles Jean de Meun working with Guillaume's material for the *Rose*. That Pygmalion subsequently fell in love with the statue was unexpected and unintended (v. 20808–10). To be sure, he foolishly tries to bestow gifts on the statue, but to no avail, and he realizes how foolish such actions are (v. 20827). Were the statue to come to life, he would marry her (v. 20984–90), not seduce her, as Amant does Rose. That is what actually transpires when, with Venus's aid, the statue becomes human. The whole affair is closer to Reason's definition of *amitié* than to that of love as *maladie*.

> S'il oppose, el se rent concluse;
> S'ele conmande, il obeïst;
> Por riens ne la contre deïst
> D'accomplir li tout son desir.
> (V. 21148–51)[55]

[If he opposes, she agrees; if she commands, he obeys; he would in no way refuse to do all she wishes of him.]

The birth of their child, Paphus, reinforces the opposition between Pygmalion and Amant, much as mutual support and response distinguish Pygmalion and his wife from the Jealous Husband and his.

Jean's narrator cuts short Mirra's story because it is not pertinent to his subject.

> Mes c'est trop loign de ma matire,
> Por c'est bien droiz qu'arriers m'an tire.
> Bien orroiz que ce senefie
> Ainz que ceste euvre soit fenie.
> (V. 21181–84)

[But this strays too far from my subject, and therefore it is right that I drop it. You will hear what this means before the conclusion of this work.]

This is a perplexing statement. Does "ce" in verse 21183 refer to the Cynaeus/Mirra story, its immediate referent, or to the entire Pygmalion exemplum, of which Mirra's incest is only an appendage? Grammatically, the former is the case; contextually the latter, since the narrative immediately tells how Venus brought Amant's statue to life with her flaming arrow, much as she did for Pygmalion's statue after his prayer to her. In a case like this, I like to apply the principle of *apo koinu*: working out the implications of both readings insofar as they are reflected in what precedes and follows in the grammatical or narrative structure. By doing so, the reader can plot through and evaluate diverse readings and contexts for the example.

The contextual referent is easy enough to discuss. Pygmalion's love for his statue anticipates Amant's love for the statue that suddenly emerges from and looms over Jealousy's castle. The resulting union of Amant and Rose is ambiguous as to impregnation (unlike Pygmalion's story) and therefore—from the point of view of Amant as narrator—irrelevant. The ambiguous line, "Si que tout le boutonet tandre / An fis ellargir et estandre" (v. 21699–700) [So that I made the small bud grow and extend], in context, suggests the arousal of Rose, not rapidly advancing pregnancy,[56] especially (as Amant imagines her) in the context of the lines that immediately follow: "Onques nul mau gré ne m'an sot / Li douz" (v. 21703–4) [The sweet thing was never resentful toward me because of it].[57] The only obvious child in Amant's complex of personifications is that produced by his attributes, Faux Semblant and Abstinence Contrainte. Their child is the Antichrist, whom they are waiting for and serving (v. 14713–15; cf. v. 11683, 11815). This "family" is analogous to that formed by Cynaeus, Mirra, and Adonis.

But the masculine "li douz" in the last citation, used to designate Rose, may well cause the reader to pause, as might the pronoun "il" in the same passage and context (v. 21706, 21707, 21710). The pronoun may refer to the "boutonet" of verse 21699 personified as well as to to Bel Acueil, while also perhaps suggesting an "unnatural" union between Amant and Rose. In the *Rose*, if intercourse is not reproductive, it is unnatural: Amant has merely spilled his seed, mixing it with that of the rosebud (v. 21697–98); his ejaculation is unreproductive. It is therefore analogous, as sin, to Mirra's incest and Orphée's sodomy. Whereupon the second interpretation of the antecedent *apo koinu* is met, taking Mirra's story as the immediate antecedent of "ce" in verse 21183. Although Mirra became pregnant, she gave birth to Adonis, Venus's lover and the unhappy victim of sexual violence.

Linking this *exemplum* to another, Genius refers to Orphée's sodomy in the context of those who impede or prevent natural reproduction. Unlike Pygmalion such lovers do not reproduce. In fact, Genius classes four sexual perversions as unproductive: incest, sodomy, castration, and virginity.[58] Orphée's perversion of sexuality, in Genius's worldview, is actually foreshadowed in Guillaume de Lorris by Narcisse. In Ovid, Narcisse is loved by both young men and young women. In Guillaume's adaptation, Echo alone tries to win his love. However, metamorphosis does not produce a flower but an allegory and a new gender; Narcisse becomes an example for haughty ladies to avoid. Similarly with Orphée, who first loved Eurydice, then turned to sodomy, Jean de Meun problematizes sexuality and sexual orientation. From examples of heterosexual love, as proposed by both Reason and Genius, emerge examples of incest, sodomy, and virginity as contrary to God's purposes with human sexuality. This brings us to Mirra's son, Adonis.

But, before discussing Adonis, I want to point out how the foregoing examples make the literal level enigmatic as to whether it relates a *somnium* or an *insomnium*, since Amant is still dreaming. As part of a dream, the literal version forces the reader to reflect on the incongruent juxtaposition of reproductive and unreproductive examples of sexuality. In the thirteenth century, such incongruity would have reminded the *Rose*'s audiences that sodomy and incest are, in fact, opposed to virginity, and that the latter virtue serves a higher purpose: salvation, both for the virgin and for those sinful mortals on whose behalf the virgin, especially the monastic virgin, may intercede by praying. To be sure, salvation is very much on Genius's mind, as the Park of the Lamb sermon shows. But his idea of salvation is ultimately won by the same natural forces at work in incest and sodomy.

Adonis, like Venus, is devoted to feminine sexuality: "Venus, qui les dames espire" (v. 15638)[59] [Venus, who arouses women]. Implied is the close cooperation between the sexual desire of men and women. Venus teaches Adonis how to hunt, recommending that Adonis pursue only timorous beasts, not those who defend themselves. But lovers do not listen to their beloved, so Adonis attacks a great boar one day: "Onc Venus ne l'an secourut, / Qu'ele n'i estoit pas presente" (v. 15710–11) [Venus never helped him because she was not present]. Without Venus, nothing can be caught, since Venus softens the objects of desire. The linking analogy to Amant's own "tournament" is obvious. Since Rose's fear resists all his efforts, Amant prudently withdraws before defeat to await the arrival of Venus. Ami's instruction is mirrored here too. No lover should disagree with his beloved; he should always defend himself by the "jeu d'amors" (v. 9786–88, 9821–22), that is, with Venus's aid (cf. v. 8222–24). This is the moral of Adonis's story as well: "Se cist s'amie eüst creüe, / Mout eüst sa vie creüe" (v. 15733–34) [If he had heeded his beloved, his life would have lasted much longer]. It seems that the lover should "hunt" only those whom Venus has "tamed"—that is, those who are as eager to be caught as he is to catch them. The conclusion to the *Rose* illustrates this in exemplary fashion.

Further clarified by *exempla* is the destructive power of the loved one, whether man or woman, as borne out by the chronicle of loves in Jean's *Rose*. There are those in which a man's love for a woman leads to the male's destruction, along with those—more frequent—in which the male overcomes or destroys his female lover. Among the former are the examples of Samson and Delilah and of Héloise and Abelard. Samson is lying asleep in the lap of Delilah when she cuts his hair, the source of his virility, as he had confessed to her (v. 16647–58). This portrait contrasts with that of Adonis, who is lying in Venus's lap when she advises him to avoid violent beasts (v. 15664–68). But Adonis is convinced he can take on anyone, like the *ribauz* who liken themselves to Roland, Samson, or Hercules (v. 9152–53) and whose opponent is the Jealous Husband. Delilah, in Venus's context, is a wild beast like the boar that emasculated Adonis. Amant, for his part, is storming Jealousy's castle and must beware lest, without Venus's help, Rose becomes his Delilah. All these images play off the same pattern, while exemplifying it in different but complementary and consistent ways.

The Adonis *exemplum* also functions to mirror Amant's story. Adonis's enemies are "wild boars" who might destroy him. In the event a boar "Contre Adonys esqueust la teste, / Ses denz en l'aine li flati, / Son groign estort, mort l'abati" (v. 15718–20) [Shook his head angrily against Adonis and, thrusting his teeth into his groin emasculated him, knocking him dead]. The reference transports us into Abelard's world. Like Adonis, Abelard suffers emasculation because he ignores his *amie*'s advice. Héloise

> requeroit que il l'amast,
> Mes que nul droit n'i reclamast,
> Fors que de grace et de franchise,
> Sanz seigneurie et sanz mestrise.
> (V. 8747–50)[60]

> [asked him to love her, but without claiming any right except those of grace and nobility, without either lordship or mastery.]

Because Abelard rejects her proposal, his fate is the same as Adonis's.

The second array, women betrayed in love, includes either the vengeance they take or their fates after betrayal. Nero's victims represent an extreme case that highlights the more commonplace examples. Indeed, Nero betrays both men and women. He puts Seneca to death (v. 6181) after having his brother killed (v. 6163) and violating his mother and sister.[61] Yet, pursued by his own people, Nero must finally commit suicide. This too works against Nature's purposes to continue the human race, since he "par ses fez tant porchaça / Que tout son lignage effaça" (v. 6435–36) [by his deeds brought about the extinction of his entire lineage]. This contrasts strikingly with the denouement of the Pygmalion *exemplum*, which is in line with Reason's plan for natural human sexuality.

> Mes conment que la besoigne aille,
> Qui veust d'amors joïr sanz faille,
> Fruit i doit querre et cil et cele,
> Quel qu'ele soit, dame ou pucele,

Ja soit ce que du deliter
Ne doivent pas leur part quiter.
(V. 4515–20; cf. 5733–58).

[But whatever happens, if one wishes to achieve true delight in love, one must seek offspring. This applies to the man and the woman, whether she be lady or maid. To be sure, they should not neglect their share of pleasure.]

All loves in the *Rose* except Pygmalion's comprise a litany of disasters, especially for women.

Chronologically, after Delilah and Samson comes Hercules, who loved Deianira, then betrayed her with Yolé; Deianira avenged her jealous rage by destroying him.[62] The Vieille's catalogue of betrayed women includes Dido, Phillis, Oenone, Medea, and herself. Jason sets the pattern. He is the first to undertake pilgrimages to strange lands, a reference for the reader rereading and therefore alert to Jean's anticipatory allegory of Amant's own first pilgrimage to Rose's shrine. Jason seeks the Golden Fleece, an apt analogue to the rose, by going overseas in search of it. In this he differs from his Golden Age ancestors.

Mes li prumier, don je vos conte,
Ne savoient que nagier[63] monte.
Trestout trovoient en leur terre
Quan que leur sembloit bon a querre;
Riche estoient tuit egaument
Et s'entramoient loiaument.
Ausinc pesiblement vivoient,
Car naturelment s'entramoient,
Les simples genz de bone vie.
Lors iert amor sanz symonie,
L'un ne demandoit riens a l'autre.
(V. 9487–97)

[But the first people I am telling you about knew nothing about sailing. They all found in their own lands whatever seemed worth seeking. They were all equally wealthy and loved one another faithfully. Thus they lived in peace, for they loved naturally, those honest people of good life. In those days there was no simony in love, no one asked anything of the other.]

Ami is evoking here a love like that which Reason locates under friendship. Jason's "pilgrimage" to foreign lands, however, prefigures Amant's kind of love after he rejects Reason, "Quant Baraz vint lance sus fautre / Et Pechiez et Male Aventure, / Qui n'ont de Soffisance cure" (v. 9498–500)

[When Fraud came with lance in place, and Sin and Misfortune who care not for Sufficiency]. Other vices and defects follow in their wake.

All the Vieille's false lovers betray their loves while sailing abroad. Jason went to Calcas where he loved Medea but betrayed her after returning to Greece with her. Paris abandoned Oenone for the foreign woman, Helen, whom he sailed away to abduct from her homeland and her husband. Demophon, while returning from the siege of Troy, loved and left Phillis. Eneas loved Dido, then abandoned her to sail on to Lavine. The results: Medea's infanticide,[64] the destruction of Troy and return of Helen to Greece, Phillis's and Dido's suicides.[65] These instances of betrayal in the context of war in fact mirror the union between Mars and Venus, reducing explicit actions—combats, voyages, pilgrimages, or whatever—to examples of the "batailles que li con esmurent" (v. 13894) [battles incited by cunts],[66] and that terminate as soon as the party is won and the champions can move on to new conquests. Women, the Vieille says, should emulate men: they should become conquerors rather than objects of conquest (v. 13235–42). All these examples rehearse the commonplace decline and disaster of love after consummation. All serve the overall intention to teach by example, while adding powerful rhetorical argument to Jean's hidden agenda: the allegory of foolish love.

Indeed, two *exempla* show the precarious state of the most excellent female virtue. Virginie and Lucrece followed willy-nilly the route to death taken by Phillis and Dido. Appius was, unlike Amant in his attempt to seduce Rose, unable to seduce Virginie (v. 5566–68). Rather than rape her outright, or call on Venus's aid, he sought a go-between, his servant, who claimed that Virginie was his own, abducted daughter: "La pucele est moie. / Por ma serve[67] la proveroie" (v. 5571–72) [The maid is mine. I'll prove she was my slave]. As judge, Appius quickly declared this servant to be Virginie's father, whereupon her true father, Virginius, committed infanticide, beheading Virginie to save her honor. This "merveilleuz apensement" (v. 5603) [marvelous reasoning] illustrates in Reason's opinion the bad judge in the specific context of lust and sexual violence. Although the *exempla* of both Virginie and Lucrece can illustrate woman's courage and constancy, as they do, for example, in Christine de Pizan's *Cité des dames*, they do not function that way in the *Rose*'s account of their fates. They rather illustrate human depravity—in this instance, male depravity—that leaves the woman no recourse except death. In human terms, Virginie and Lucrece are analogous to Socrates and Seneca, who also accept death for the sake of virtue. The turn of fortune and moral depravity destroy them all. Their only consolation is that proposed by Boethius: virtue.[68]

In response to such events, the Jealous Husband, for his part, refuses to believe there are any more Penelopes or Lucreces among women. Lucrece, for example, was raped by Tarquinius's son. Both her husband and her family supported her, exonerating her of any blame. But, unable to pardon herself, she committed suicide, her punishment, she said, for the sin. She died asking for vengeance. The examples of Virginie and Lucrece are analogous to those of Dido and Phillis, and, *mutatis mutandis*, that of Abelard. The one common denominator is that love and lust are irrational and violent, and should be eschewed. Only love conducive to child-bearing is sanctioned, a love like Pygmalion's when blessed by Hymeneus and Juno with offspring (cf. v. 20981–90). Yet, as Tarquinius and the Jealous Husband prove, even a good marriage offers no refuge from violence. All these examples prefigure potentially nightmarish sequels to Amant's dream, had he not awoke.

There is no suggestion that Amant intends anything like Pygmalion. He is operating with the blessing of Venus alone, not that of Juno or Hymeneus. His sole preoccupation is sexual conquest, both before and after he seduces Rose, and his story contains the potential of all the mythical examples except for Pygmalion's. Jean has clearly chosen examples that relate an ironic preservation or enhancement of love (*conservatio* or *augmentum amoris*)—ironic because they preserve nothing and illustrate only a serious decline and end of love (*deminutio* or *finis amoris*)[69]—an array of deaths and vengeances, summed up in Lucrece's appeal " . . . qu'il travaillassent / Tant por lui que sa mort venchassent" (v. 8611–12) [that they strive to avenge her death], for "Je ne m'en pardoig pas la peine" (v. 8607) [I don't pardon myself the punishment for it]. A powerful argument, no doubt, except for the woman like Rose who projects her life into Lucrece's.

But, in addition, the story of Lucrece mirrors two other examples directly linked to Amant's "pilgrimage": the Jealous Husband's and the Vieille's. Both belong to the *conservatio/deminutio* phase of love. When the assiduous lover becomes the Jealous Husband, the wife will soon notice the difference:

> cil qui seut servir cele
> Conmande que cele le serve
> Ausinc con s'ele fust sa serve,
> Et la tient courte et li conmande
> Que de ses fez conte li rande,
> Et sa dame ainceis l'apela!
> (V. 9438–43)

> [He who used to serve her now orders her to serve him as if she were his slave, keeping her on short leash and demanding that she account for her conduct—and he used to call her his lady!]

The decline from "lady" to "serf" or "slave" marks the narrative change in Material Style from the mythological and historical examples cited above to more down-to-earth experience in the contemporary world of Ami and the Vieille. In medieval terminology the foregoing examples are all women's tragedies, briefly related, in the sense of the tragedies told by the Monk in Chaucer's *Canterbury Tales.*

> Tragedie is to seyn a certeyn storie,
> As olde bookes maken us memorie,
> Of hym that stood in greet prosperitee,
> And is yfallen out of heigh degree
> Into myserie, and endeth wrecchedly.
> (V. 1973–77/*3163–67)[70]

However, medieval tragedy, as John of Garland's example of a tragedy makes obvious, could range from Medea to women performing the services of camp concubines and washer women (*Parisiana Poetria* 7.1–153). This is reflected in the *Rose*'s "lower class" loves, like Ami's and the Vieille's. They know the same fate as gods and goddesses, heroes and heroines.

With Ami and the Vieille, the Material Style has changed. They evoke the "middle" or "working class" denizens of urban milieux who dwell in apartments, not in the palaces of princes.[71] When Ami tells how the Jealous Husband abuses his wife, her screams bring in neighbors from her own building and those nearby, along with passersby from the street. Similarly, in a variation of the Jealous Husband's marriage, Nature tells how a wife seduces her husband into telling his secrets. But the setting is the same. The description of their bedroom includes neighbors on the other side of the wall and passersby just outside the window (v. 16381–95).

The Vieille's world is no more loving or lovable than Ami's. It is peopled by the same shopgirls and hustlers, pimps, gamblers, and drifters whom Villon would still find in medieval city streets. Her love fails too. Like their aristocratic exemplars, the inhabitants of the Vieille's world live for sex and thrive on deceit and mutual pilfering. It is a world in which love is synonymous with avarice and greed.

On the other hand, the *dramatis personae* of Ami's conjugal world includes three principal personages: the Jealous Husband, his wife, and her seducer.[72] In this setup, the Jealous Husband's wife may or may not be unfaithful. Since she says nothing during his tirade, we may read his jealousy as either justified or unfounded; the only certainty in Ami's depiction of him is his change after marriage from a loving, willing servant of his lady to the domineering slave master his tirade bespeaks.

The Vieille, however, offers a counter-model. The wife of such men or even of a less abusive husband balances lovers, frantically manipulating the men for her own gain, security, vengeance, and independence before her looks fail her and she is left alone, as with the Vieille after that transformation in her own life. But the men she hates have no more secure future, as we may judge by Ami, who suffered financial ruin while trying to splurge his way into the arms of the woman he desired, and the Vieille's *ribaut*, who died somewhere among gambling *crapule*, leaving her nothing.

This summary statement of the various tragedies exemplified in the *Rose* includes an array of depressing scenarios.[73] In the marriage the husband is a jealous, abusive tyrant whose wife may be faithful or not. In either case, the husband who trusts his wife enough to tell her his secrets will either be betrayed by her or become her victim out of fear that she will betray him. His secrets in the *Rose* are crimes he has committed or intends to commit. Whether in or out of marriage, *ribauz* and *ribaudes* proliferate everywhere. Seeking free love (*amor carnalis*) or profit from love (*amor mundialis*), to recall Aelred of Rievaulx's terminology, they destroy one another and many marriages. In this scenario, the Jealous Husband and his wife exemplify marriage, Ami and the Vieille represent the free love of *ribauts*. All show love and marriage without friendship or *amitié*.

Like Guillaume de Lorris's dream that announced to him a love yet to be experienced, these examples tell Amant and Rose what to expect after he plucks the rose. The enjoyment of the rose—or what passes for it in Amant's clinical description of the act—is small indeed. As Amant contemplates his potential postcoital life, he reduces women to *cons* of various sizes and ages, and himself to a walking phallus. Amant expounds on the advantages of young ones and old ones, ditches and holes, confident that Rose has not made a similar study of *coilles* and *viz* (v. 21630–37). If he is right, of course, Rose's relationship to Amant will be as miserable as those of other women abused in love, the Vieille and the Jealous Husband's wife as well as Phillis and Dido, Oenone and Medea. Or, if Rose has followed the Vieille's advice and explored the world of male sexuality, her and Amant's relationship will surely duplicate the frenzy and violence that characterize the war of the sexes in the Jealous Husband's house or the Vieille's relationship. Thus, Amant's *gradus amoris* interlaces with numerous *conservationes/deminutiones amoris* that admonish the thoughtful audience. Whatever the perspective, all these examples teach the same lesson: Amant's kind of love, like most other kinds, leads to misery and disaster.

The two gods who dominate the *Rose* put all this into the perspective of universal history and its succeeding ages. Venus—mother of Love/Cupid, wife of Vulcan, and lover of many men—and Jupiter—who castrated his father and was an unfaithful husband and abductor of many women—are the *Rose*'s patron deities. Venus was born from Jupiter's castration of Saturn (v. 19824–34), an act that put an end to the Golden Age (v. 5505–20, 20002–6, 20155–78). The descent into the Iron Age (v. 20053–178) is signaled by Jupiter himself, when he established pleasure as the highest good, divided land into properties, created enmity among humans as well as between them and animals and among animals, produced the four seasons, and invented the arts. In the midst of these tribulations, Jupiter established the pleasure principle, as implied by Venus when she rose up from Saturn's testicles. Delight is the goal of life, and deceit is the art used to acquire it (v. 20079–84). Jupiter's new world order fits Reason's definition of that Love whose minions love for carnal pleasure.

Reason

Pour acoler et pour besier
Pour els charnelment aesier.
Amant autre chose n'entant,
Ainz s'art et se delite en tant.
(V. 4353–56)

[to embrace, kiss, and sexually gratify
themselves. A Lover seeks nothing else,
that's all he burns for and delights in.]

Jupiter

Jupiter, qui le monde regle,
Conmande et establist por regle
Que chascuns pense d'estre aese;
Et s'il set chose qui li plese,
Qu'il la face, s'il la peust fere,
Por soulaz a son queur atrere.
(V. 20065–70)

[Jupiter who governs the world
commands and establishes by law that
each think how to ease him- or herself.
And if he or she knows some source of
pleasure, do it if it's possible, to solace
the heart.]

Similarly, both Amant and Jupiter see pleasure as the supreme good.

Amant

Atropos mourir ne me doigne
Fors en fesant vostre besoigne,
Ainz me praigne en meïsmes l'euvre
Don Venus plus volentiers euvre,
Car nus n'a, ce ne dout je point,
Tant de delit conme an ce point.
(V. 10341–46)

Jupiter

Car deliz, si conme il disoit,
C'est la meilleur chose qui soit
Et li souverains biens en vie.
(V. 20075–77)

[May Atropos let me die only while performing your act. May she take me in the very act in which Venus most willingly operates; for no one has as much pleasure as at that time—I have no doubt about it.]

[For, as he said, delight is the best thing there is and the supreme good in life.]

In the context of the *Rose*'s examples, the greatest good and pleasure in life becomes truly morbid.

Although Venus is the God of Love's mother, the two do not always see eye to eye. Love says he calls on his mother only when necessary because he does not approve of all her activities, notably prostitution and other forms of sex for sale (v. 10719–96). In the *Rose*'s plot, Venus provides Genius with the burning candle that, at the conclusion of his sermon, sets afire the assembled hosts of Love. She in turn fires the burning arrow that inflames Jealousy's castle, causes its capitulation, and leads to Bel Acueil's surrender of the rose.

Since the sounding board for Jupiter and Venus is Amant's malady, as defined by Reason's adaptation of Andreas Capellanus's definition of love, the decline from the Golden Age to the Iron Age prefigures Amant's own decline from the constant generous love advocated by Love in Guillaume de Lorris to the quest for carnal pleasure that Amant exemplifies at the end of his dream. The castration, or rather the severing of the testicles, removes that part of the male genitalia that permits conception, leaving only the penis to experience and give delight. It is apt in this context that Amant expresses little awareness of delight during his wet dream. It also suggests his assimilation to a castrate.

Amant's moral decline fits as well the model of Fortune's Wheel. Indeed, Reason links the image of the Wheel with those of the two rivers of good and bad fortune and of Fortune's teetering house to announce Amant's inevitable fall. That fall in Amant's and Rose's case is also prefigured by the Sleepwalker digression, at the end of which the sick dreamer falls to the ground (v. 18297–394). At the end of the *Rose*, Amant also falls before Rose after her defenses have burned to the ground and her image has collapsed. As Nature explains, only Reason can counter the diverse effects of fortune, but neither Amant nor Rose pays any attention to Reason. Thus, their story together, which is just beginning with the "fall" at the end of the *Rose* (*ordo artificialis*), anticipates the calamities typical of the exemplary misfortunes recounted during their *gradus amoris* in *ordo naturalis*. To fall into one another's arms in their case is to fall into the muck and mire under Fortune's Wheel.

To summarize, all these examples begin chronologically with the castration of Saturn. This act puts an end to the Golden Age, gives birth to Venus, and inaugurates the arts with which humans seek pleasure as the supreme good. The ensuing history of pleasure-seeking couples and triangles illustrates corruption and disaster as ages succeed one another up to the current Iron Age, over time and throughout human history. Indeed, if we gather these examples of love adventures together in a catalogue,[74] we discover an implicit chronological sequence that extends from the mythographic age of partially euhemerized Saturn, Jupiter, and Venus to current events like Manfred's defeat and the love lives of Ami and the Vieille.[75] That is, the catalogue illustrates in rough chronological order Jean's minihistory as a species of *forma tractandi* by exemplification:

Divinities
- Saturn's castration and Jupiter's promulgation of the pleasure principle
- Jupiter + Juno + Io: triangle
- Venus + Vulcan + Mars: triangle
    - + Adonis[76]

History or Euhemerized Mythology
- Samson betrayed by Delilah
- Orphée as sodomite
- Narcisse + Echo + Narcisse's own image: triangle
- Jason + Medea + another, unnamed woman: triangle
- Hercules + Deianira + Yolé: triangle
- Paris + Oenone + Helen: triangle
- Eneas + Dido + Lavine: triangle
- Demophon betrays Phillis
- Socrates's suicide, put to death by Athenians
- Appius + Virginius + Virginie triangle: unjust judge and infanticide
- Tarquin + Husband + Lucrece triangle: rape and suicide
- Croesus + Phanie: moral blindness
- Nero + Mother + sister triangle: incest, murder, suicide
    - + Seneca: murder, suicide
- Pygmalion + statue: love marriage
    - Paphus: child of their love marriage
    - Capaneus + Mirra: incest
        - Adonis: child of their incest, gored to death[77]
- Abelard + Héloise: castration and forced separation
- Manfred, Charles of Anjou, and Conradin: assassination
- Ami + *ribaudes*: seduction and impoverishment

Vieille + her special *ribaut* + other *ribauts*: abuse, lust, and prostitution
Amant + Rose: deceit, seduction, and infidelity as cycle of betrayal promises to repeat itself

This "universal history" prefigures Christine de Pizan's *Mutacion de Fortune*, although it functions as a catalogue of disasters. The context of most of the *Rose* examples is the kind of love which Reason condemns. The positive lesson of this history, whether moral or *événementielle*, is that Amant's and Rose's kind of love is disastrous because they scorn the one agent, Reason, able to circumvent fortune and orient them toward a friendship founded on sufficiency, fidelity, and generosity.

Reason's own rationality, however, grates a bit on sensibilities since her language borders on the obscene. But is not such obscenity inherent in language itself, which is corrupt, thereby mirroring the twin corruption of mores and moral language during the decline from the Golden Age to the Iron Age? That Reason uses the words *coilles* and *andoilles* is rhetorically incorrect when addressing a *fol amoureux*. She had other, more decent language at her disposal, as we have seen. Yet, it is not the language as much as the associations that are at fault. Literal, proper language has been twisted into obscenity such that it cannot be used objectively. Human language, which Reason personifies as much as she does the mental faculty, is corrupt. Her language makes this obvious, especially when the literal comparison of *coilles* and *andoilles*, itself merely humorous, becomes obscene when the thirteenth-century (and modern) connotations of these words color the language, as they inevitably do. Nonetheless, although Reason here personifies the reason of Iron Age man and woman, she (and, therefore, they) still knows enough to orient Amant's conduct and redirect his desires. That is, as the personification of Amant's own rational faculty, Reason also shows that he has the capacity to correct himself. His decision not to heed his reason by rejecting Reason's lesson is a moral decision and must be evaluated as such. In Jean's world, a human who rejects reason is unreasonable and, consequently, out of control.

Yet, Reason has been judged a defective purveyor of examples. Indeed, Marc Pelen has found Reason wrongheaded and even comic in her choice of them.[78] He notes that the castration of Saturn is awkwardly close to the decapitation of Virginie, that Socrates's and Seneca's wisdom leads to violent death, and that Abelard's misfortune is hardly more pleasant. The *ribauts de Greve*—whose name and actions mirror the amorous *ribauts* who populate other *Rose* examples and eventually absorb Amant himself—Reason casts as models of Boethian sufficiency.

Icarus and Dedalus show how men may escape by flight, yet we must wonder whether Jean's audience knew of Icarus's "fall" after flying too high. Finally, Manfred's fate is an implicit warning for Charles d'Anjou on the turns of fortune.

Although Reason's use of language and examples is at times dubious, one of Reason's examples may help put her thought in another perspective, or at least serve as a warning to the reader. Phanie, the prophetic daughter of Croesus, delineates the truth in her father's dream as a caveat on impending misfortune.[79] Croesus refuses to accept her integumental reading. Rather, he insists on the literal truth of the dream, convinced that he is a favorite of the gods. He may very well be, because the gods' favorites do not fare well in the *Rose*. This fact in itself cautions Jean's readers—and may make them squirm a little too.

It seems obvious that we must bear in mind Phanie's example when reading Reason's other examples. Croesus's imagination, like Amant's, is a literally attuned imagination. He is not interested in his daughter's integuments because the letter itself looks rosy. Amant does not wish to inquire into Reason's interpretations either. He takes the chaff—*coilles* as a word he can accept and use—and leaves the grain—that which can permit reproduction. "Mes des poetes les sentances, / Les fables et les methaphores / Ne bé je pas a gloser ores" (v. 7160–62) [But I'm not now interested in glossing poets' meanings, fables, and metaphors]. For Amant, the *Roman de la rose* is a book only about plucking roses. Its examples sustain his reading on the literal level. For the reader, they also point to its disastrous consequences.

We may now appreciate the skill with which Jean de Meun consistently uses examples to illustrate both his rhetorical intent and the romance's double instruction. The pleasure principle dominates the letter of Amant's story, and literal readers will, perhaps, promise one another the same rewards from the gods which Croesus imagined for himself. But the profitable instruction of the *Rose*, which is also part of Jean's intention as poet, points to an allegorical *integumentum* that contradicts the literal meaning, serving as a reminder that Phanie's quite different reading of her father's dream was the right one. The letter and its allegory are *contraires choses*. The allegorical reading actually emerges from the first story, which, like Guillaume's *Rose*, is also incomplete in Jean's version. Yet, also like Guillaume's version, Jean's contains embedded signals as to what would have happened had Amant gone on dreaming. The signals are the examples. In this scenario, an erotic wish fulfillment dream becomes a nightmare. The reader who reads only once, completing the *Rose* when Amant awakens, repeats Croesus's error. One knows the truth of the plot both by mentally following the literal story to the conclusion implied by its examples, and by understanding and applying the Boethian statements about true and false goods and true and false loves.

All the so-called scientific and philosophical modes point Jean's reader toward a Boethian satire on foolish love. Whatever pleasures such love may offer, experience and written authority argue powerfully and persuasively that they are transitory, meager, and false. The argument is sustained throughout Jean's part of the *Rose* by his use of definitions and digressions that restate the terms of Guillaume's art of love and by the debate and examples that either demonstrate the morbid drift of false loves toward disaster and violence, or show indirectly how the logic of seduction is false or foolish.

4

The Poetic and Rhetorical Modes of Treatment

Sed aliter credo quod Siton magnus philosophus fuit qui considerando metaforice superclestia que activa dicuntur in eis peritus fuit et sic fuit homo, sed quia etiam peritus fuit in philosophia naturali conscidarando speram activorum et paxivorum et in hiis peritissimus fuit ideo dictus est femina.

—Vatican lat. ms. 2877

[But otherwise I believe that Siton was a great philosopher, who, when considering metaphorically supercelestial phenomena which are called active, became an expert in such matters and thus was a man; but because he was also knowledgeable about natural philosophy, when considering the sphere of active and passive things and being an expert in these matters, he is called a woman.]

The epigraph[1] to this chapter illustrates one of its main topics as well as a crucial issue in *Rose* scholarship today: sex and gender in allegory. Siton is both a man and a woman according to his or her role and activities. The male activities take his mind into the realm of ideas, whereas Siton's female studies concern her with sublunar phenomena. This curious, even crude and forced allegory—is the man closer to God or has he lost his head in the clouds, is the woman on a lower level or is she more down-to-earth and rational?—is less important than the poetic fiction which uses commonplace, traditional sex roles and hierarchies to define levels of philosophical investigation which, of and by themselves, are entirely legitimate and honorable. More specifically, literal sex and gender function here metaphorically to characterize a person who, literally, does not have the sex attributed to him or her. Ovid played with such metamorphoses, authorizing Christine de Pizan's own allegory of her fictional metamorphosis into a man in the *Mutacion de Fortune*. In so doing, she defines not her sex, but her role in terms of commonplace, traditional gender roles. Jean de Meun does much the same for Amant, but with an entirely different intent. These are features of description, one of the poetic and rhetorical *modi tractandi.*

INTRODUCTIONS TO MEDIEVAL WRITINGS (II)

As Jean de Meun describes them, the poetic and rhetorical modes belong to the poet's office. They are not argumentative in nature but rather serve to delineate and to amplify forcefully upon a given matter. In this chapter, I shall continue following the Froissart model by rereading the *Rose* to discern its poetic and rhetorical treatment of the *gradus amoris* of Amant and Rose.

The poetic and rhetorical modes include devices common in medieval poetics, especially for purposes of amplification. *Poeticus*, or "poetic," identifies not only writings in verse but also the artificial order of treatment as distinguished from natural order. Natural order usually refers to chronological order of events in narrative; but it may also designate a commonplace topical sequence like the *gradus amoris*, or the stages of falling in love from sight to consummation. Artificial order, in contrast, occurs when a normal or expected chronological or topical sequence is set out in a different order. Important here, in an allegory like the *Rose*, is the fact that the literal level may follow one order, while the allegorical level or levels may represent a different, "artificial" order.[2] On the other hand, *fictivus*, or "fictive," refers to the use of fictional matter that is nonetheless a convincing or moving illustration of a proposition. *Descriptivus*—usually called "descriptive" but more properly termed "topical" or "commonplace"—refers in medieval terminology to the elaboration of circumstantial topoi (for example, *sexus*) so as to make things conform to signification, context, or commonplace expectations. *Digressivus*, or "digressive," may include the three or four principal kinds of digression common in medieval rhetoric or poetics: digression from natural order to another part of the subject matter, digression to a topic outside the subject matter, either to bring in something useful for the case being made (*digressio utilis*) or simply to vary presentation—much like an interlude—which is typical of poetic style (*digressio inutilis*).[3] Finally, *transumptivus*, or "metaphorical," includes allegory. The modes of irony and personification fit, respectively, under the metaphorical and descriptive modes.

The poetic and rhetorical modes move us closer toward the *Rose*'s allegorical meanings. The poetic mode, defined by the poet's office, encompasses the rewriting characteristic of the medieval poet. That rewriting turns Guillaume de Lorris's allegorical autobiography, recounted in the mode of a true dream exemplifying an art of love, into a false dream representing an art of seduction. Hence, the true biography becomes a fiction and is recounted in the fictional mode. Amant himself changes from lover to seducer. Accordingly, the descriptive mode metamorphoses Guillaume's Amant into a new character. Perhaps the most astonishing feature of Amant's metamorphosis is his assumption of feminine attributes and actions that are commonplace in medieval misogyny. In this way, Jean adopts in the descriptive mode the features of human sex difference and orientation to grammatical gender and its anomalies. Topical digressions support these new contexts while contributing to the rewriting, especially by the *mise en abyme* of the Sleepwalker in Nature's complaint. Finally, the metaphorical mode sets forth clearly the two main lines of argument advanced by Jean's allegory: the art of seduction and the foolishness and irrationality, the fundamental inhumanity, of such deceit. The reader is thus squarely confronted by the issue of morality in the *Rose* and by his or her moral response to the plot and the exemplary lessons it teaches on its literal and allegorical levels.

THE POETIC MODE (*Modus poeticus*)

The poetic mode has two facets: versification and the traditional office of the *poeta* in medieval poetics. In the first sense Jean de Meun is a poet because he uses verse and rhyme; and the *Rose* is a poem because it is written in rhymed octosyllabic couplets. Versification in the *Rose* cannot be described otherwise and, as such, has no significance for the interpretation of the poem, unlike *terza rima* in Dante's *Divine Comedy*.

The other sense of the poetic mode is significant here. In chapter 1 we examined briefly the two passages in which Jean refers to the office of the poet and likens his task to it. (see pp. 14–15). In the first passage he refers to the use of *integumenta* in poetic discourse and thus to the use of allegory to elicit truth from exemplary matter. The *Rose* is, consequently, a poem because it is an allegory. I shall examine the allegorical mode in this chapter's section on the metaphorical mode and its interpretation in chapter 5. I shall say here only that the two or more levels of interpretation in allegory, the literal and others, contribute to the poetic intention Jean refers to in his second reference to the poet's office of providing "profiz et delectacion" (v. 15211), a translation of the Horatian "Aut prodesse volunt aut delectare poetae, / Aut simul et iucunda et idonea dicere vitae"[4] [poets wish to give profit or pleasure, or express what is pleasing and, at the same time, suitable in life], to which I shall also return in chapter 5. The *Rose* certainly can fit at least one of Horace's three categories, depending on how it is read: it pleases, it instructs, or it both pleases and instructs. Jean's words imply that it should do both: "profiz *et* delectacion."

Beyond this general poet's *dictum*, Jean also says that the poet recites or reports ancient authorities, only occasionally adding something new to them. It is important that reporting as relating—*reciter*—is not copying. Amplifications and abbreviations are permissible; indeed, they are almost requisite. Since the art is Horatian, what follows is a brief sketch of this particular notion of the poet who "recites" ancient authority as preserved in sources.

Perhaps most fundamentally, Horace prefers that the poet treat well-known rather than new matter.[5] Matthew of Vendôme expresses the same preference by dividing *materia* into two kinds: *materia pertractata*, or *executa*, that is, material like the Trojan War that poets have already written about, and *materia illibata*, material which has not been treated before and may be entirely new—"created," as it were.[6] Matthew echoes Horace in urging that the former is harder to treat, and, hence, success more estimable.

Geoffrey of Vinsauf also takes up Horace's admonitions in his *Documentum*: "Est notandum quod difficile est materiam communem et usitatam convenienter et bene tractare. Et quanto difficilius, tanto laudabilius est bene tractare materiam talem, scilicet communem et usitatam, quam materiam aliam, scilicet novam et inusitatam."[7] [Note that it is difficult to treat a commonplace, familiar subject matter aptly and well, much more difficult, and thus praiseworthy if treated well, than another subject which is new and unfamiliar.] Geoffrey bases his admonition on Horace's *Ad Pisones*, in *Opera*, verse 128–30: "Difficile est proprie communia dicere; tuque / Rectius Iliacum carmen deducis in actus, / Quam si proferres ignota indictaque primus" [It is difficult to treat common matter well. You would do better to narrate the Trojan War rather than treat unknown, unheard subjects].

The commentary tradition which Matthew and Geoffrey probably drew on followed the Horatian recommendation while schematizing it for pedagogical purposes.[8] A particularly interesting development on verse 128–30 is found in the *scholia* attributed to Heiric of Auxerre (second half of the ninth century).[9] The commentator insists that it is more difficult to treat extant matter, criticizing on the basis of Horace's authority those who have argued for greater originality in choice of subject matter. Originality, then, exists in achieving what Horace and the other commentators call making a *materia communis* become *propria*. Anticipating Matthew and other glossators and commentators,[10] Heiric says that the new version should not merely translate or paraphrase the old one (cf. *Ad Pisones* v. 135). Taking Vergil as an example, he continues:

> Si quis diceret illas easdem sententias quas Vergilius dicit, licet aliis verbis, tamen non esset proprie sua materia; sed si eandem materiam haberet et alias sententias et alia verba[11] ex toto poneret, tunc de communi faceret propriam materiam, quod facere difficile est. (*Scholia in Horatium* 4:465)[12]

> [If one were to express the same meanings as Vergil, albeit by paraphrase, then it would not properly speaking be that person's matter. But if one used the same matter, but lay it out with totally different meanings and language, then one would have made one's own work with matter that is known and generally shared. This is difficult to do!]

According to these traditional distinctions between two kinds of *materia*, Guillaume de Lorris, unlike Jean, considered his *Rose* as fashioning *materia illibata* (v. 39, 2064). Jean de Meun himself treats *materia* largely *pertractata*, by rewriting it, but also includes some *materia illibata*, by continuing the *Rose* onto a different conclusion from the one Guillaume announces. Of course, Jean also uses secondary sources, or *materia pertractata*, to do so, as in the Pygmalion example. In other words, Jean rewrote Guillaume's *Rose*, giving new shape and meaning to his predecessor's version with descriptions, debates, digressions, and other modes of treatment. Then, at precisely the point where Guillaume's *Rose* ended, he introduced "quelque parole," profoundly altering the content and meaning of the *Rose* as Guillaume began it. Jean's new twist that prepares for the rest of the poem makes Guillaume's incomplete *Rose* new. He did so, in Horatian terms, by inventing a new person. That new person emerges when Amant decides to practice deceit.

Now, Horace says that if one "dares" to invent a new person, one should be consistent from beginning to end. Horace is explicit, as are his glossators, Matthew and Geoffrey: "Si quid inexpertum scaenae[13] committis et audes / Personam formare novam, servetur ad imum / Qualis ab incepto processerit, et sibi constet" (*Ad Pisones*, in *Opera*, v. 125–27) [If you publish and dare to fashion an unknown, new person, let that person conform to his or her beginnings and be consistent to the end]. The change in Amant's character is consistent with these recommendations. Guillaume's Amant too illustrates changes in character as his seduction of Rose progresses, including deceit as a stage in the *gradus amoris* following on Ami's recommendation that Amant hide his true feelings. Following on Guillaume's example, which already demonstrated a tendency to alter the conception of love from adventure to adventure, Jean let Amant descend into carnality. Thus, Amant backslides into the stage he occupied when, in the first adventure in Guillaume, he asked for the rose outright. Thus, Jean adopts Guillaume's strategy for character variation, but adapts it along new lines.

In chapter 1, I summarized my interpretation of Guillaume's Amant, whereby Amant evinces and anticipates an elevation in the quality of his sentiments from carnal desire toward a less possessive love.[14] Nonetheless, the two encounters between Amant and the rose in Guillaume are erotic enough to allow Jean to let Amant slide back into the carnality characterizing his first adventure in Guillaume. With Venus's aid, as in Amant's second and last adventure in Guillaume's *Rose*, Amant can subsequently sink to carnality, then to deceit. In short, Jean rewrites Amant's trajectory in Guillaume as "backslide," making the decision to practice deceit a credible stage in the *gradus amoris* as decline in quality (*deminutio amoris*) by integrating Amant's earlier mutability in Guillaume into his own continuation and conclusion. Jean's version is therefore an allegory of Guillaume's plot because the first author's conception of Amant and his love is rewritten in terms of seduction and deceit.

THE FICTIONAL MODE (*Modus fictivus*)

The fictional mode transforms Guillaume de Lorris's autobiographical allegory into a fiction—a false life and a false dream, with an allegory whose truth lies beyond and outside what the fictional plot seems to exemplify literally.

The fictional mode is both prominent and complex in the *Rose*. It has ramifications in the three remaining modes to be discussed in this chapter. A fable (*fabula*) is a fiction, that is, literally, a lie. But it may also blanket a truth and hence function as an *integumentum*.[15] Reason explains this to Amant while justifying her literal account of the castration of Saturn.

> Qui bien entendroit la letre,
> Le sen verroit en l'escriture,
> Qui esclarcist la fable occure.
> La verité dedenz reposte
> Seroit clere, s'el iert esposte;
> Bien l'entendras, se bien repetes
> Les integumanz aus poetes.
> (V. 7132–38)

> [If one properly understood the letter, one would perceive the text's meaning, which would clarify the obscure fable. The truth hidden in it would be clear if it were revealed. You will get it right if you consult the poets' integuments.]

Thereafter Reason anticipates Jean's own allusion to the Horatian *delectare* and *prodesse* by explaining how the fable and its hidden truth bring both pleasure and profit (v. 7143–50). Amant's disinterest in hidden meanings shows his unwillingness to learn the truth of Reason's fable.

The integumental fable reveals its kernel, or hidden truth, through the form of its shell, or surface letter. These two aspects of the fable, kernel and shell, will be taken up successively in the following sections on descriptive, digressive, and metaphorical modes. Here I propose to consider the true as opposed to the false fable in the context of true and false dreams, and then show how this distinction relates to the poet's original treatment of commonplace matter.

Traditionally, a *fabula* is a fiction containing the outline or lineaments of a truth. As such it is an *imago*,[16] which is true or false according to whether it accurately represents that outline or not. An *imago* is, in other words, like a mirror. Of course, there may be disagreement as to what is perceived. The good life for Reason, based on attention to Boethian *sufficientia*, is not Genius's good life based on a very active sex life. Which image of the good life is in fact true may ultimately depend on authority—in the last analysis, divine authority. But appeal to authority is not so simple as it may appear today.

A passage in the *Rose* illustrates appeal to authority and, at the same time, the problems such appeal may raise. Jean appeals to authority in his debate with women in his audience who were offended by his representation of them. It focuses on the issue of true and false images and hence of truth and falsity.

> D'autre part, dames honorables,
> S'il vos samble que je di fables,
> Por manteür ne m'an tenez,
> Mes aus aucteurs vos an prenez
> Qui an leur livres ont escrites
> Les paroles que g'en ai dites,
> Et ceus avec que g'en dirai;
> Ne ja de riens n'an mentirai,[17]
> Se li preudome n'en mentirent
> Qui les anciens livres firent.
> (V. 15185–94)

[On the other hand, worthy ladies, if you think I am making up stories don't take me for a liar. Criticize the authors who put into their books the words I have said and will say on the subject. I shall in no way speak falsehoods unless the worthy men did who wrote the old books.]

As is well know, Christine de Pizan responded by questioning authorities who are only "preudome," not "preudes femes": "Je leur respons que les livres ne firent / Pas les femmes, ne les choses n'i mirent / Que l'en y list contre elles et leurs meurs" (*Epistre au dieu d'Amours*,[18] v. 409–11) [But I answer that woman did not write the books or include the attacks one reads there against women and their ways]. Noteworthy here is that Christine's attack is directed against the literal authorities, not Jean's integument. If one seeks the integument, then one must go beyond the literal misogynist language to find its kernel of allegorical truth. As allegory, that truth cannot be the "truth" in the fabulous letter of the text because the allegorical meaning must be "other" than the literal meaning.

In many instances, there may be uncertainty regarding the fable's hidden meaning, with the result that a variety of images of the same fable and within the same narrative may oblige the reader to make his or her own evaluation. In the *Rose*, the best example might be the different readings of the passage from the Golden Age to the Iron Age pursuant to the castration of Saturn. Amant refuses to listen to Reason's explanation, although he is attentive to Ami's and Genius's. Rose too, as Bel Acueil, listens to the Vieille's gloss of the Golden Age and its sequels.

Reason tells Amant that study of integumental fables is necessary to know their truth (v. 7137–38). We recall the artificial way in which the postcoital *conservatio/deminutio amoris* serves to warn the apprentice in the art of love of the disaster that ensues from plucking roses: the misfortunes of fabulous and historical lovers recorded in the poem's examples. These examples develop in the reader the habit of reading integumentally by almost automatically glossing the text while reading. That mental gloss is necessary in order to perceive the truth or falsehood of the fictional images. Although the lineaments of the *integumentum* are sought and begin to emerge in the first reading, rereading is necessary in order to confirm the consistency and the validity of the initial mental gloss.

In this context, the major fable in the *Rose* is Amant's dream itself, which extends uninterrupted (except for author or narrator interventions like Jean's self-defense) from Amant's falling asleep at verse 25, "me dormoie mout forment" [I was sleeping soundly], at the beginning of Guillaume's second prologue, and the beginning of the actual dream in verse 45, "Avis m'iere qu'il estoit mais" [it seemed to me that it was May], until he awakens in the last line of Jean's continuation "Atant fu jorz, et je m'esveille" (v. 21750) [at daybreak I wake up]. According to Guillaume's prologue, the dream is true. It is a true dream, or *somnium* in Macrobius's sense, not only because the love story it tells came true five or more years later (v. 21–30, 46),[19] but also because it does not show the future literally and requires interpretation. That interpretation—the integumental reading—will reveal an art of love, according to the same prologue (v. 38).

Guillaume's literal assertion is credible.[20] Although some have claimed that he is referring to the Virgin Mary, the claim is one of convenience and has no textual or contextual justification.[21] On the other hand, the interpretation of Rose as the beloved would not preclude a rejection of that love along the lines of the palinode suggested by C. S. Lewis.[22] Similar rejections are not unknown in medieval lyric, which itself functions as one of the intertextual models for the *Rose* as a transformed *chanson courtoise*. Similarly, Jean Froissart wrote an analogous palinode in the *Joli buisson de jonece*, turning from his lady to a new lady—the Virgin Mary.[23] But this particular change of heart is textually explicit. There is no evidence that Guillaume intended anything of the kind.

Jean replaces Guillaume's expressed intention with a new one of his own invention. To be sure, Jean's *Rose* is also an art of love, although his story requires little effort to understand, so close is it to being literal. But in an important digression, Jean departs from Guillaume's prologue by suggesting that dreams like Amant's are not true (v. 18334–94). Amant's dream changes from a *somnium* to an *insomnium*. The false dream of a lover gaining, enjoying, and keeping his beloved's embrace requires glossing that will reveal the lineaments of the truth that make the mendacious surface dream into a true image. The old fable, as Jean relates it, acquires a new integument. Description reveals its outline to the imagination.

In all this, Jean is being a poet in his sense of the word. He is using the common matter of a dream told in the incomplete *matière* of his first author. His allegory turns that autobiographical allegory into fiction. But he is also making that matter fit his own meaning, not (only) Guillaume's, through additions or adjustments. His continuation of Guillaume reorients the story in a new direction to fit his new intention. This is what a poet, in Jean's sense of the word, was supposed to do.

THE DESCRIPTIVE MODE (*Modus descriptivus*)

Description is perhaps the single most important device Jean uses to rewrite Guillaume de Lorris. Amant is metamorphosed into a deceitful seducer. Rose assumes greater specificity, becoming much more prominent and active in her response to the seduction. The specific features Jean chooses to characterize the two and the attribution of the corresponding features to other exemplary figures in the *Rose* make obvious the redefinition of Amant's love as Guillaume describes it. Similar modifications occur in Amant's and Rose's actions within the three commonplace schemes of the *gradus amoris*, the *conservatio/deminutio amoris*, and the *scala amorum* as I defined them in the previous chapter. The most important distinguishing characteristic for Amant and Rose is their sex. But literal sexual difference is less important here than sexual and gender allegory analogous to that used to describe and distinguish Siton's philosophical activities. We shall see Rose assume male traits under the guise of Bel Acueil, a masculine noun, while Amant takes on the attributes of the woman of misogyny in his quest for Olympian "ease," or *mollities*.

Description is the first mode Reason uses to explain Amant's love to him: "Or i met bien l'entencion, / Voiz an ci la descripcion" (v. 4261–62) [Now pay attention, here's the description]. In medieval rhetoric and poetics, description is a technique. It elucidates an object, however concrete or abstract that object may be, doing so by topical invention. Since I have discussed this basic principle of invention elsewhere,[24] I shall only summarize briefly the features relevant to the specific context of true and false images in literary dreams like the *Rose*.

Description elucidates by first identifying in the object of description "places" (loci, topoi) which are common to all examples of such objects, then assigning them specific attributes that show the observer how the describer construes the object. For example, all human beings have a sexual gender, male or female. The attributes will conjoin to constitute the informing image and the subject matter of the new work.[25] Whether the image is true or false depends on its conformity to the thing actually represented. Of course, there may be differences of opinion, as, for example, between Christine de Pizan and the Jealous Husband about women's ways. If so, different descriptions become an issue. In forensic oratory, the choices made in a description may form the basis for a trial and verdict as to the merit of opposing accounts of a case. In the *Rose*, clearly at issue is the quality or worth of love—good or bad—as exemplified by Amant and Rose as well as by other speakers and exemplary figures in the poem. Thus, when Reason describes Amant's love, she emphasizes the contradictions inherent in foolish love in order to show how foolish Amant is.

Reason's description of Amant's love contains a series of oxymorons that suggest the contradictory core of his love experience. "Amors, ce est pez haïneuse, / Amors, c'est haïne amoureuse" (v. 4263–64) [Love is hate-filled calm and loving hate]. In contrast to this one, other descriptions use different devices. In the descriptions of the Golden Age or of Paradise, for example, each speaker emphasizes descriptive elements that underscore his or her conception of the commonplace image in the context of his or her view of love in that age and after. For example, the time later identified as the Golden Age was for Reason a time of honest human love, but for the Vieille it was the heyday of free love. Both Ami and the Vieille evoke the freedom, especially the sexual freedom, of those who lived in the Golden Age prior to the castration of Saturn. There are similar examples of selective attribution in description elsewhere. As Genius reads Nature's decree to Love's army, heavenly bliss is the reward for vigorous, even strenuous sexual activity. Similarly, he describes and contrasts two different paradises in the Park of the Lamb and the Garden of Deduit, blending heavenly bliss and carnality in an amplified oxymoron. For Nature, the fundamental difference between sex for reproduction and sex for delight alone is the locus for differentiating between good and bad love.[26]

An important feature of description in allegory is the semantic range of the attributes designating or contextualizing the person, place, or action represented. Since semantic range is important in explaining sexuality, let us examine here pertinent features of the defining mode. Jean took over Guillaume de Lorris's use of the technique; under the *modus diffinitivus*, for example, we saw how he used semantic range to suggest different kinds of love and *franchise* (see pp. 56–65). On the level of vocabulary, semantic range shows in one of the exemplary characters of the *Rose*: the *ribaut*. Jean identifies three major types for this character. The first is the "ribaut de Grieve" (v. 5250; cf. v. 5018–19). Reason finds this day laborer remarkable for his *soffisance*, or Boethian sufficiency; he lives unmolested by fortune and is therefore carefree and self-sufficient (v. 5018–32, 5250–54). The second group, the amorous *ribauts*, is not admirable. They make up the swarms of men who prey on women; their counterparts among women, the *ribaudes*, hustle men for profit. The Jealous Husband refers to them and his wife in the same terms (cf. v. 8521 and 8528, 9084 and 9095), as does Ami to any woman who sells her love (cf. v. 8246). Finally, in an even broader context, Amant calls Reason herself a *ribaude* because of her language (v. 6952, 7040); Franchise belongs to this species, according to Dangier (v. 15331), as do the Furies, according to Nature (v. 19803).

When the God of Love receives Faux Semblant into his army, he names him overseer of the *ribauts*. "Tu me seras rois des ribauz" (v. 10908; cf. v. 11953–54) [You will be my king of the lewd]. This "king of the *ribauts*" was an actual office in the French court and elsewhere. The functionary was charged with administering justice in the royal retinue; he was also responsible for regulating prostitutes, gambling houses, and games and sports in general.[27] In the *Rose*, his office is to oversee, among other games, the *jeu d'amors*. There are affinities between Faux Semblant and the Vieille's former lover, a *ribaut* adept at both gambling and lovemaking (v. 14446–509), who played the game of love to pacify the young Vieille, as Ami advises Amant to do when in difficulty (v. 9731–32, 9786–88, 9821–22); Bel Acueil, says the Vieille, is to use his (= her) wits in the same game (v. 12972–77, 13815–16, 14289–92). This is the love Reason decries as "li geus qui n'est point estables, / Estaz trop fers et trop muables" (v. 4289–90) [the game with no fixed rules, a status at once very firm and highly mutable]. The games foreseen by Ami and the Vieille sustain this description, as do the protean features of Faux Semblant, *roi des ribauts*.

Like Abstinence Contrainte, Bel Acueil, and Male Bouche, Faux Semblant has an attribute that controls his role in the plot. He personifies *Faux* Semblant, which necessarily excludes the *Vrai* Semblant, otherwise called in Old French *simplece* and related semantically to *franchise* as candor.[28] However, to be effective, Faux Semblant's falsity must be hidden, just as Abstinence must not reveal her constraints. Thus, when he and his companion approach Male Bouche, they are identified only as Male Bouche perceives them: Semblant and Abstinence (v. 12081, 12089, and so on). A personification is only an exterior appearance. Actions, not words, reveal the interior intent, as Faux Semblant says in speaking about the deceitful behavior he personifies.

> Les euvres regarder devez,
> Se vos n'avez les euz crevez,
> Car s'i font el que il ne dient,
> Certainement il vos conchient,
> Quelconques robes que il aient,
> De quelconques estat qu'il saient,
> Soit clers, soit lais, soit hon, soit fame,
> Sires, serjanz, baiasse ou dame.
> (V. 11045–52)

[You must observe their actions—unless you're as blind as a bat! For if their acts differ from their words, they've shafted you for sure, however they dress and whatever their social standing, cleric or layman, man or woman, lord, soldier, servant, or lady.]

Male Bouche learns this when Faux Semblant cuts his tongue out while apparently shriving him.

We now have two controls on reading personifications and their attributes in the *Rose*. One is the actual semantic range of the word personified as we can best determine it from surviving documents and, more specifically, the sense or senses drawn upon in describing the personification. The other is the choice of attributes and actions that qualify and delimit the semantic range as well as provide a moral or social evaluation of the word, as in the case of Faux Semblant, Male Bouche, and Bel Acueil. We may illustrate this further with Amour, or the God of Love, and Venus.

Reason sets forth an array of meanings for love. Furthermore, she variously evaluates the kinds of love as good, bad, or, in the case of the desire to procreate, neutral. Amant's particular love is personified by the God of Love. That love may slip from one sense or level to another. It is therefore susceptible of being differently evaluated as its attributes change. Amant's decision to practice *traïson* revises the commandments of Love in Guillaume, commandments Amant recites for the God of Love in Jean in a capital instance of Faux Semblant, that is, of saying one thing and doing or intending to do another. The God of Love implicitly acquiesces in the amendment to his commandments by receiving Faux Semblant into his army. On the other side, the rose complex follows suit when the Vieille advises Bel Acueil to ignore the commandments to be faithful and to be reasonably generous (v. 13007–8). Amant himself puts his new kind of love into practice, as he informs us at various points, including the conclusion, where he evokes his subsequent adventures with old and young women in the context of deceit (cf. v. 14719–22, 21367–97, 21515–31).

Jean describes Venus as the personification of female sexuality. Either she invokes sexual arousal, as in the burning of Jealousy's castle, or she excites male sexuality, as when Venus gives Genius the burning candle with which he inflames the God of Love's army. She may also represent female prostitution or seduction for gain or reward. The God of Love is unwilling to accept his mother in this role (v. 10735–96; cf. v. 4739–52), although Amant would have had Richesse consented. There is a role for Venus in the Pygmalion episode as well. But here her intervention leads to marriage and children, which recalls the traditional good Venus of conjugal sexuality (see above pp. 76–77).[29]

After the castration of Saturn, Venus signals the passing of the Golden Age. Feminine sexuality emerges from the male member—or, more accurately in the *Rose*, the testicles—much as Eve did from Adam's rib. As a transformation of male genitalia, Venus also points to the issue of male and female identity in the *Rose*. The issue is complex. It is also important, and therefore requires separate treatment in two contexts: the one, under division as mode of representation, is treated above (pp. 65–70); the other, under allegory, will be taken up in chapter 5. Together with the ambiguous relation between male and female sexuality represented by the birth of Venus from Saturn's testicles is the issue of the allegorical representation of man and woman. Insofar as Amant the man is an allegory, he must also be something else, for he cannot still be a man on the allegorical level. The woman is a rose—or, more accurately, a rosebush in Jean. She is also personified by her attributes on the literal level. She appears as a woman on one allegorical level, while parts or aspects of her nature appear elsewhere. For example, in analogy with Guillaume's strategy of applying the Narcisse *exemplum* to a certain class of women, feminine traits are ascribed to a man like Amant himself or to masculine personifications like Bel Acueil. Importantly, allegory permits gender transfer. It is the topos of gender that Venus problematizes and that we must examine here.

Sexus as topos or commonplace may be simple or complex. It is simple where it merely designates a person as male or female according to their sexual organs. It become complex when sexuality takes on other commonplace or received traits usually attributed to either the male or female human being. *Sexus* and its corollary activities form a complex mosaic in the *Rose*. As topos, it raises issues of sexual and grammatical gender and propriety. Jean uses such issues to introduce both contrasting male and female mores as well as different kinds of sexual orientation into contexts like constancy and fidelity, marriage and adultery, and natural and unnatural love. In what follows, I shall discuss both sexual and grammatical gender. This discussion will lead to Jean's vision of human mores, including male and female mores, and cross-gender assignment of mores: the assignment of mores customarily attributed to one sexual gender to members of the opposite gender. In all this, Jean evinces a basic misanthropy as he plays with the general and special, or narrower, meanings of sodomy, finally branding all human conduct that is unnatural as sodomitic. He includes Amant's kind of love in this category.

Gender is a human commonplace. Circumstantial topoi have always included sexual gender as a commonplace human attribute. It appears in obvious ways in the *Rose*. For example, Ami advises Amant to use force if necessary and in this way prove himself a man (v. 7660–61), thereby identifying the male as one who uses force to gain desired goals. Nature and Genius use the gender topos as well when they assert that women cannot keep secrets (v. 16317–551, 16661–76, 18659–62, 19188–207).[30] These particular articulations of the gender topos draw on specific commonplace attributes assigned to the topos. The issues they raise are taken up, for example, by Christine de Pizan in her attack on the *Rose*. Why the use of force, she asks ironically: "A foible lieu fault il dont grant assault?" (*Epistre* v. 397) [Does one have to mount such a grand assault on a weak site?] But the *Rose* raises even more complex gender problems than these.

The dominant images in the *Rose* are Amant and Rose themselves. Each takes on a complex of attributes that are mostly personified and put into action at various stages in their *gradus amoris*. Along with his topical attributes, Amant gathers personifications about himself that describe him as a lover and delineate what we might call his "self."[31] His complex of attributes changes as Amant himself changes. The most striking example is the aforementioned appearance of Faux Semblant and Abstinence Contrainte after Amant decides to practice deceit and seduce Rose. His decision shows him following Ami's advice (v. 7845–48), patterning his comportment both on Ami's Ovidian lessons and Ami's own experience. It also colors the moral and social significance of Love's barons before the attack and of the agents, weapons, and armor used during it. Thus, Faux Semblant and Abstinence Contrainte actually personify the increasing degeneration of Amant's love. When he rejects the God of Love's two tenets on fidelity and generosity, Love acquiesces in the change by receiving Faux Semblant and Abstinence Contrainte among the barons who make up his war counsel and by implicitly accepting the lesson the new members teach. Love has changed. As with Nature and Genius, so with Faux Semblant and Love—the lower wields the higher. With Faux Semblant, Love becomes false love; with Abstinence Contrainte, love becomes constrained and sexuality unnatural.

As I have argued elsewhere, Rose is entirely passive in the female complex in Guillaume de Lorris, being nothing but a botanical rose subject to various implicit allegorical readings.[32] In Jean, however, the rose quickly reduces to a single, more or less obvious object and meaning, female genitalia as stimulus for male orgasm. Rose herself in the end is likened to a rosebush, suggesting that rose in the sense of virginity no longer obtains (Rose's virginity, signaled by the hymen, is represented allegorically by a defensive barrier, v. 21577–612). And the rose allegory proliferates. Each rose on the rosebush is a potential source of carnal pleasure. But Rose also gathers about herself a "fictional person," thus offering a suitable image for Amant's own person in the literal plot. Her body emerges as the great statue surmounting Jealousy's castle just after the Pygmalion digression. And like Pygmalion's statue, it comes to life, that is, it is aroused by Venus. The final scene shows Amant and Rose talking, touching, kissing, and having intercourse. Prior to Rose's emergence among the *dramatis personae*, she is, as in Guillaume, only a complex of personifications that speak and act for her.

Moreover, in evaluating the implied lessons of the *Rose* as an art of love and applying them to the reader's own conduct, it is more useful to read the personifications as attributes of either Amant or Rose[33] that come to the fore in certain stages of the *gradus amoris*, rather than as independent agents—that is, additional actors on the stage of love, as it were. Amant is his own best friend in pursuing sexual delight; hence, Ami is Amant telling himself what he wants to hear by teaching a false love that permits Amant to seduce Rose and gratify himself.[34] In this, he fits the Narcisse pattern: just as Narcisse turned from Echo to self-love, so Amant turns from Reason to Ami, so much does he love himself and the pleasures he hopes to win for himself.[35] Similarly, the Vieille's lecture to

Bel Acueil becomes the, as it were, inherited experience of every woman; much like instinct, she teaches how a woman's Bel Acueil may gain pleasure and profit from men. In this, the Vieille derives, as guardian, from Jealousy and is part of the protective wall Rose throws up around herself, and not from Jealousy as a presumed father or husband. Rose may well fear "rivals" for Amant's affection, but more cogently, she fears that she is not really loved. Fear of not being loved is a commonplace meaning of jealousy in medieval love literature.[36] In Jean's *Rose*, her fears are justified.

In these instances, broader reading of personifications explains more coherently the letter and allegory of the text while permitting, in specific readings, local adaptation to personal circumstances.[37] Thus, the principal objects of topical description in the *Rose* are the man Amant and the woman Rose and their attributes whether personified or not. Given the pervasive male-female antinomy in the *Rose*, and its subset, masculine-feminine, the major topos or locus will obviously be that of *sexus*. However, the ways by which the text represents this topos are problematic because of the different levels and contexts in which it is deployed. *Sexus* is at once sexual gender as male and female and grammatical gender as masculine and feminine.

However, this duality is even more problematic, not only because human conduct may confuse traditional gender roles as defined by sexual gender, but also because of the very nature of the allegorical mode of representation. Allegory requires more than a simple letter with an obvious other meaning.[38] Sexuality problematizes matters further. When sex and gender extend beyond the surface or literal "genitally focused sexual act," then 'gender' refers "not to biologically determined sex ('male' and 'female') but to sexual identities that are socially constructed ideas ('masculine' and 'feminine')." Deconstructed masculine and feminine roles may, however, identify "positions" and "functions that can be taken up, occupied, or performed by either sex, male or female. . . . "[39] This rather obvious state of affairs becomes highly complex and problematic in allegory that describes social mores and evaluates moral decisions.

This ambivalence of gender terminology is very much in evidence in the *Roman de la rose*.[40] Guillaume de Lorris illustrates it in two obvious ways. First, the masculine gender of Bel Acueil as agent of feminine consent seems to impose a masculinity on the rose complex, a masculinity that has disturbed some modern readers.[41] Second, as we have observed, Guillaume's moral to the Narcisse fable applies to women, not to men. These two examples raise questions of both grammatical correctness—or, at least, acceptable or proper usage—and of sexual identity. However, Guillaume does not problematize them nearly so much as Jean de Meun does. But before turning to Jean's use of the gender topos, I should like to review two issues: gender in language in general and gender change as syllepsis in particular.

English no longer has noun gender. Consequently, native speakers of English must make some effort to understand gender in gender-specific languages like French. Long and short vowels and syllables in Latin present an analogous problem. English speakers usually express vowel length in Latin by accent. Similarly, confronted by grammatical gender, the same speakers translate it into sexual gender. To be sure, the terminology of Latin grammar, from which English usage derives, facilitates the translation. Masculine, feminine, and neuter authorize attaching male or female sexuality to nouns of masculine and feminine gender, whereas neuter leaves the nouns, as in English, as sexless as cupids in Victorian art. In fact, noun gender usually determines the sexual gender of personifications of the noun in gender-marked languages like French.

The problem of personifications of one grammatical gender that refer to a person of the other sexual gender seems less acute for native speakers of gender-marked languages than it does for speakers of languages like English that are no longer so marked. French allows for such anomalies, as did Latin before it. An acceptable departure from the grammatical norm in agreement is termed syllepsis. Syllepsis is defined as follows in Webster's unabridged: "The use of a word (as an adjective or verb) to modify or govern syntactically two (sometimes more) words, with only one of which it formally agrees in gender, number, etc." An example: "Miss Bolo went home in a flood of tears and a sedan chair."[42] Similarly, in French, modification in gender may occur when a word modifies or governs only one word (*Petit Robert*, s.v. *syllepse*): "accord selon le sens et non selon les règles grammaticales," with two examples, the first of number—"minuit sonnèrent"—and the second of gender: "C'est *la sentinelle* qui *le premier* s'inquiète" (emphasis mine). Grevisse defines this type of syllepsis as occurring when a pronoun agrees not with its antecedent but with another word that substitutes in thought for the antecedent,[43] as in this example: "*La pauvre Barbe-bleue* se doutait bien de quelque chose, mais *il* ne savait pas de quoi" (emphasis mine). French grammar recognizes the relation between sex and gender, even if it is not unduly troubled when the relationship seems to be violated.[44] This in itself authorizes Jean's incorporation into his continuation of the ambivalence evoked but not problematized by Guillaume.

Bouche or "mouth" has always been a feminine noun in French. An adjective modifying it will accordingly assume the feminine form, as in the *Rose*'s personification Mal*e* Bouche (cf. "la pauvre Barbe-bleue").

Yet, Male Bouche is a sentinel, one of the four guardians posted at the gates of Jealousy's castle to protect its roses. In Guillaume de Lorris, pronominal reference to Male Bouche is at first "gender correct": "Male Bouche, *la* jangleor, / Et avec *li* Honte et Peor" (v. 2819–20, cf. 3020; emphasis mine) [Male Bouche the prattler {feminine adjective}, and with *her* Shame and Fear]. But shortly after Bel Acueil allows Amant to kiss the rose, syllepsis takes over. Henceforth Male Bouche is consistently marked by the masculine for pronouns, gender flectional modifiers except *male*, which is part of her/his name, predicate adjectives, and synonyms.[45]

> Male Bouche, qui la covine
> De mainz amanz pense et devine
> Et tot le mal qu'*il* set retret,
> Se prist garde du bel atret
> Que Bel Acueil me deignoit fere,
> Et tant que *il* ne se pot tere,
> Qu'*il* fu *fiuz* d'une vielle irese,
> . . . .
> Et dit que *il* metroit son oil
> Que entre moi et Bel Acueil
> A un mauvés acointement.
> Tant parla *li gloz* folement
> De moi et dou fil Cortoisie
> Qu'*il* fist esveiller Jalousie,
> Qui se leva en esfreor
> Quant ele oï *le* jangleor.[46]
> (V. 3493–99, 3505–12; emphasis mine)

> [Male Bouche who suspects and divines the affairs of many lovers, reporting all the slander *he* can about them, took note of the friendly manner with which Bel Acueil deigned to receive me, so much so that *he* couldn't keep still, for *he* was *son* of a quick-tempered old woman . . . and *he* said *he* would bet an eye that there was some hanky-panky going on between me and Bel Acueil. The pig {masculine!} raved on about me and Courtesy's son so much that *he* awakened Jealousy, who rose up in a fright when she heard the prattler {masculine!}.]

Two facts stand out regarding the Male Bouche syllepsis. First, it occurs only for Male Bouche. The other guardians, Dangier (masculine), Honte, and Peur (both feminine), are sexually marked by their grammatical genders throughout, even in the tournament in Jean de Meun. Second, not even Jealousy, who has been equated with a putative husband or paternal authority,[47] undergoes syllepsis. Nor does Bel Acueil. Could not

Bel Acueil have become a "she" just as Male Bouche became a "he"?[48] Why did both Guillaume and Jean single out Male Bouche for such syllepsis?

Answers may be found in Jean's well-known intervention to answer charges from his audiences about his use of language and representation of women and the religious. It is useful to assess the general thrust of the self-defense rather than treat the three topics only separately. In treating language, Jean advances general propositions about how one speaks about anything, including the moral context that determines how one may speak about women and religious in allegory. As we have seen, Jean argues that his language fits the matter being treated and the speakers. In Material Style (see above, p. 46), the language chosen should be appropriate—cousin to the deed, as Jean puts it—regardless of the author's opinions on the matter. The justification is traditional and applicable in any context and subject, not just that of naming genitalia with words like *coilles* and *vits*, at which Amant—and apparently members of Jean's thirteenth-century audiences—took offense. The argument applies equally well to the representation of women and the religious as Jean defines and variously differentiates these two groups.

In the intervention, then, Jean divides his topic in two ways: first he says his arrows are aimed at bad women and bad religious only, not at everyone in these groups or any specific member of them. Faux Semblant himself is quite adept at making such distinctions. He uses and abuses them time and again by the diverse false robes he wears.

> Qui Faus Semblant vodra connoistre,
> Si le quiere au siecle ou en cloistre;
> Nul leu fors en ces .II. ne mains,
> Mes en l'un plus, en l'autre mains.
> (V. 10977–80)

> [Whoever wants to know Faux Semblant should seek him out in the secular and religious spheres. I dwell nowhere except in these two, although I am more in the one than in the other.]

He is expert at taking on the outer mores suitable to the infinite number of dwellings he occupies and robes he dons. What he scrupulously hides is the falsity of his appearances.

Second, Jean insists that he attacks the mores of false women and false men only, not those of all men and women. Thus, his barbs hit certain kinds of conduct described by learned authorities. On their authority, he describes what he terms "meurs femenins" (v. 15170, 15196, 15199), or feminine mores, as these were consigned to writing;[49] he does not single out any specific woman. In the case of the religious, he reports what is known from written testimony and experience, or demonstrable by reason (V. 15265–68), but names no specific offender. "Dames honorables" (V. 15185) [honorable ladies] and "home . . . / Sainte religion sivant" (v. 15223–24) [those leading a holy religious life] are specifically excluded. In other words, Jean's topic is mores. He uses stereotyped representations of women and religious that, he says, have some basis in experience. Mores are customary actions that betray true or false appearances, as Faux Semblant points out. Jean reminds those who find the representations objectionable that he is merely observing decorum. In any case, he adds, general representation applies only to those persons it actually fits, that is, to those whose actual mores fit the stereotypes, and to no one else. This includes both women and religious (like Abstinence Contrainte as a personification). Specifically, it can include men who manifest *meurs femenins* and heretical opinions and sinful conduct. Just as Guillaume uses a male model for the mores of haughty women, Jean uses female models to identify certain kinds of men.

This brings us back to the *sexus* topos in the *modus tractandi descriptivus*. Jean claims that his appeal to authority in the depiction of *meurs femenins* is unimpeachable, based on experience, exact in the retelling, instructive, and poetic (v. 15185–212). Since, as we noted above, Jean's implied audience is unlettered, its members would have had to reconstruct the voices of authority and experience from his own words, being mindful—as he cautions them—to correlate the language used with the person, personifications, settings, and actions it refers to. For example, although the Jealous Husband cites at length misogynist authorities in conformity with his persona, Jean's narrator suppresses Pygmalion's misogyny in retelling Ovid,[50] a rewriting which supports the positive reading of this example I propose above (pp. 76–78). The word *meurs* itself underscores this fact while focusing on the significance of the mores depicted. Thus, in representing *meurs*, Jean no more focuses on the agents per se than, for example, La Fontaine specifically attacks foxes or crows as a species in his fable. His lesson is for readers, not for foxes or crows, notably for those readers who mirror the stereotypical mores of his bestiary. The same holds for those readers of the *Rose* whose conduct mirrors stereotypical *meurs femenins*.

Problematic in this dynamic is how misogyny operates on the literal level to identify the "normal" mores of women prior to Jean's intervention. Jean's ultimate appeal in the intervention on women is to ancient authority, that is, the bookish authority Christine de Pizan was to reject as biased. Women, she reminded Jean's readers, did not write the ancient books which Jean used to authorize misogynist statements. Application of the commonplace roles of one sex to the other is not misogyny by any definition I know except in those cases where one role is made superior to the other. That is what Jean does by identifying male mores as good and female mores as bad. But he goes on to equate such mores not only with sexual gender but also with grammatical gender. That equation permits him to reread traditional, literal authority on misogyny in terms of human types—male and female—which can assume the attributes of the other as sexual change in allegory.

Women's alleged moral weakness, which ancient authorities castigated, has two corollaries that are of some importance in the *Rose*. One is that women may rise above their alleged weakness. Such women, who illustrate the *fortis mulier*,[51] like Phanie, Héloise, and Penelope, show forth intelligence, independence, and fortitude among Jean's examples of women. Second, the man who sinks into feminine weakness—the *vir mollis*—becomes effeminate. This happens to Amant after his decision to reject Reason. We shall see that Amant takes on almost all the attributes of the misogynist authority's description of women. As a *vir mollis*, he actually personifies *meurs femenins*. In the moral sphere, these gender modifications of male/female and masculine/feminine fit the phenomena Carolyn Dinshaw describes in the quote cited above (p. 107).

Before proceeding, we may stop to ask what a human being is in Jean's poem, and, more specifically, what mores are typical of a representative human being in the *Rose*, whom they describe, how they fit into the *Rose*'s plot, and what lesson they teach there. By mirroring ourselves in these mores we may come to know ourselves better, as do Socrates, the women whom Jean addresses in his intervention, and La Fontaine's readers. In doing so, we must also consider the corollary contexts of male mores and female mores. And, for reasons that will emerge more clearly further on, the reader must bear in mind that the *Rose*'s allegory makes the literal male and female bespeak something other than their literal sense.

In the *Rose*, two attributes are generally affirmed of humans, both men and women. They have a "reasonable soul" and therefore have at their disposal God-given reason (v. 19581–88); they also have genitalia and, thus, a sexual drive (v. 19513–30). That this is true of Amant is illustrated in the Reason episode. It follows that Reason's words to Amant are applicable to Rose, although Reason does not appear to her, thwarted, one might suppose, by the presence of the Vieille. Nonetheless, Reason's presence is perceptible during the tournament, in which Peur and Honte dominate Rose's defense. In Guillaume de Lorris, Honte is Reason's daughter (v. 2824), and Amant associates both Honte and Peur as belonging to Reason's lineage (v. 14929–32). Moreover, male sexuality responds to and complements that of the female, as the conclusion of the poem shows. Hence, the *Rose* has a lesson for all humans, a lesson that is the same for both men and women because they share reason and sexuality.[52]

Since, however, evil is a defect, its "presence" in humans means a lack of humanity, such that, following Boethius, Reason can proclaim that "li mauvés ne sunt pas home" (v. 6292) [the evil are not human]. Evil, and thus defective humanity, are the object of Reason's and Nature's complaints. Nature echoes Reason by cataloguing an array of vices which she attributes to all men, whether we take "man" to include women or not:

> Orgueilleus est, murtriers et lierres,
> Fel, couvoiteus, avers, trichierres,
> Desesperez, gloz, mesdisanz,
> Et haïneus et despisanz,
> Mescreanz, anvieus, mantierres,
> Parjurs, fausaires, fos, vantierres,
> Et inconstanz et foloiables,
> Ydolatres, desagraables,
> Traïstres et faus ypocrites,
> Et pareceus et sodomites:
> Briefmant tant est chetis et nices
> Qu'il est sers a tretouz les vices
> Et tretouz an soi les herberge.
> (V. 19195–207)

> [He's proud, murderous, and a thief, felonious, covetous, avaricious, deceptive, wracked by despair, piggish, slanderous, hateful and scornful, suspicious, envious, lying, a perjurer, falsifier, fool, and boaster, inconstant and mad, idolotrous, surly, a traitor and lying hypocrite, lazy and a sodomite. In short, he is so wretched and dumb that he's a slave to all vices, harboring everyone of them in himself.]

I quote the passage not only because it succinctly evokes the evils of (hu)mankind, but also because it summarizes *meurs femenins*, as we shall see. But first let us note two striking features of Nature's catalogue of human vices. First, the only explicitly sexual vice she names is sodomy. As we have seen, this term is polyvalent, referring to any unnatural sexuality, that is, any sexual activity that does not serve Nature's purpose to continue the species. Second, she describes evil men while speaking as a woman. Nature is referring to men—"homes"—in this passage. But such men, as humanity, may include women. By the same token, women's ways may describe any part of humanity they fit, including male men. They do so in Jean's *Rose*.

But let us first place sodomy in its medieval context. Medieval writings do not represent sodomy very frequently or openly. Examples include: Aelred of Rievaulx's sublimation of his homosexuality,[53] the play on bad grammar and homosexuality in Alain de Lille's *De planctu Naturae*, and the location of Brunetto Latini among the sodomites in Dante's *Inferno*. Jean's use of "sodomite" is less problematic, but more suggestive. In Old French a sodomite is *hérétique*.[54] In the context of the *Rose*, it includes anyone who practices any kind of sexual activity not performed for procreation, thereby comprehending Amant's kind of love. Genius for his part condemns sodomites to castration in some of the most vicious language in the *Rose* (v. 19636–56). As castrates they would assume *meurs femenins*, like all sodomites (cf. v. 19627–38, 20028–30)—the very mores, moreover, Jean castigates in his intervention on women.

Reason anticipates Genius's excommunication of sodomites because of the wrong they do to nature (v. 4313–15). Reason also lumps sodomites and lovers like Amant together (v. 4316–25) because sodomy precludes procreation (v. 19599–632). Similarly, Nature recalls the God of Love's analogous condemnation of those who do not practice sexual activity as she sums up man's vices:[55]

> Mes por ceus dom Amors se plaint,
> Car g'en ai bien oï le plaint,
> Je meïsmes, tant con je puis,
> M'an plaing et m'an doi plaindre, puis
> Qu'il me renient le treü
> Que tretuit home m'ont deü
> Et tourjorz doivent et devront
> Tant con mes oustilz recevront.
> (V. 19297–304)

[But as for those Love complains of—for I have heard his complaint very well—I myself complain of them as forcefully as I can, and I must do so since they deny me the tribute all men have owed me, and always do and will as long as they receive my tools.]

This passage equates lovers like Amant, virgins, and chaste persons with sodomites, and would surely have caused some perplexity in Jean's medieval audiences. Genius also evokes Nature's tools in condemning those who, like Orphée, "vont conme maleüreus / Arer en la terre deserte / Ou leur semance vet a perte" (v. 19614–16) [go about like wretches sowing in barren land where their seed goes to waste]. The image corresponds to Amant's self-description at the end of the *Rose*, when we see him probe the ruts, ditches, and holes along his sterile sexual itinerary (v. 21367–77). Amant and sodomites alike ignore Nature's rules, perverting their sexuality to carnality. They are therefore excommunicated, additionally condemned to castration of their masculine sign, we might say today; as Jean phrases it in the "improper" language of metaphor, they should be bereft of their hammers and stylet, plow and ploughshare, staff and skrip, because they use them improperly.

This is an astonishing punishment, recalling Jupiter's castration of Saturn, which functions as a problematic example throughout Jean's *Rose*. But it fits Jupiter's example insofar as Genius preaches "ease," the goal of human life after the castration of Saturn. Genius himself mentions the castration soon after the passage quoted above, condemning the harm emasculation does to both lover and reproduction: "Granz pechiez est d'ome escoillier" (v. 20020) [It's a great sin to castrate a man]. Castration deprives man of human mores, notably courage—"hardemant et meurs humains / Qui doivent estre en vaillanz homes" (v. 20026–27)[56] [courage and human mores which ought to be in worthy men]. Indeed, castrates, or eunuchs, take on *meurs femenins* (v. 20028–30). Curiously, they are the same mores as those that prevail after Jupiter usurps his father's throne and gives the world over to a life of "ease" (v. 20067). Such ease occurs in unreproductive sexuality. In Jean, such sexuality is sodomy.

Perhaps we have here a clue as to Male Bouche's masculine gender and thus to his virility or virtue. In the context of identifying a *fol amoureux*, a bad mouth can only be good in protecting that kind of love's potential victim. His tongue is not only his defining member, it is his means of protecting roses from ravishment. It therefore follows that to "castrate" Male Bouche, that is, to deprive him of his defining member and let him die, is to open the Rose complex to the same "effeminacy" or *meurs femenins* Amant has adopted. With this discussion serving as context, what, we may ask, are *meurs femenins* in Jean's *Rose*? The phrase itself is used in various ways in the poem. First, it applies to the two complexes represented by the male Amant and the female Rose. Second, it refers to the conduct of any number of grammatical "feminines" in the *Rose*. Finally, it describes all human beings who have rejected reason. I shall examine each of these in turn.

Above I suggested that a useful way to read the assemblage of personifications and other figures in Amant's dream is in terms of complexes—specifically, a male complex centering on Amant and a female complex deployed around the rose. Jean retains Guillaume's system while problematizing it in the instance of *meurs femenins*. In addition, he allows the demands of allegory to problematize the male complex. Guillaume de Lorris may again have served as touchstone here. As we have observed, Narcisse is an allegory not because of his self-love but because of the pride of haughty ladies; similarly, the masculine Bel Acueil is the receptive agent in the rose complex. As an allegory, the question arises, could Amant be a woman because he evinces *meurs femenins* as the ancient authorities have described them?

We are now on the edge of explicit and implicit allegory (see above, pp. 19–21). As in the *Queste del saint graal*, if an implicit reading sustains an explicit reading, it is admissible as an interpretive commentary in allegories. How explicitly feminine are Amant's *mores* as *meurs femenins*? Sodomites and castrates are said to exhibit *meurs femenins*. Since Amant is sometimes assimilated to these two groups, without being a literal, but only an allegorical sodomite or castrate, and since some men can exhibit feminine mores, it seems we may apply the attributes of *meurs femenins* to men who are "effeminate" in analogous ways.

The encasement of amplifications in various contexts allows for both men and women, as well as for virile and effeminate along with womanly or mannish figures. Such hybrids may manifest themselves in various ways, according to context, speaker, or plot. For example, two prominent features of *meurs femenins* in Jean's *Rose* are garrulousness and the inability to keep secrets (v. 16317–58, 18269–73, 19188–91). Genius and Nature agree on this, but their agreement in fact problematizes the issue. Genius illustrates his views through the husband who confesses his secrets to his wife. He

> a fet espoir quelque chose,
> Ou veust par aventure fere
> Quelque murtre ou quelque contrere,
> Don il craint la mort recevoir
> Se l'an le peut apercevoir.
> (V. 16362–66)

[has perhaps done something, or wishes perchance to commit some murder or crime, for which he fears death if caught.]

If the wife made known the murder or other crimes her husband committed or intended to commit, would she be "garrulous"? Elsewhere Nature apologizes for her own garrulousness in her complaint about men's vices.

> Fame sui, si ne me puis tere,
> Ainz veill des ja tout reveler,
> Car fame ne peut riens celer,
> N'onques ne fu mieuz ledangiez.
> Mar s'est de moi tant estrangiez,
> Si vice i seront recité
> Et dirai de tout verité.
> (V. 19188–94)[57]

[I'm a woman and I can't keep still; rather I want to reveal everything right away because a woman can hide nothing, nor was he, man, ever more effectively vilified. Woe betake him for having become so unnatural. His vices will be set forth and I shall tell the whole truth.]

Yet, she is speaking the truth (v. 18273) about man's sins and crimes against her. Man and woman, like the criminal, must fear death or shame because of their vices, a point made by both Reason and Nature (v. 4403–8, 19208–92), each a voluble feminine personification. Yet, they are Amant's own reason and nature speaking. Without Reason neither Nature nor Genius can discriminate between *meurs femenins* as they would construe them and honesty based on love and mutual concern.

These models of crime and vice and of revelation and punishment fit the larger paradigm the *Rose* displays in the examples of what transpires after Amant's oniric consummation. If we place Amant into that scheme, we also observe him garrulously revealing the intimate details of his sex act, just like any woman telling the whole truth about her husband's wrongs. As Reason remarks: "Nus fols ne set sa langue tere" (v. 4704) [no fool can hold his tongue]. The fool displays *meurs femenins*. So does, *a fortiori*, the *fol amoureux*. Indeed, as I have pointed out elsewhere,[58] Amant prattles right through the sex act, scarcely stopping to acknowledge or recall—or experience?—the pleasure he presumably knew, so busy is he telling the truth about this and other acts. The irony is underscored by a *jeu-parti* on the same issue:

je vous vueill demander
Quant fins amis a plus de seignorie,
Ou quant il velt le soulas recorder
Qu'il a eü et d'amours et d'amie,
Ou a ce point que le deduit em prent.
(*Recueil général des Jeux-partis français* LXXXIII, v. 1–5)

[I want to ask you when a lover is more on top: when he desires to recall his pleasure with love and his beloved, or at the moment of orgasm?]

In Amant's case, recalling past conquests interests him more than the actual experience of pleasure.

Amant contrasts with friends of either sex who, male or female, know how to keep their friends' secrets while admonishing them to mend their ways if they have done wrong. That is, for example, what the wife as friend might have done on hearing her husband's confession. In this context, a woman like Rose who is capable of friendship as Reason defines it would assume *meurs humains*. For Nature too, "humanity" is possible through the proper use of reason—reason as mental faculty and as speech. This applies to both men and women, since both are endowed with reason as human beings—that is, the capacity to choose right conduct while resisting both fortune and impulse.

This in no way excuses Jean's use of "femenine" to describe mores that, properly speaking, are characteristic of any irrational, immoral, or morally defective conduct and sentiments. To be sure, he attempts to justify his language by appealing to conventional authority, an authority which even Christine de Pizan still recognized as applicable to some women's conduct. That authority expresses the biblical and patristic misogyny of the Middle Ages.[59] But Jean also argues that all humanity is fallen and defective because of attachment to false goods in the Boethian sense of the expression. By use of reason—even in its fallen, defective state in Iron Age France—men and women can correct themselves.[60] In doing so, they may cooperate with one another along the lines Reason suggests: friendship, charity, love of reason. That they will do so seems doubtful. This is because humans, in their weakness (*mollities*), prefer ease to fortitude. This pessimistic prospect signals Jean de Meun's misanthropy.

Jean's description of "fallen" woman has three parts: her bodyparts, her dress, and her typical actions. To describe the woman's body, Jean arranges borrowings from Ovid and other sources according to the head-to-toes stereotype of corporal descriptions in the Middle Ages as part of the Vieille's harangue to Bel Acueil.[61] The result foreshadows, to illustrate with a well-known example, Villon's dual portrait of the Belle Heaumière first young, then old. The Vieille's description, however, focuses on hiding or making up for defects. In so doing, she turns the stereotype into a *faux semblant*.

The *faux semblant* is accommodated by dress, the second part of the medieval model. "S'el n'est bele, si se cointait, / La plus lede atour plus cointe ait" (v. 13251–52) [If she isn't beautiful, let her fix herself up: let the ugliest woman have the most beautiful outfit]. *Cointerie* is necessary for lovers in Guillaume de Lorris, although there it suggests the man's stylish elegance more than his natural physical beauty (v. 2121–62). Faux Semblant himself may take the guise of either man or woman, and, in doing so, conform his appearance to a hypocritical role rather than to the hidden truth. "Autre eure vest robe de fame, / Or sui damoisele, or sui dame" (v. 11177–78) [On other occasions I wear woman's dress, now as a damsel, now a lady]. We have already observed this in a number of the sexual metamorphoses adumbrated in Guillaume's Narcisse, features which Jean carries over into his continuation: Male Bouche's syllepsis and Bel Acueil as a masculine manifestation of a feminine complex, as well as in Orphée. The Vieille likens the woman who falls asleep at table to Palinurus falling overboard and drowning. Sodomites castrated take on feminine traits and actions. So do lovers like Amant: "O extrema libidinis turpitudo, que . . . mentem effeminat."[62] [Oh! most abject lust that makes the mind effeminate!]

In evaluating the mores of one sex or the other, the degree of prejudice in praise or blame depends on how universal or exclusive the praise or blame is. In fact, the catalogue of man's vices read out by Nature and cited above (p. 113) refers to them not only in males but also among women. But *meurs femenins* as such are treated in the *Rose* in a misogynistic way: according to the masculine Genius: "En fame a tant de vice / Que nus ne peut les meurs parvers / Conter par rimes ne par vers" (v. 16304–6) [there is so much vice in women that no one can relate in rhyme or verse their perverse ways]. Yet, according to Nature, a feminine personification, man too "est sers a tretouz les vices / Et tretouz an soi les herberge" (v. 19206–7) [is slave to all vices and harbors all of them in himself]. The different vices listed by Nature are exemplified for both men and women at various places in the *Rose*. For example, just as women lure men into their traps, so men hunt in the same deceptive ways in the war of sexes (cf. v. 13559–60 and 15108–12). Both men and women lie, hate, perjure themselves, boast, betray, and waste their time. Both are sodomites because both are effeminate.[63] If Jean de Meun is a misogynist, he is also a hater of males. There is a measure of "misandry" alongside the *Rose*'s misogyny.

These parallels are not entirely accurate; nor are they meant to underscore a systematic correlation between *meurs femenins* as defined by the "authors" and man's vices summarized by Nature. They are complexes of attributes that, taken together, constitute commonplace images of a good or bad type.[64] The common or largely overlapping semantic fields evoked by topical elaboration of human vice and *meurs femenins* direct our attention to a common fault in human conduct, a fault represented by unnatural sex, which in the *Rose* includes any human sexuality not governed by reason.

The vice and sin is *mollities*, which includes *meurs femenins*, sodomy, and bestiality. It was associated with women, effeminacy, weakness, and softness even before Isidore of Seville offered the following definition of *mollis*: "Mollis, quod vigorem sexus enerviati corpore dedecoret, et quasi mulier emolliatur" (Isidore of Seville, *Etymologiarum libri*, X. 179)[65] ["soft" because it disfigures the body by sapping the strength of unmanned sex, and softens it like a woman's]. The Vulgate makes this explicit in relation to *mollities*: "Nolite errare: neque fornicari, neque idolis servientes, neque adulteri, neque molles, neque masculorum concubitores . . . regnum Dei possidebunt" (*Biblia sacra*, I Corinthians 6.9–10)[66] [Make no mistake about it: neither fornicators nor idolators, adulterers nor the soft nor sodomites . . . will enter the kingdom of God]. Fornicators, like the *molles* in whichever of the many senses this word had in medieval Latin, are practicing the sin of *mollities*. That is, they are living Jupiter's life of ease.

The distinctions among different types of *mollities* are descriptive, but they are not confined in usage to one sex or the other. Anyone may follow the "mollitiem voluptatum huius seculi" (Hrabanus Maurus, "Epistolae," 34.8–9, on p. 469)[67] [ease of temporal pleasure seeking], just as anyone may rise above it. "Illa . . . mollitiem iam deponens muliebrem / Et sumens vires prudenti corde viriles" (Hrotsvitha of Gandersheim, *Opera*, p. 183, v. 168–69) [she sets aside womanly weakness, assuming the virile strength with a prudent heart], exclaimed Hrotsvitha von Gandersheim of a woman in her *Vita Basilii*. Similarly, Guillaume de Saint Thierry glosses the Vulgate Canticum: "*Pulchra*, inquit, *inter mulieres*, fortis inter molles" (*Exposé sur le cantique*, p. 162, strophe 5, §63) [Beautiful among women, he says, strong among the soft]. Etymologically, he continues, "a mollitie quippe mulier dicitur" ["woman" is in fact derived from "softness"]. Adam of Bremen, like Reason, faults a man for sinking into "mollitiem animi" [softness of soul] because, like Amant in Reason's estimation, "ignorabat . . . modum" (Adam of Bremen, *Gesta Hammaburgensis ecclesiae*, p. 121, 3.36) [he does not know the mean].

A good "courtly" example is this judgment regarding Foulques d'Angers's submission to his former wife, the remarkable Bertrade de Montfort, who "ita mollificaverat" [had so softened] her former husband "ut eam tanquam dominam veneraretur et scabello pedum eius sepius residens, ac si prestigio fieret, voluntati ejus omnino obsequeretur"[68] [that he adored her as his lady, often sitting on her footstool as if out of respect for her, and acquiescing in her wishes in every way]. Amant's similar postures in Guillaume de Lorris may have inspired disapproval, leading to the writing of Jean's continuation. Archbishop Suger, who describes this scene with disapproval, grudgingly acknowledges in the same place that Bertrade is a "virago," or *mulier fortis*, because of her beauty, learning, and feminine wit.

Mollis itself ranges in meaning from "soft, effeminate, listless" through "impressionable" to "vain."[69] These attributes include the human vices which Nature's catalogue amplifies by *frequentatio*. As a substantive, *mollities* includes sodomy, effeminacy (that is, anyone who evinces *meurs femenins*), and lechery in both sexes. "The celibate, the courtly lover, the pederast, the evil man culminate in the figure of Orpheus . . . , who established evil rules against Nature for his false followers . . . : the rules he creates contrary to Nature are false and artificial."[70] Perhaps the most cogent illustration of Amant's kind of *mollities* comes from a *summa* on Gratian's *Decretum*. Saint Ambrose is said to have claimed that a man may practice incest, but not a woman, a statement the commentator finds literally absurd, so that he interprets it allegorically. The man and woman are so named not because of their sexual gender, but because of their virtue: "Virum ibi appellant non a sexu sed ab animi virtute, mulierem etiam non ob sexum sed ab mentis mollitie"[71] [They designate a man thus not by sex but by moral virtue, a woman not on account of sex but moral weakness]. Many more examples are available.[72] But these are sufficient to suggest, cumulatively, that virtue or vice, but not sexual gender, might govern the allegorical reading of a literal person. Nonetheless, the authority for the commonplace description of *meurs femenins* is a misogynist authority not subject to refutation in the Middle Ages without a major, general change in religious mentality that has hardly been completed even today. Yet, as the epigraph to this chapter shows, the man or woman, in allegory, can exemplify any kind of conduct, good, bad, complementary, or neutral.

In the light of divine authority, secular authorities, and human language, moral judgment is based on traditional sexual attributes, not on one's actual sexual gender. The Vulgate's condemnation of fornicators, adulterers, sodomites, and the *molles* all together certainly demolishes the lesson of Genius's sermon. The implicit condemnation is reinforced, insofar as Amant is concerned, by Ephesians 5.5: "Hoc enim scitote intelligentes: quod omnis fornicator, aut immundus, aut avarus, quod est idolorum servitus, non habet haereditatem in regno Christi et Dei" [Know then this, you who have understanding: every fornicator, or impure person, or miser, because he or she is an idolator, will not inherit the kingdom of heaven].

In telling Amant that he must hide his identity by assuming a feminine *senhal*, Ami reinforces a traditional courtly justification for gender ambivalence like that which marks Amant's kind of love in the *Rose*.

Mes ja n'i metez propre non,
Ja cil n'i soit se cele non,
Cele resoit cil apelee;
La chose en iert trop mieuz celee.
Cil soit dame, cele soit sires,[73]
Ainsinc escrivez voz matires.
(V. 7461–66)

[But never use a proper name, let him be only she, and she be called he. Their affair will be concealed much better in this way. Let him be a lady, she a lord—write what you have to say in this way.]

This is what Jean de Meun did. In doing so, he gave Amant a *faux semblant*.

After so much has been written on Jean de Meun's misogyny, it is surprising, yet credible in allegory, to find it directed at Amant's characteristic features.

In assimilating the attributes of the woman that are commonplace in the literature of misogyny, Amant also takes on the *meurs* those attributes describe. The moral implications of the mutation are striking. No one has, I think, put them so clearly yet so movingly as Emmanuèle Baumgartner. I quote the passage here because it was the point of departure for my research into the matter (although Professor Baumgartner is in no way responsible for where it has led me).

> Ne serait-ce pas plutôt, mais il faudrait encore bien des pages pour conclure sur ce point, que la mysogynie de Jean de Meun ou des personnages qu'il met en scène, mysogynie qui s'exprime souvent de façon brutale et pénible pour l'amour-propre féminin, est moins une condamnation globale et systématique des femmes qu'une dénonciation de ce qui, en elles, et peut-être par la faute des hommes, témoigne d'une dissonance entre leur être véritable et les semblances trompeuses et multiples qu'elles donnent d'elles-mêmes. Besoin de paraître, recherche de l'artifice, goût immodéré du luxe, de la parure, hypocrisie du désir, vénalité des sentiments, recours à la ruse, au mensonge, etc., autant de preuves de leur conduite inauthentique, donc condamnable. Conduite qu'elles partagent d'ailleurs avec les hommes, même si, semble-t-il, elles en assument la plus grosse part!
>
> *Sanz faille ausinc est il des homes* (v. 9033), avoue le mari jaloux dans un rare éclair de perspicacité et de franchise . . . .[74]

We are all *ribauts* when we evince such *meurs femenins*. As astonishing, even as repugnant as the allegory may strike us today, it was, as *mollities*, a commonplace image in moral discourse in the twelfth and thirteenth centuries.

Here too, perhaps, we may discover an explanation for the masculine Male Bouche. By the second half of the thirteenth century, preconsonantal "*s*-" ceased to be pronounced in Francien. "*Masle*," "male," was a homonym of "*male*," "bad."[75] Amant and his *meurs femenins* would indeed assimilate Rose's *male bouche*—the male/bad mouth of his garrulousness and of his articulated misogyny. He had, after all, refused *amitié* as much as did the Jealous Husband. In the last analysis, these figures travesty the immoral mores imputed authoritatively to the feminine sex.[76] Such travesty, in the context of *mollities*, is a metaphor for moral perversity in men and women.

THE DIGRESSIVE MODE (*Modus digressivus*)

Digression highlights description by setting the described image in a new matter or a new context. It is similar to allegory, except that in digression two different matters reveal the same truth, whereas in allegory, one matter reveals two different meanings. In the *Rose*, digression tends to set the plot into new and unexpected contexts, contexts that show forcefully and clearly the significance or meaninglessness of Amant's fictional seduction, as when Reason sets Amant's love into the context of fortune. However, this mode is more complex in medieval rhetoric than it might first appear. I shall therefore discuss digression under its four traditional varieties in medieval poetics, all of which are prominent in the *Rose*: description as such, transition from one part of a matter to another, passage to a topic outside the given matter but pertinent to it (this includes comparisons), and passage to a topic not pertinent to the matter in a free-ranging excursus.[77]

Description is taken to be disgressive because the text departs from narrative to introduce a topical passage not necessary for the tale alone. It consequently departs from the matter in order to introduce context: descriptions construe matter. We have discussed the art of description under the descriptive mode. Here I am concerned with its contribution to the matter it is grafted onto. The only so-called head-to-toe description (so common in Guillaume's *Rose*) in Jean is that which orders the Vieille's instruction on how Rose should adorn herself in order to seduce Amant and others like him and to hide her blemishes. Let us look at that description again as an example of digression.

The description is digressive in that a survey of body parts is not called for. Yet the survey, topically adapted to the intent to seduce, does set the context for the Vieille's instruction on Rose's role as seductive woman. It also includes a circumstantial analysis of comportment that both seduces the man and protects the woman. The treatment of the topic "hair" will suffice to illustrate how the stereotypical array is made to illustrate the Vieille's lesson. If a woman like Rose notices that her blond hair is falling out, or that some illness obliges her to cut it off, or again if some *ribaut* has pulled her hair out in anger, drastic steps must be taken to hide the damage and restore her beauty. If she can no longer use her beautiful hair as allure,

> Por grosses treces recovrer,
> Face tant que l'en li aporte
> Cheveus de quelque fame morte,
> Ou de saie blonde borreaus,
> Et boute tout en ses forreaus.
> (V. 13262–66)

[in order to recover large plaits of hair let her get the hair from some dead woman, or fillets of blond silk, and shove it all into their false shapes.]

Note as well how the description re-enters the narrative in passing to that constant threat for the seductive woman, the violence of *ribauts*, that is, of those Amant is beginning to resemble, or jealous husbands who, in anger, pull out their wives' hair while beating them (see v. 9331–39, 13259–61).

The second kind of digression anticipates or flashes back to another part of a plot. The most striking illustration in the *Rose* is the prefiguration of Amant's and Rose's postcoital life in the numerous examples of love gone wrong that punctuate the lessons of Reason, Ami, the Vieille, and Nature. In effect, the second part of the diptych "before and after" filters through the first. If, in addition, we take Ami and the Vieille as attributes of Amant and Rose respectively, their personal stories become continuations of Amant's and Rose's, whether their union remains free or whether it results in marriage.

Digression to another part of the plot also occurs with the introduction of Nature and Genius. Amant has already become a passive observer of the vast field of operations opening up to parallel strategies, combats, and skirmishes during the siege.

> Je, qui estoie pris ou laz
> Ou Amors les autres enlace,
> Sanz moi remuer de la place,
> Regardai le tournoiement
> Qui conmença trop asprement.
> (V. 15078–82)[78]

> [I, trapped in the snares Love catches others with, stayed to watch the tournament that began very harshly.]

When the *mêlée* ends inconclusively, but also unsuccessfully for Amant, messengers are sent to Venus imploring her aid. At the same time, Nature's complaint to Genius begins. Ultimately, the bifurcation of narrative lines leading away from Amant's observation post rejoins for the final assault in which Amant and Rose are inflamed by Genius and Venus.

The third kind of digression is the excursus to another relevant topic. Reason's excursus on fortune; Ami's on the Jealous Husband; the different amplifications on the end of the Golden Age; Faux Semblant's lengthy analysis of true and false religious, begging, and academic quarrels at the University of Paris; Nature's excursuses on predestination, dreams, mirrors and lenses; and Genius's description of Heaven—these developments take up a new subject matter or theme which is then integrated into the main plot and its concerns. Such digressions put into context the principal topic. Amant's submission to the God of Love carries with it submission to fortune. The Jealous Husband's violent, tyrannical *seigneurie* contrasts with Ami's policy of laissez-faire in love, yet each represents an attempt to manipulate the object of love for his own satisfaction. Mirrors, like eyes and dreams, may deceive, showing distorted or false images—as does a lover's imagination when uninformed by the definitions and descriptions of Reason. Genius's separation of the Park of the Lamb from the Garden of Deduit obscures the fact that his life of sexual pleasure takes place in the Garden of Deduit, an obfuscation that suggests the vanity of the promised paradise. Sexual pleasure is momentary, not eternal.

The fourth kind of digression, the so-called *digressio inutilis* into matters having nothing to do with the subject,[79] is not uncommon in poetry and historiography. Yet, it can be ironic. Nature's concern with procreation and her long complaint are in the last analysis of no interest to Amant or Rose; pregnancy is the last thing on their minds. Indeed, childbirth and children occur rarely among the *Rose*'s examples, and those children who do appear hardly illustrate family values: Nero, Medea, Jupiter, Mirra, Adonis. Parenthood is not reassuring either. Virginius prefers that his daughter lose her head rather than her virginity. Croesus, Phanie's father, ignores her advice. Mirra lures her unsuspecting father into incest. These examples are as depressing as most of the others cited in the *Rose*. Moreover, they are truly digressive in the context Nature would impose since they mean nothing to Amant and serve to illustrate corrupt children and childhood.

In the *Queste del saint graal*, one must interpret a *semblance* in order to understand what it images. The author chooses descriptive attributes and configurations which, as *semblance*, reveal the meaningful, identifying form beneath the fictional matter. In the *Rose*, such vision fits the role of extramission in sight as Nature describes it. In medieval science, extramission refers to the beam of light which emerges from the eye and, meeting light coming from an external object, carries the image of the object back to the viewer. If nothing opaque reflects light from the eye's beam, sight passes through the object of vision and sees nothing (v. 16825–64). Faux Semblant is especially anxious to pass unrecognized so as not to reveal his essential falseness. Lovers like Amant act in the same way. Just as the variable transparency and opaqueness of the moon causes us to perceive shapes of a man, a tree, and a serpent, so too the distorted vision of persons like Amant and Rose makes them misconstrue the objects of their vision.[80]

Jean suggests how this is so by a digression that functions as a *mise en abyme* modeled on an analogous structure in Guillaume. Whereas the God of Love in Guillaume outlines a love ennobled by the sublimation of the lover's desire from passionate possessiveness to contemplation of Rose's beauty,[81] in Jean, the author incorporates the image of the Sleepwalker into Nature's complaint so as to suggest the overall scheme of his version of the *Rose* and its new conclusion (v. 18274–418). In Jean's digression, *maladie de pensée* and the desire to possess lead through promenade, conflicts, towers, and imprisonment to bushes before which the Sleepwalker collapses and is astonished to find himself upon waking. The digression reveals Amant's dream to be an *insomnium*, which Macrobius defines in part as the wish fulfillment dream of the "amator deliciis suis aut fruentem . . . aut carentem" (*Somnium* 1.3.4) [lover enjoying or missing out on his or her pleasures]. Everything about such dreams is untrue.

> Si li avoit la maladie
> Sa veüe mout afoiblie,
> Et li airs iert occurs et troubles,
> Et dit que par ces resons doubles
> Vit il en l'air, de place en place,
> Aler par devant soi sa face.
> Briefmant miraill, s'il n'ont obstacles,
> Font apparoir trop de miracles.
> (V. 18171–78)

> [His illness had greatly weakened his power of vision, as did the dark and troubled atmosphere; and he says that for these two reasons he saw here and there his own face pass before him. In short, mirrors, if they have no obstacles, cause a great number of extraordinary things to appear.]

These are useless digressions that fill the minds of lovers bereft of critical reason. That is Amant's fate from the moment Reason, and thus discernment, takes leave of him. There are no more "obstacles" to his vision. But, as Nature argues,

> resonable creature,
> Soit mortex hom, soit divins anges,
> Qui tuit doivent a Dieu loanges,
> S'el se mesconnoit conme nice,
> Cist defauz li vient de son vice,
> Que li sans li trouble et anivre,
> Car il pot bien reson ansivre
> Et pot de franc voloir user,
> N'est riens qui l'an puisse escuser.
> (V. 17832–40)

> [if a creature endowed with reason, whether mortal or angel, all of whom owe praise to God, foolishly fails to recognize who he or she is, the fault

comes from vice which confuses and befuddles the mind; for he or she can in fact follow reason and use free will—and there is no excuse for failing to do so.]

Jean insists on human responsibility. The individual errs by abdicating responsibility and deliberately rejecting self-knowledge.

THE METAPHORICAL MODE (*Modus transumptivus*)

The entire *Roman de la rose* is an extended metaphor and thus an allegory. The metaphorical mode serves to contrast literal and allegorical readings of its plot, as we have seen. Yet it does not articulate a single meaning or evaluation of either the literal plot or its allegory. It offers no definitive gloss, moral, or interpretation. Here I shall briefly discuss the artistry of Jean's metaphorical mode, saving the larger issues of interpretation for chapter 5.

Metaphor is an explicit or implicit comparison between two different things. If extended, the metaphor becomes an allegory. In the prologue to his part of the *Rose*, Guillaume sets up three levels of his allegory: the enigmatic "other" dream that predicts the biographical love story and articulates the art of love. Rose, the name he invents for his lady, allegorically restates the rose Amant desires in the dream. But Guillaume's *Rose* is not just another way to tell a real-life love story. As an art of love, the dream becomes an exemplary lesson on how to be a lover, how to act, think, and feel—and how not to—when in love. The instruction is primarily directed at Amant, although the lady is not excluded, as the moral to the Narcisse exemplum shows. But, in Guillaume, the rose complex is only passive or reactive.

Jean changes all that. In the first place, he redefines the dream as a false dream. The Sleepwalker digression actually redefines Guillaume's *somnium*, or true dream in need of explanation and thus an integument or allegorical structure (v. 1–30), as *insomnium* (cf. v. 18274–484). This invalidates it as an art of noble love. The *Rose* becomes a new handbook on deceitful love. The deceit comes to the literal surface in Ami's section of Jean's continuation. It is then accepted by Amant and personified by Faux Semblant. The Vieille extends the context to the rose complex in her art of feigned love for women. This means the truth of the dream is either nonexistent or "elsewhere" in the allegory. If it is nonexistent, the dream enters into the category of nonsense, or "truffes," meant only to produce laughter.[82] As such, the *Rose* would be a fabliau or fabula recounting a ludicrous, oniric seduction. If the truth is elsewhere, the locus of that truth must be identified in order to permit an allegorical reading.

This is where Jean's art is most effective. As we have noted above (pp. 38–40), his rewriting of the dream is analogous to and thus a refraction of Boethius's encounter with Philosophy. The analogy begins at the point Jean takes up Amant's story. The Boethian image locates all that precedes, and thus all of Guillaume's *Rose*, in the category of the idle songs Boethius tried to console himself with before Philosophy descended upon him. Philosophy's counterpart in the *Rose* is Reason. The true beginning of Jean's *Rose* is, therefore, Jean's own beginning, not Guillaume's. For that is the point at which Reason redefines Amant's love as malady and tries to reorient his thinking and conduct along Boethian lines.

The artificial order begins therefore between the midpoint of the entire work and Guillaume's actual beginning. Guillaume's *Rose* is redrawn as an image of love as *maladie*, and Reason invites Amant to reject it. The invitation is turned down, and the potential development along Boethian lines aborts. Amant turns to Ami for consolation and counsel, then embarks on the deceit that will lead him successfully through a rough *gradus amoris*. In the context of Reason, his malady becomes more acute and, as the anticipated conquests in the *batailles des cons jeunes et vieux* suggest, chronic. The allegory could not be more antithetical on its two layers: happy-go-lucky Amant sick with folly. An oxymoron typical of the love described by Reason in lines like, "C'est reson toute forsenable, / C'est forcenerie resnable" (v. 4269–70) [it's reason gone quite mad, reasonable madness], or, "C'est langueur toute santeïve, / C'est santé toute maladive" (v. 4275–76) [it's sickness in full health, health completely ill].

Does this mean Reason provides the corrective gloss, or at least the right context, for Amant? She certainly provides one context, albeit, as we have seen, she lacks the dignity and consistency of Boethius's Philosophy. But there are other contexts which counterpoint Reason's and cannot be excluded or ignored in an analysis of the *Rose*'s metaphorical mode. Ami and the Vieille have their readings of Amant's quest for the rose. These must be taken into account as possible readings of the romance, adapted respectively to a male or female reader—or rather to a certain kind of male and female reader. In addition, that reader may reflect on the scope of the different contexts. Just as Reason points out several different kinds of love besides the one Amant chooses, so Ami and the Vieille reject a love not illustrated by Amant, that characterized by fidelity and generosity. The reader may ask how one should choose, or indeed whether it is necessary to choose, between Ami's and the Vieille's readings, as well as among other available readings, and to what extent Amant's conduct fits or departs from any of them. This is the kind of personal allegoresis Jean actually invites in his self-defense. Such "internal difference," to recall Emily Dickinson's expression, is the locus of understanding and multiple meanings. These are implicitly suggested when Amant sets aside some of the God of Love's commandments, thereby allowing for a narrative that would retain those commandments, as Guillaume's does. The reader might then ask if Pygmalion's love does not illustrate the fidelity and generosity Amant now lacks.

However, Faux Semblant takes over for Amant and orients the plot in his direction.[83] Stakel has ably demonstrated how deceit, the notion Faux Semblant personifies, imbues Jean's *Rose* from beginning to end: lexicography, personifications, love—all these features of the plot are illuminated by Faux Semblant's words and glossed by his message. The metaphors of clothing, religious, heresy, and gluttony all interface in his discourse with deceit and fraud. These attributes are then brought to bear on Amant's love. Just as Male Bouche is taken in by Faux Semblant's *semblant*—an empty shape—so the Vieille, for all her cynicism and experience, lauds Amant as a perfect lover. According to the Vieille, who, judging by her instruction and experience, should know better, Amant is "li plus cortais vallez du monde, / Qui de toutes graces habonde" (v. 12557–58) [the most courteous valet in the world, and as gracious as can be]. "Il vos aime," she assures her ward, "n'en doutez mie, / De bone amor sanz vilenie" (v. 12603–4) [he loves you for sure with a good love, not a villainous one]. "Bien nous i poon fier" (v. 12607) [We can trust him] because he is "sages" (v. 12611) [prudent], "leaus" (v. 12617) [faithful], "de meurs bien ordenez" (v. 12621) [proper in conduct]. "Cil qui sa compaignie sivent / L'en ont torjorz porté tesmoign, / Et je meïsmes le tesmoign" (v. 12618–20) [Those who are with him have always vouched for him, and so do I]. Those in Amant's suite include Faux Semblant and Abstinence Contrainte. Either the Vieille is duped as easily as Male Bouche was, or as easily as her *ribaut* once duped her, or she is betraying Bel Acueil for the "largece" (v. 12636) Amant promises her. Both readings are possible. In the last analysis, Rose is duping herself or seeking her own profit, or both.

Indeed, Faux Semblant remains active almost to the end of the *Rose*. Though he does not participate personally in the tournament, his presence is felt on Amant's side in all the combats. We have seen Franchise weapon Chuerie, or "cajoling." Pitié is armed with a misericord, a treacherous weapon, of tears. Bien Celer fights with silence and hidden places as weapons. Hardement, which I would translate in this context as "reckless daring," comes armed with "security," or Seürtez, and "self-assurance," or Assurance, and so on. The arms of deceit and seduction are everywhere. But Rose is more than a match for them. More disarming action is needed on Amant's part to prevent her from fearing the worst and thus fending off his attack.

Deceit also enters into the Nature-Genius section. Although Nature seeks only continuation of the species, which she places under the aegis of

Reason, Reason is, in fact, absent and Genius alone assumes responsibility. This shifts the focus from Nature's concern with procreation back to love as *maladie* whose only goal is carnal delight. When both Amant and Rose have mutually consented, Faux Semblant departs, followed quickly enough by Abstinence Contrainte. Genius's equation of heaven and delight, a common erotic metaphor here reduced *ad absurdum*,[84] is sustained metaphorically in Amant's words on pilgrimages and shrines, relics and staffs. He has not entirely forgotten Reason's words.

These examples show that the metaphorical mode does indeed permeate the *Rose*. This is hardly a novel discovery,[85] but it also suggests the ambiguity of the metaphor as it slides from one explicit or implicit integumental context and gloss to another. How, then, does the audience respond to such metaphor, especially that rather uneducated, perhaps less attentive, easily bored, or displeased lay audience Jean seems to include in his publics? How, for example, would Reason's *ribauts de Grève* have reacted upon hearing the *Rose* after a hard day, during a long evening spent consuming their day's earnings in the pub?

> Il balent et tripent et saillent[86]
> Et vont a Seint Marcel aus tripes
> Ne ne prisent tresors .III. pipes,
> Ainz despendent en la taverne
> Tout leur gaaign et leur esperne,[87]
> Puis revont porter les fardeaus
> Par leesces, non pas par deaus,
> Et leaument leur pein gaaignent
> Quant enbler ne tolir ne daignent,
> Puis revont au tonel et boivent
> Et vivent si con vivre doivent.
> (V. 5022–32)

[They dance, skip, and jump, heading for tripe at Saint Marcel; they don't give a damn for banked wealth, but spend all they earned and saved at the tavern. Then—hi ho!—back to work they go again, where they earn their daily bread without grief, by hard labor, desdaining theft and robbery, then back again to the keg drinking and living as they must.]

There seems to me little difference between Reason's *ribauts* who return to their tripe and tun and those who go from *con* to *con*, especially those willing, again like Amant and the *ribauts de Grève*, to spend all they have earned to do so. Indeed, such models of *soffisance* seem to have been of one mind with Amant at the end of the *Rose*. What a quandary for the reader!

5

Allegories, Moral Issues, and Audiences

Ad nostrum dogma convertimus.
—Hrabanus Maurus,
De clericorum institutione

[We convert to fit our faith.]

Ceste parole n'est pas mienne,
Car onques n'amai par tel art.
—Jean Froissart, *Méliador*

[I reject what you have said for I never loved in that way.]

THE PRECEPTIVE MODE (*Modus praeceptivus* or *docendi*)

A *modus* not included in the Can Grande catalogue is the *modus praeceptivus* or *modus docendi*: the teaching mode.[1] Both Guillaume and Jean use it. For Guillaume, the *Rose* is a work in which "l'art d'Amors est tote enclose" (v. 38) [the whole art of love is contained]. As we have seen, on the literal level of the *Rose*, Jean wrote in order to show how one might succeed in plucking roses. Further examination reveals that he also sought on the allegorical level to dissuade his readers from that goal by representing Amant as a *fol amoureux*. This discrepancy raises the final question of ethical intent.

If allegory becomes irony, the literal level or surface may become false. Thus, the surface image of a dream or fable is false when it hides a truth. In this sense, the *Rose* as a book on how to pluck roses is a false semblance or image; it shows itself to be mendacious and fabulous as the reader glosses it. As a Macrobian *insomnium*, the dream is only an erotic dream. This means that the letter must be carefully read so as to identify the true image of the work, then reread with that image in mind. The true image as allegory will be "other." Without it we may, like Love's barons before Genius's sermon, snicker and nudge one another as we listen to the literal fable's "diffinitive santance" (v. 19474), but we will have no more than a snickering "read": "Et cil, qui ses paroles plesent, / S'antreguignent et s'antreboutent" (v. 19470–71) [and they who like what he says poke one another, and exchange knowing glances]. Such words have their effect: "Amen, amen, fiaz, fiaz!" (v. 20664) [Amen! amen! do it! do it!]. To such an audience, the religious metaphors, the relics, shrines, and genuflection of intercourse, are an adequate expression of what requires little "soutiveté de glose," or subtle glossing, to be understood. Such interlace of truth and falsehood is characteristic of Faux Semblant.[2]

READING THE *ROSE*

For Genius, the road to heaven is, literally, a primrose path. Yet, Reason argues that images of love like Genius's are false, leaving doubt as to whether Reason or Genius has the last word. We do not, of course, hear Rose's views. Nor does Amant himself express much interest in them. But Jean invites the women in his audience to consider the conclusion of the *Rose*. What will their reaction be? Women like the Vieille or the Wife of Bath (in any of the diverse ways she is being read these days) will have their reactions. We know Christine de Pizan's opinion of that "orde et tres abhominable et honteuse conclusion . . . deshoneste" (*Débat*, p. 56.254–55) [filthy, most abhominable and shameful, ignoble conclusion]. On one level, Nature's intent has been achieved if, willy-nilly, Amant has made Rose pregnant. Moreover, as with the maiden quoted at the beginning of this chapter, there is room for the reader who finds the *Rose* well written, but the lesson unacceptable. Multiple interlacing narratives on the literal level of the *Rose*—Amant's and Rose's story, those of counsellors like Ami and the Vieille, and numerous exemplary stories—punctuate the dream while suggesting both potential variants on Amant's *gradus amoris* and foreseeable continuations beyond its conclusion.

In approaching the allegorical levels that inform these stories, we must confront centuries-old criticism of the *Rose*. Three facets of that criticism bear consideration in our evaluation of the poem's allegories and their lessons. First, as we have observed, there was general agreement, even in a controversy as sharp as the "Querelle" of 1401–2, that Amant is a *fol amoureux*. Second, there are numerous interpretive voices in the *Rose*, any one of which provides a reading of the story it tells and thus a potential allegorical, even ironical, level of meaning. Third and last, the notion of the rhetorical case, or *cas*, which Matilda Bruckner has applied to Chrétien de Troyes's *Charrette* and its critical reception is equally useful in evaluating

Rose criticism. That is, the romance's potential readers are themselves so many mirrors of the text they read. What the reader perceives in the *Rose*, and especially which authority he or she accepts for the work's "definitive meaning," reveals the reader's own stance toward the plot and thus how he or she would apply it to moral issues like the seduction as well as related acts like changing confessors, following reason, and exercising free will. I propose to review these matters and then, with that review as foundation, discuss the poem's perceptible intention and *modus praeceptivus*.

Jean de Meun himself discloses the earliest instance of medieval reception of the *Rose*. Even before he had completed the poem, he felt compelled to defend it. In the intervention in v. 15105–272, in which he justifies the *Rose*'s language and its representation of women and the religious, Jean is responding to what must have seemed potential or truly significant objections to these features of the *Rose* even while it was being written and, perhaps, published or at least read serially.

Jean opens the intervention on the level of the literal dream. To that dream he assigns the metaphor of the hunt. "Or antandez, leal amant, / Que li dieu d'Amors vos amant / Et doint de voz amors joïr" (v. 15105–7) [Now listen, true lovers, may the God of Love advance your cause and grant that you find joy in love]. *Leal* is clearly meant to be ironic: Amant has already decided to use deceit to seduce Rose. But the plan of attack is hardly that envisaged by the God of Love in Guillaume de Lorris. Jean makes this more explicit as he continues.

> En ce bois ci poez oïr
> Les chiens glatir, s'ous m'antandez,
> Au connin prendre ou vos tandez,
> Et le fuiret, qui sanz faillir
> Le doit fere es raiseauz saillir.
> Notez ce que ci vois disant,
> D'amors avrez art souffisant.
> (V. 15108–14)[3]

> [In this woods you can hear the dogs yapping, if you get my point, after the coney you yourself are trying to catch, and the ferret which is to make sure it springs into your snares. Mark my words and you will have an adequate art of love.]

These words relate metaphorically the literal intention of the *Rose*; both hunt and rose-gathering are metaphors of seduction and sexual conquest. The hunt's images of genitalia and sexual intercourse are as thinly veiled as is the religious vocabulary at the end of the poem.

This is underscored by Jean's words following the hunt metaphor in his self-defense. He assures his audience that they will be able to answer any objections to his poem once he has glossed it: "Quant le texte m'orrez gloser" (v. 15120) [when you hear me gloss the text]. Since a gloss adds an explanation to the one already suggested by the preceding "s'ous m'antandez" (v. 15109) [if you get my point], we have two major readings. They are the double allegory *aliud . . . aliud* based on opposition.

As a hypothesis, let's take seriously Jean's statements about the *Roman de la rose* here and in other works attributed to him. Here the *Rose* is an art of snaring. Elsewhere, in the prologue to his translation of Boethius, it is an art of plucking. Jean's retraction and penance in his *Testament* might well be construed to include the *Rose*.

> J'ai fait en ma jeunesce maint dit par vanité,[4]
> Ou maintes gens se sont plusieurs foiz delité;
> Or m'en doint Diex un faire par vraie charité
> Pour amender les autres qui poi m'ont proufité.
> (V. 5–8)

> [In my youth I wrote many a vain work which lots of people enjoyed on numerous occasions. May God now grant that I write one out of pure charity to atone for those others which have profited me little.]

A last will announces the approach of death. The *Testament*, written toward the end of Jean's life, bespeaks real anxiety, if not terror, at the prospect of hellfire.[5]

Le codicile, also attributed to Jean de Meun, is not so explicit as the *Testament*. Nonetheless, like the *Testament*, it mirrors with unmistakably serious intent some topics in the *Rose* in such a way as to undermine the morality of seduction implicit in the statement, "In the *Rose* I taught how to pluck the rose." For example, it rehearses Faux Semblant's warnings by chastising those who pretend to be poor but are in fact quite prosperous, concluding: "Ce est escript, je le recors" (*Rose*, ed. Méon, 4:118)[6] [This is written, I report it]. It is written, among other places, in the *Rose* (V. 11014–19, 11207–8, 11645–48). Further on, the author reminds us that all will die, "Aussi des homs comme des fames" (*Rose*, ed. Méon, 4:120) [both men and women], thus enlarging the implied *Rose* audience, whether male or female, fruit or flower. All will die, and the rewards are not those Genius promises. Not to heed this warning is to be deceived—"A tart vous en repentirez" (*Rose*, ed. Méon, 4:121) [it will be too late when you repent of it]. These statements are warnings to anyone who would take the lesson of the *Rose* literally. Even more obviously, they correct Genius's view of Paradise and the means of access to it.

Reading through the *Rose* in the context of these statements produces the following argument. If you study the romance, you will learn how to pluck roses. But in following that instruction, you must betray your love. That is, you require the assistance of Faux Semblant, the agent who deceives by pretending, among other things, to be a needy and worthy beggar all the while he is wealthy, living at ease on the profits of his deceit.[7] But Faux Semblant and his kind will receive their due after death if they do not repent. In fact, all men and women will stand before God at the Last Judgment. For sinful souls—original sin was man's attempt to deceive God (*Rose* v. 19118–22)—it will be too late. Unrepentant deceivers will be deceived. Modern readers of medieval literature must never underestimate the reality and immanence of hell and damnation for medieval audiences.

These words permit two allegories: the allegory of seduction and the allegory of sin. To read the *Rose* on the first level is to learn an art of seduction. But, as such, it is also an art of sinning. To read the *Rose* on the second level is to learn how foolish artful lovers are. It is the reading by which Amant can be designated a *fol amoureux*. Put this way, the moral of the *Rose* is as harsh and uncompromising as, say, that in the *Queste del saint graal*, in which any infringement on virginity or chastity is irredeemable except by the most radical change of life and harsh penance. Although there is abundant evidence that the *Rose* was read as an allegory on a *fol amoureux*, the reception in the Middle Ages does not indicate the sober realism suggested by this stark contrast between the two allegories. One reason for this is its humor—a humor that many have found objectionable.

THE *FOL AMOUREUX*

In the "Querelle," *fol amoureux* is a negative appellation. In medieval literature prior to Jean de Meun, love's fools are not absent. Some were dreadfully ill—for example, those who were victims of "hero's disease"—whereas others appear only to go through the throes of young love.[8] The chronicles and moral treatises give evidence not only of widespread sin, including sexual licentiousness, they also suggest that sinners wrote poems in praise of their alleged sins.[9] Thus, the expression *fol amoureux* is not always negative. In many cases, it is one stage in a *gradus amoris* that can be consummated in sanctified marriage.

In Chrétien de Troyes's *Cligés*, for example, Alexandre makes a fool of himself over a single strand of Soredamors's hair, just as Lancelot does for a comb-full of Guenevere's in the *Charrette*. Yet both perform better because of the same love, thus exemplifying the contention that "de rien blasmer ne le vuel / S'il lait ce qu'Amors li desfant / Et la ou ele vialt antant" (*Charrette*, V. 1252–54) [I don't wish to blame him if he relinquishes what Love forbids while following her wishes]. Such a paradox may be received literally as betterment or ironically as foolishness to be avoided. Criticism and condemnation of "courtly" literature treating such topics in the twelfth and thirteenth centuries hardly support such a contention.[10] That the romances *could* be read as moral caution is, of and by itself, not proof that they were written or always read in that way. If the righteous wanted to show that love is a sin, they could call on the examples of Lancelot and Guenevere or Tristan and Iseut to prove it. But that means they condemn their love precisely because it was perceived as a good by lovers in terms of the foregoing quote from the *Charrette*. Criticism of romance and other kinds of narrative is quite explicit on these points, as are counsels to eschew the vanity these texts represent (like Jean's early writings recalled in his *Testament*) in favor of morally rewarding reading, as suggested in this passage from the anonymous thirteenth-century *Vies des pères*:

> Les autres dames de cest mont,
> Qui plus pensent aval qu'amont,
> Si font les mençonges rimer
> Et les paroles alimer
> Pour les cuers mielz enrooillier
> Et pour honesté avillier.
> Dame, de ce n'avez vos cure:
> De mençonge qui cuers oscure,
> Corrompant la clarté de l'ame,
> N'en aiez cure, douce dame.
> Leissiez Cliges et Perceval,
> Qui les cuers tue et met a mal,
> Et les romans de vanité.
> (Mölk, *Französische Literarästhetik* §75.23–35)

[The other ladies here below whose thoughts are directed down rather than up have lies set to verse and words strung out in order more effectively to corrupt hearts and vilify honorable conduct. Lady, take no heed of such things! Pay no attention to falsehoods that darken the heart by diminishing the light of the soul. Set aside Cligés and Perceval, works which slay and harm the heart, and romances on vain subjects.]

Such romances, by internal glosses like that quoted above from the *Charrette*, provide their audiences with an issue. The issue seems to have led to diverse judgments during the twelfth and thirteenth centuries. Nor did the year 1400 mark a sudden change in tastes and modes such that the strictures of a Jean Gerson and the criticism of a Christine de Pizan became possible for the first time.[11] Specific objections to the *Rose* emerged even before it was completed, as Jean's own inserted defense of the poem demonstrates. Since then, the work was transmitted and received in diverse ways.[12]

Criticism of love implies that there was unrest. In numerous twelfth- and thirteenth-century texts, a sexual love is idealized as a source of worth, although such love is not compatible with conservative Christian morality. This is because it admits adultery and allows for fornication without intent to conceive. To confound such claims, including those by Guillaume de Lorris, Jean wrote the *Rose* continuation, just as the author or authors of the complete Lancelot-Grail cycle corrected Chrétien's *Charrette* and, no doubt, the *Noncyclic Lancelot* and even, perhaps, the first authors or scribes of the cycle itself.[13] Yet Christine de Pizan and Gerson argue that Jean errs by presenting too one-sided a view of love; he does not, they assert, seek to correct explicitly his *fol amoureux* or show the reader clear examples of alternative routes to love beyond some explicit allusions, or the implicit possibilities suggested to different kinds of readers who reflect on themselves in relation to the plot.

> Et diras que maistre Jehan de Meung entendoit de ceulx qui en sont oultreement foulx: je te respons que de toutes choses, mesmement qui sunt bones, puet on mal user; mais puis qu'il vouloit descripre entierement amours, il ne la deust mettre si extreme a une seule fin. (*Débat*, pp. 129.470–130.475)[14]
>
> [You will assert that master Jean de Meun meant those who are wholly mad. I respond that one can misuse everything, even things that are good. But since he wanted to give a full description of love, he shouldn't have been so extreme in setting it only one single goal.]

Jean seems to argue, that is, that, for all lovers, "toute leur felicité soit de tendre a couchier avec leurs dames" (*Débat*, p. 129.457) [their only happiness comes from trying to get their ladies to bed]. To be sure, Christine overlooks the negative examples of postcoital love that punctuate the *Rose*. Still, her argument makes sense, not only if one reads the *Rose* as a strict moral allegory with a clear program, but also as a work an older Jean de Meun might have come to regret from the sober point of view of the *Testament* and *Codicile*. According to Christine, Jean might have developed some of Reason's suggestions by contrasting more clearly Amant with an "honourable amoureux" (*Débat* p. 130.496)[15] [honorable lover], perhaps one in line with Guillaume de Lorris's original intention, which even Gerson finds almost acceptable.[16] As we have seen, Reason evokes a kind of friendship between men and women that would avoid the deceit Amant surrenders to after he leaves Reason. Christine de Pizan too had something like this in mind when she wrote that je croy que plusseurs ont amey loyaument et parfaitement qui onques n'y couchierent, ne onques ne deseurent ne furent deceu, de qui estoit principale entencion que leurs meurs en vaucissent mieulx,—et pour celle amour devenoyent vaillans et bien renommés, et tant que en leur viellesce ilz louoient Dieu qu'ilz avoient esté amoureux. (*Débat*, p. 129.458–64)[17]

[I believe that a number of people have loved faithfully and perfectly who never bedded down together, nor did they ever deceive or be deceived in love; their primary goal was to improve their conduct. And their love made them valiant and renowned, so much so that in their old age they praised God for having been lovers.]

To be sure, to make an old *matière* new, Jean had to rewrite Guillaume. But, as Stakel has shown, his most profound and far-reaching change came with the emergence of deceit at the approximate midpoint of the total work. That *mutation brusque* transformed the love taught in Guillaume and the friendship authorized by Reason, a friendship that seems by and large compatible with the kind of courtesy outlined by Guillaume's God of Love. The instruction of the Vieille on picking fruit mirrors Amant's image of plucking roses: "Le fruiz[18] d'amors, se fame est sage, / Cueille an la fleur de son aage" (v. 13453–54) [let the smart woman pluck the fruit of love while she is still in bloom]. (See above pp. 15–16). In doing so, she will eschew gift-giving (but not gift-taking) and fidelity, which shows that the female side of the game follows the same game plan as the male. Bad cat, bad rat! "L'un vault l'autre, c'est a mau chat mau rat," as Villon puts it. (*Testament* v. 1624)[19] As in fables, the words do not condemn cats and rats, only men and women like Amant and Rose. The *Rose* becomes thereby a mirror of deceptive love. Anyone who believes in the "goodness" of such love is, in Jean's *Rose*, a *fol amoureux*. Everyone in the "Querelle" agrees. What they do not agree on are some features of the treatment, or *modus tractandi*. On issues of decorum, there never has been agreement. No doubt, there never will be. Jean is showing us how people act so that we may enjoy the comedy while reflecting on human *mores*. Such comedies can be unsettling. They have always been controversial.

INTERPRETIVE VOICES

Useful here is Payen's notion of the "carrefour idéologique," which I would rename in medieval terms a "carrefour moral"—a moral intersection and crossroads.

Tout se passe comme si le texte se trouvait en quelque sorte à l'intersection d'un certain nombre d'ensembles. Chacun de ces ensembles est constitué par

> une série de données intellectuelles (système de valeurs, code linguistique, référents métaphoriques ou mythiques) qui sont précisément les éléments fondamentaux d'idéologies [moralités] diverses.[20]

The different readings of the hypothetical case of Amant and Rose raise the issue of the morality of their interaction and the levels upon which, and the modes in which, their case is played out and argued.

Susan Stakel has lucidly analyzed the major voices that gloss Amant's actions and thoughts in Jean's part of the *Rose*. She convincingly shows how the plot centers on Faux Semblant, who emerges from Amant's decision to practice deceit. The insatiable appetite of Faux Semblant's companion, Abstinence Contrainte, both allegorizes and anticipates Amant's voracious sexual appetite evoked at the end of the poem. Ami's advice to pretend indifference to the rose anticipates the appearance of Abstinence Contrainte and prepares for the Vieille's subscribing to deceit for self-defense in the female register. Embracing the Ami-Vieille pair is the group of Reason and Nature. For Stakel, Reason and Nature are as defective as Ami and the Vieille: they are all tainted by Faux Semblant. I have no quarrel with her analysis of Nature except to recall that one of Nature's avowed problems is the absence of Reason. Therefore, I shall focus here only on Reason.[21]

Reason is crucial to any reading of the *Rose*. Although Guillaume marginalizes her voice—hers is a brief intervention, like a dash of cold water after a depressing refusal[22]—Reason assumes a central role in Jean de Meun, where she is present and voluble for over three thousand lines. Furthermore, she is the cause of important interventions, notably by the God of Love who, like Amant, expresses the ongoing enmity between himself and Reason, and by Nature, who underscores the role and purpose of reason in human conduct. If Reason's reasoning is faulty, as it can be,[23] this must be taken into account in any reading of Amant's rejection of her counsel. Many readers have found defects in Reason's arguments. All references to her authority, including her own, are suspect, they argue, and are consequently subject to review. We must therefore evaluate Reason's interpretive voice in the light of such criticism.

Two kinds of faults have been imputed to Jean's Reason: those that are placed there by the author himself and those that the author failed as an artist to represent according to the standards he himself enunciates.[24] Marc Pelen, Susan Stakel, and Donald Rowe pair and contrast Reason and Nature. All agree that these personifications complement one another in the instruction they impart yet betray limitations that ultimately misdirect Amant. Reason subordinates all to reason without allowing for the larger implications of charity that point to God and realms that lie beyond her ken. She also seems incapable of properly confronting her pupil. She loses his interest by dwelling on topics like fortune rather than on love. She fails to understand sympathetically a person overwhelmed by love, a force so universal, yet sweet, that some allowance should be made for it. She should have accommodated Amant's shortcomings, bringing up more interesting matters in order to lead him to a more human and humane love. Her examples are perplexing. Does Reason really believe that infanticide is a suitable response to unjust sexual empowerment, as in the Virginie exemplum? "Could Reason be suggesting that, in a fallen world, Amant himself should protect his own chastity at all costs, including murder, suicide and castration . . . ?"[25] Since, however, Reason is an opposite of love, she can hardly represent the mean she extols; she teaches by paradox, a rhetorical strategy out of place for her audience, a *fol amoureux*; she relies on numerous examples that illustrate sexual violence and appear to condone suicide, notably in the case of Lucrece; and her lengthy description of Fortune's house is useless. Reason "ultimately undermine[s] the credibility of [her] own words."[26]

According to this interpretation, Reason is an unsympathetic instructor who does not fully grasp the lessons she teaches, nor is she aware of the rhetorical and linguistic decorum required in moral instruction. The defects attributed to Reason focus on her allegedly inadequate logic, examples, and language. Jean may have intended to show that Reason, using *raison* in the sense of human language,[27] cannot speak properly. Insofar as Reason exteriorizes Amant's own addlepated reasoning powers, a state evident in his lamentation just before her appearance, she could actually be intended to personify his defective thought and language, not Reason of divine emanation.

I find these arguments compelling but unconvincing. Jean's *Rose* is an allegory, whereby personifications act out their semantic potential, not their humanity. This is as evident in the intractable violence of Prudentius's personified virtues[28] as in the indomitable strength of Jean's Peur while defending the rose. Jean de Meun represents Reason as a God-given faculty. She represents and extols the mean between two forms of folly, love as Amant loves and hate.[29] She envisages and explains several kinds of love to Amant; it is his fault for rejecting them, not hers. Amant represents a human being; he is not a personification. He possesses reason and, therefore, the wherewithal to understand and act reasonably or to argue convincingly against her view. Because Reason personifies Amant's own reason, just as the God of Love personifies his love, she actually tells Amant what he already knows, even if he refuses to understand her words or act on them. In this, Amant is partially analogous to Boethius when Philosophy finds out what he has forgotten in Book I of the *Consolation*. Amant's choice is willful, however, and for that he is responsible. Insofar as Reason represents Amant's own reason, he effectively rejects his own argument in an interior dialogue with himself. Reason's problem is not inherent in herself. As we observed above with respect to her language, she problematizes her role precisely because Reason is trying to do right in a world fallen from a lost paradise and with humanity—Amant's—which, like Jean's very audience, cannot always see through its fallen language into a truth and rectitude that the language may recall only dimly. There is no better example than what the word *coilles* signified before the Fall and what it came to connote afterward. Thus, Reason functions, as it were, as a mirror of Jean de Meun's own approach to language. Her speech is offensive because the decline of humanity from the Golden Age has made language connote what it does today.

Nature's intervention underscores these issues which are at the heart of Jean's allegory. Nature's long complaint identifies Reason as the God-given faculty (v. 18842–45, 19062–63) that discovers truth by logical argument (v. 16800–801, 17113–16, 17254–59, 17267–68), communicates it clearly and effectively (v. 17766–67), and directs conduct (v. 16592–93, 17053–70, 17233–36, 17523–26).[30] This is entirely consistent with Reason's efforts to convince Amant to follow her counsel. She argues, for the most part eloquently, that her conception of truth is correct. She seeks to direct Amant's conduct away from loving in the way he does and cannot be blamed for his failure to heed her words.

> Mes resonable creature,
> Soit mortex hom, soit divins anges,
> Qui tuit doivent a Dieu loanges,
> S'el se mesconnoit conme nice,
> Cist defauz li vient de son vice,
> Qui le sans li trouble et anivre,
> Car il pot bien reson ansivre
> Et pot de franc voloir user,
> N'est riens qui l'an puisse escuser.
> (V. 17832–40)

[But if a reasonable person—whether mortal or angel, who all owe praise to God—foolishly fails to recognize his or her true worth, the fault is attributable to that person's vice, which troubles and inebriates his or her wits. For that person could follow reason and exercise free will—and there are no excuses for failing to do so!]

By separating Nature and Reason in the *Rose*, Jean mirrors the actual separation between the two in Amant.

Nature emphasizes three points about her relation to Reason. First, Nature lacks the God-given capacity for *antandement*, or understanding, conferred on Reason alone (v. 17053, 19019–20, 19025–27, 19116). Second, Nature and Reason must cooperate for one to achieve the good human life and to avoid the original sin of deceit.[31] Third, Reason includes language in its semantic field: she has the power to name the things Nature makes.[32] But, in the *Rose*, Reason is absent at the moment Nature speaks. Nature, bereft of reason, is reduced to following her own course, in the event, that dictated by Genius as personification of male sexuality. In the *Rose*, Nature functions only as reproductive agent. Genius "Anjoint li qu'ele demourast / Dedanz sa forge et labourast / Si conme ainz labourer souloit" (v. 19389–91) [enjoins her to remain in her smithy, laboring as she labored before]. For his part, Genius sets off "si con s'il alast queroler" (v. 19407) [as if going a-caroling] while Nature returns to her hammers and anvil.

Nature's proper understanding of her task comes from a different authority. God appointed Nature, she tells Genius, to provide man with his physical self, life, and senses (v. 19008), gifts he shares with stones, plants, and animals, respectively. As such, man is a microcosm (v. 19023). Yet, although the understanding or *antandement* Nature cannot give comes from Reason, Reason has her own limits too. For example, she cannot comprehend revelation. Nature points this out, in remarks based on Plato's *Timaeus*, while expounding on the scope and limitations of ancient philosophy, which relied solely on reason. The triune deity no more fell within Plato's ken (v. 19089–117) than it does Nature's or Reason's. Nonetheless, in the realm of human morality, Nature and Reason must cooperate lest, deprived of truth and direction, the human being go astray.

> Car quant, de sa propre nature,
> Contre bien et contre droiture
> Se veust home ou fame atourner,
> Reson l'an peut bien destourner,
> Por qu'il la croie seulement.
> (V. 17057–61)

[For if a man or woman following his or her natural inclination turns against what is good and right, Reason can dissuade that person from doing so provided only that he or she heed her words.]

The words apply to both Amant and Rose. Nature paraphrases them more than once (v. 17228–36, 17520–42, 17832–40, 18839–47). It is obvious that Nature knows something Amant does not know, or that he has forgotten or ignored. Amant did not heed Reason nor is he prepared to seek her counsel at this stage in his seduction. In his topsy-turvy world, one follows Nature down Genius's path toward the paradise of corruptible nature and carnal delight. But, as Nature also states, at the same time Amant abandons Reason, he also submits to Fortune, that is, to the *destinees* that rule the life of irrational humanity (v. 17029–156). Amant's ignorance of his own rationality never flags. At the end "de Reson ne me souvint, / qui tant en moi gasta de peine" (v. 21730–31) [I forgot Reason who wasted so much effort on me].

Genius's sermon (in Nature's church) to Love's army also raises problems.[33] Genius is no more capable than Nature or Reason of comprehending the divinity. He proves it by preaching a sexual crusade bent on attaining the paradise of Rose's relics. He paints a picture of the Park of the Lamb, touted as the opposite of the Garden of Deduit. In the Park, the "white sheep" are saved to live with God in everlasting joy. Yet salvation depends on work in Nature's smithy: "Pensez de Nature honorer, / Servez la par bien laborer" (v. 20607–8) [think to honor Nature, serve her by laboring well]. No wonder Amant confuses religious and sexual imagery in the consummation of his pilgrimage on the altar of Nature's church. He is only following the lead of Genius's false sexual allegory of a literal image of heavenly bliss.

But Genius personifies not only male sexuality. He may also personify the faculty of imagination. Since imagination may be true or false, Genius may err and even run wild. For example, he fails to perceive that, while contrasting the Park of the Lamb and the Garden of Deduit, he is actually preaching in and contributing to the realization of the perishable garden.[34] Since Amant rejected Reason—who could have explained the proper and integumental meaning of images and thus allow him to get them right—he is in no position to understand celestial delight other than as an everlasting orgasm. To imagine heaven as a reward for sexual activity is such blatant heresy that the promise of heavenly rewards in Genius's sermon is nothing short of laughable, as in all likelihood was intended. Genius's sermon shows how foolish Amant has become. Rather than cooperating in the reproductive act, the God of Love, who had acquiesced in the treachery personified by Faux Semblant, joins Nature in following Genius, or the impulse of male sexuality. Amant is living in a topsy-turvy world of his own imagination.

There remains the issue of Reason herself as Jean de Meun represents her. The propriety of the word *coilles* has already been discussed. Her use of the word becomes even more interesting in the light of the proximity of the castration of Saturn and the decapitation of Virginie.

Pelen notes the virtual juxtaposition of the castration of Saturn and the decapitation of Virginie and suggests that, in a Christian context, Virginius "is still a murderer . . . , so that his action is perhaps a less than appropriate example of righteous defense against corruption."[35] The further link Pelen makes between the murder of Virginie and Lucrece's suicide also supports his interpretation, since Lucrece's suicide was also condemned, notably by Augustine.[36] Jean would again appear to make Reason sin against decorum. The impression is enhanced by the poem's conclusion, which offended the opponents of the *Rose*, but which Pierre Col found appropriate in terms of encouraging the continuation of the human race:

> Ne Nature ne Genius n'enortent pas c'on soit fol amoureux, mais ilz enortent suyvre les euvres de Nature, lesquelz sont licites aux fins auxquelz ilz les ennortent d'exerciter, c'est assavoir pour continuer l'espesse humainne et pour delaissier l'euvre contraire a nature, qui est abhominable a plus exprimer. (*Débat*, p. 107.640–45)[37]

> [Neither Nature nor Genius urges one to be a foolish lover, but they do urge people to do Nature's works; these are permissible in achieving the goals for which they are arguing, that is to say, the continuation of the human race and abstention from the unnatural act which it is abhorent to speak about any more.]

This would certainly be the definitive meaning according to Nature's excommunication and Genius's proclamation.

However, missing from Genius's sermon and from Amant's and Rose's concerns afterward is any thought of reproduction. In fact, pregnancy appears irrelevant to them. In this, the defenders of the *Rose* err regarding the conclusion, which focuses only on sexual intercourse, not on conception. There is, to be sure, the passage about Rose's sexual response to Amant.

> Si fis lors si meller les greines
> Qu'el se desmellassent a peines,
> Si que tout le boutonet tandre
> An fis ellargir et estandre.
> Vez ci tout quan que g'i forfis.
> Mes de tant fui je bien lor fis
> C'onques nul mau gré ne m'an sot
> Li douz,[38] qui nul mal n'i pansot,
> Ainz me consant et seuffre a fere

Quan qu'il set qui me doie plere.
Si m'apele il de couvenant,
Et li faz grant desavenant,
Et suis trop outrageus, ce dit.
Mes il n'i met nul contredit
Que ne preigne et debaille et cueille
Rosier et rains et fleur et fueille.
(V. 21697–712)

[Then I made the seeds mix so that they would hardly be separated, with the result that I caused the tender bud to open and extend. That's all the harm I did. But I was then quite sure that the sweet boy didn't hold it against me—and I didn't intend any harm—rather he grants and tolerates whatever it pleases me to do. And he calls upon me to keep my word, saying I am very discourteous and outrageous. But he doesn't object to my taking, handling, and plucking rosebush and branches, flower and leaf.]

Like Pelen, I think this passage refers to Rose's arousal. In the perfunctory events of the conclusion, it hardly seems to mean anything else. In any case, there is no amplification on Nature's goal of reproduction, only Genius's of sexual climax.

THE *ROSE* AS "CASE"

The issues raised by the conclusion actually transform the *Rose* into a Case, or a kind of trial in which its various prolocutors argue several interpretations of Amant's and Rose's thoughts and actions.

Li qels fait mieus a prisier,
U cil qui onques n'ama
Par amour jour de sa vie,
U chil qui par trecherie
Aime et tous jours a amé
Sans foi et sans loiauté?
(*Recueil des Jeux-partis français*, LXVIII, v. 3–8)

[Who is more estimable, the person who never loved at any time, or the one who loves deceitfully and has always loved unfaithfully and inconstantly?]

Is this not like asking who is more estimable in La Fontaine's fable, the ant or the cicada?

The foregoing issues fundamentally ask, What is the moral of the *Rose*? No answer is vouchsafed, although Jean, like Guillaume before him, seems to promise a gloss or commentary that would "explain"

Amant's dream. Thus Guillaume: "La verité, qui est coverte, / vos sera lores toute overte / quant espondre m'oroiz le songe" (v. 2071–73)[39] [The truth which is hidden will then be fully revealed when you will hear me explain the dream]. This corresponds in Jean to:

> Bien savrez lors d'amors respondre,
> S'il est qui an sache opposer,
> Quant le texte m'orrez gloser;
> Et savrez lors par cel escrit
> Quant que j'avrai devant escrit
> Et quant que je bé a escrire.
> (V. 15118–23)[40]

[When you hear me gloss the text you will be able to explain what love is should someone object to the doctrine as set forth here. By that text you will then know all that I have written heretofore and what I still intend to write.]

Neither Guillaume nor Jean has left a "gloss" or "commentary" in the sense we usually give to these terms: an interpretation *separate from* the *Rose*. No auctorial commentary glosses the *Rose*'s allegory.[41]

I do not know whether either author actually intended to write a commentary or gloss to the *Rose* such as, for example, the prose commentary written to accompany the verse *Échecs amoureux*; nor whether either Jean or Guillaume intended marginal glosses that would clarify different passages and direct the reader or audience in the direction intended by the authors.[42] Rather I find the suggestion convincing, and historically likely, that the gloss was actually imbedded in the text.[43] According to this view, the explanation or exposition unfolds as one reads by cross-references to what has already been written ("quant que j'avrai devant escrit," [v. 15122]). This implies that the gloss is in *cel escrit*, just as it will be in *cel escrit* which remains to be written ("quant que je bé a escrire," [v. 15123]). "Cel escrit," that is, refers to "le texte" of the *Rose*, not to a separate gloss. By reading the entire romance, Jean asserts, the reader will know all there is to know about love and have the wherewithal to answer any objections to its lesson.

Other medieval texts also gloss internally. Gui de Mori did so in his adaptation of both Guillaume and Jean.[44] The *Ovide moralisé* incorporated glosses into its octosyllabic couplets, albeit in a manner more systematic than either Guillaume or Jean.[45] The gloss is, furthermore, both literal and allegorical. The reader or audience would also comprehend literally and allegorically, as Jean's words suggest (see chapter 2).

Part of the *Rose*'s allegory, as we have observed, includes two mutually exclusive evaluations of Amant in the dream as a *fol amoureux*. Either his folly is good—and his silly or amusing antics are typical of people in love, including those who, like Pygmalion, would marry and have children—or his folly is reprehensible and to be eschewed. Pygmalion may not seem to be the best example. To be sure, he begins acting foolish. Yet, unlike Amant, he does realize that he is foolish and finally forms an acceptable marriage and family with his lady. This is acceptable in the moral context of both Reason and Nature. There are narrative voices speaking for both evaluations, with variations in perspective and spectrum, which function as lenses through which the conduct of Amant and Rose is reflected, refracted, and deformed. The reader is therefore encouraged to choose among the readings the text proposes and mirrors, but Jean as narrator offers no *explicit* indication of which reading is preferable.

Matilda Bruckner offers a useful way out of the impasse.

> In the Case, a situation arises in which we cannot measure only the conduct of an individual; we must also measure the norm by which we usually judge his conduct. As an incident unfolds,[46] for example, a given law may be shown to produce good and bad results: the weight itself is not giving true weight. One must then judge between norms, evaluating each in turn by a superior one. But the Case does not conclude; it poses a question: when are the weight and the norm necessary for that evaluation? While it imposes on us the obligation to decide, the Case does not contain the decision itself. If it does contain such a decision, it ceases to be a Case and becomes a different form, the Nouvelle, in which the positive decision abolishes the necessity to decide.[47]

These words offer a superb program for reading the *Rose*. But—the question is historically important—does Jolles's notion of the Case hold for the Middle Ages? Does the notion of the Case as argument without conclusion, as Bruckner so ably applies it to Chrétien's *Charrette*, correspond to any medieval evidence that would suggest people read and might be expected to read the *Rose* or any other medieval work in that way?

In traditional rhetoric, the Case is an "issue" (*causa*). The Issue leads to the formulation of hypotheses based on interpretation of data. A hypothesis is an exemplary reading that must be decided upon, by a judge, jury, or—in literary works like, say, the *jeu-parti*—an audience. The decision followed disputation. Several *jeux-partis* illustrate issues raised or implied in the *Rose*. For example, Amant and Rose, as faithful disciples of Ami and the Vieille, are reflected in the following Case:

> Uns faux amans faussement proie
> Une qui faussement otroie.

Li queus doit estre puis blasmez,
Ou il ou elle? Or i gardez.
(*Recueil général des jeux-partis français*, CXXV, v. 5–8)[48]

[A faithless lover asks for the love of a woman who faithlessly grants her love. Which one should one criticize, him or her? Consider the issues.]

Is there any hope that such lovers might change?[49] Are the redeeming features of good human love operable in their case, as Aelred of Rievaulx might suggest?

In fact, disputation always presumes opposing interpretations that are to be evaluated and judged, whether in forensic, deliberative, and epideictic oratory, sermons, or quodlibetal disputations and recitations of lessons like those Jean evokes literally and in debates and discussions among the *Rose* speakers. By reading the *Rose*, Jean assures his audience, everyone will be able to answer objections to the lessons he teaches. Those lessons are the *Rose*'s hypotheses. They make the Case, in Bruckner's sense of the word. The problem is, of course, that so many lessons are being taught that the reader is unsure of which Jean is expounding. In this sense the *Rose* is truly a Case as *jeu-parti*.

The difference between the *Rose* and Bruckner's definition of the Case and illustration of it in Chrétien's *Charrette* is that the *Rose*'s Case is not univocal. That is, it is not limited to a single Case. The romance is a patchwork of opposing Cases made by different voices. While some voices speak directly to Amant, like Reason, Ami, and the God of Love, another voice, the Vieille's, performs an analogous role with Bel Acueil, as does Faux Semblant with the God of Love, Nature with Genius, Genius with Love's army, and, finally, Amant with Rose. Only the reader or audience hears all the speakers. In eminently rhetorical fashion, only the reader or audience can decide whose voice is convincing. Reason's decisions will not reveal to readers what Jean de Meun thinks, but it will make them aware of their own moral identity.

Several choices are therefore possible among the *Rose*'s voices. Indeed, all have a certain claim to authority as potential allegorical readings. Amant's and Rose's interlocutors offer opposing moralities that constrain the reader to decide among them. As allegory, each of them must be read on at least two levels. One is primary in allegory: the literal level. The other is the reader as mirror and lens, that is, the eyes and mind of the reader. The eyes transmit as lenses the messages to the inner self as mirror, faithful or not, of what is imagined through the act of reading.

Allegory cannot exist for either ancient or medieval authorities without a letter. That letter is Amant's story, the plot of his dream. Amant's plot has two major moments, as Stakel has shown.[50] First, in Guillaume de Lorris, Amant falls in love and agrees to live by Love's commandments. Then, at the approximate midpoint of the entire *Rose*, Amant decides that, in order to win the rose, he must reject two of those commandments, generosity and fidelity, in favor of deceit. The God of Love mirrors the change by receiving Faux Semblant into his army. Later Bel Acueil, at the instigation of the Vieille, agrees to love on the same terms. The fundamental thrust of the plot is deceit and prevarication on both sides—the whole range of manifestations that Stakel identifies in the semantic web of deceit. This love fits neither that which Guillaume describes nor is it friendship between man and woman as Reason defines it. The love of Amant and Rose is neither generous nor honest.

Amplifications in monologues and dialogues constitute interpretative glosses imbedded in the plot to explain it, or, more accurately, to elaborate upon it. Thus, Amant decides to practice *traïson*, whereupon Faux Semblant emerges to expand upon deceit and to put it into action by the murder of Male Bouche.[51] Similarly, in the conclusion, Amant and Rose represent male and female sexual arousal as they grow "hot" when Genius enflames Love's army and Venus sets the castle afire. Nothing here indicates Nature's reproductive goals being met.[52]

But let us take the matter further to see if Jean has imbedded more clues in his Case. To know the truth, we are told to apply the principle of *contraires choses*, the basis of irony. Such irony occurs when Amant's opposition of "old" and "young" is ridiculously applied to the truth of *cons* as pleasure-giving organs. Now, in Latin, irony is *dissimulatio*, which means both the deceit that Faux Semblant personifies and the oppositions it veils in incongruities like love as heavenly bliss or love as dissimulation. Jean's allegory has stretched itself to the very limits of allegory, while extending the metaphor to force the reader to decide on the juxtaposition of opposites represented by Reason's and Love's evaluation of the *Rose*.[53]

The Case is Amant's and its letter illustrates love as deceit. One may take various views regarding that love. There are Amant's interlocutors like Reason and Ami, the Vieille and Venus for Rose. Jean's intervention shows that audiences too were becoming involved, notably, those who found offensive the *Rose*'s language, descriptions of women, and representation of religious. All these reactions are consistent with Bruckner's conception of the Case. They are also consistent with Jean's conception of the *Rose* as a *Miroër aus Amoureus* that presents more than one Case.

THE MIRROR AND "CASES"

The mirror is doubtless the major image in the *Rose*. Amant's own story is mirrored by a *mise en abyme* which, like a similar device in Guillaume,[54] reflects obliquely and briefly Amant's plot. This is the exemplum of the Sleepwalker.

The Sleepwalker is set forth in two parts. Each contains elements that rehearse then anticipate the ensuing plot of the *Rose*. Men, Nature says, are so deceived that, while asleep, they prepare their equipment—including "bourdons" and "escharpes," later clearly identified as genitalia[55]—and set out on a long road, albeit ignorant of where they are going. During this time their senses are awake, but they are not conscious. Aroused, yet asleep, they finally reach strange places (*leus*[56]). Suddenly awakened, they tell everyone with great astonishment that devils must have borne them off, although, in truth, "il meïsmes s'i porterent" (v. 18296) [they got themselves there on their own].

A special kind of Sleepwalker is the person who is ill. "Maladie" and "frenesie" (v. 18299–300) take him or her off to wild places as well where they "se lessent . . . choair" (v. 18307) [collapse]. Even healthy people, "de trop panser . . . curieus" (v. 18317) [of overwrought thought] or the excessively fearful,[57] may sleepwalk. Sleepwalkers include both men and women. Various and diverse apparitions come before their eyes, apparently outside themselves:

> Qui mainte diverse figure
> Se font parair en eus meïsmes
> . . . .
> Et de tout ce leur samble lores
> Qu'il sait ainsinc por voir defores.[58]
> (V. 18320–21, 18325–26)

[which cause many a diverse shape to appear in their minds . . . and all this seems to them at that time to be truly outside of them.]

The state conforms to the *insomnium* as Macrobius defines it, as Nature reminds us obliquely in a reference to Scipio's dream (V. 18337). Such dreams seem to show, among other things, "esperituex sustances" (v. 18336) [spiritual substances], "anfer et paradys" (V. 18338) [hell and paradise]—indeed, much of what Nature evokes in her complaint and Genius in his sermon—as well as the construction of castles, lovemaking in chambers, wars and tournaments, dances and caroles. Finally, the Sleepwalker dreams he is lying in his beloved's arms while Jealousy comes to the attack incited by Male Bouche (v. 18327–94). That this is an *insomnium* is borne out by Jean's second example. People dream of the dangers and anxieties that threaten them or which they fear in waking life (v. 18371–74). Just so, Macrobius illustrates the *insomnium* as the false enigmatic dream:

Quotiens cura oppressi animi corporisve sive fortunae, qualis vigilantem fatigaverat, talem se ingerit dormienti: animi, si amator deliciis suis aut fruentem se videat aut carentem, si metuens quis imminentem sibi vel insidiis vel potestate personam aut incurrisse hanc ex imagine cogitationum suarum aut effugisse videatur.

(*Commentarii in Somnium* 1.3.4)

[Often mental or physical anxiety, or misfortunes, that wearied the waking person oppress the sleeper. Mental preoccupations, for example a lover observing him- or herself enjoying or failing to enjoy delight, or another person in fear of impending traps or forces that might befall him or her, seems to be in flight from these imaginings.]

Here are Amant and Rose, respectively. Taught by "foles vielles" (v. 18459) [mad old women] and under the guidance of Dame Habonde,[59] they are lured into folly and madness. Since the dream is enigmatic, it resembles the *somnium*—the kind Guillaume evokes in his prologue. However, in the *insomnium*, "quia in ipso somnio tantum modo esse creditur dum videtur, post somnium nullam sui utilitatem vel significationem relinquit" (*Commentarii in Somnium* 1.3.5) [because in the dream itself everything seems to be as it appears, there remains nothing useful or meaningful after the dream is over]. It is only a dream—the *insomnium* common among lovers (*Commentarii in Somnium* 1.3.6). Jean is asserting the exact opposite of Guillaume: Amant's dream is false and deceptive. The Sleepwalker provides an example of it and becomes thereby, in his turn, the informing model or image for Amant and his dream.

But neither Amant nor Rose is the reader or listener. We are. To that extent the true lenses are our own eyes and the way we respond—with hilarity, pious indignation, or squirming—to the plot we read and the actions we visualize and reflect or imagine ourselves in. Even the reader who cannot or will not go beyond the surface letter and its devices betrays a certain moral superficiality, as Amant does in refusing to inquire into poetic integuments. Our response, the kind of identification or distancing we experience, tells us who we are. It tells us how faithfully or distortedly we reflect, in both senses of the word, Amant's dream in our own minds and lives.

Conclusion: Jean de Meun as *Moraliste*

Mes ausi come vous veez que li hons forsvoie aucune foiz en son chemin quant il s'endort et il revient arriere si tost com il est esveilliez. . . .

(*Queste*, p. 65.9–11)

[But just as you see someone occasionally go astray after falling asleep, then return to the right path upon awakening. . . .]

Ride di quella bestia d'uccellino che non ricorda la disperazione, vicino alla quale è vissuto certi giorni, perché egli stesso non ne fu toccato. Ma dopo di aver riso si pensa all'impassibile aspetto della natura quando fa i suoi esperimenti, e si rabbrividisce.

(Italo Svevo, "Una burla riuscita")

[He laughs at that beastly little bird which does not recall the despair he lived so close to at times because it was not affected by it itself. But after laughing he considers Nature's impassive appearance while conducting her experiments—and he shudders.]

The word *moraliste* enters the French language during the late seventeenth century. It distinguishes an author who observes *mores* from a *moralisateur* who evaluates them according to some authority. The notion, if not the word, was current in the thirteenth century: *moralité* is found as early as the twelfth century.[1] *Meurs* (*mœurs*) seems to have a long life in the language, stemming as it does from centuries-informed Latin *mores*. For Jean de Meun, the word *meurs* refers to the customary activities of various kinds of persons. For example, those who love out of true friendship have no fear of speaking openly with a friend or beloved since friends keep one another's secrets,

Que l'un quan qu'il ose penser
Puisse a son ami recenser

> Conme a soi seul seüremant,
> Sanz soupeçon d'ancusemant.
> Tels *meurs* avoir doivent et seulent
> Qui parfetemant amer veulent.
> (V. 4667–72; emphasis mine)

[so that one might tell a friend or beloved whatever one dare think, without fear of denunciation and with all the confidence one would have in oneself. Such manners ought to and usually do characterize those who wish to love perfectly.]

Meurs can be natural or unnatural; they may also vary with external circumstances, be controlled or uncontrolled, good or bad. We may therefore use the modern word *moraliste* whose semantic range was at least available in the thirteenth century to refer to the observer of human conduct. As poet, Jean de Meun was a *moraliste* because he described *meurs*.

Lionel J. Friedman has posed an intriguing question regarding the lessons taught by the various voices in the *Rose*. "Are any of the ideas expressed in the *Roman de la rose* the opinions of Jean de Meung?"[2] The question is analogous to what might be asked about characters in La Fontaine or Molière. Do the "Bourgeois gentilhomme" or the Fox and Crow express opinions of their authors in the way that, for example, Julie de Wolmar and Saint-Preux express Rousseau's or Oreste Sartre's morality?

The answer is, of course, that we cannot know for sure. On the other hand, as we have seen, medieval authors perceived an intention in writing serious works. Jean himself admits such an intention: to please and to instruct. But the instruction is not discursive, it is heuristic. Jean wants his readers to know themselves. We do learn something about ourselves individually by reading the *Roman de la rose*.

What we perceive in La Fontaine, Molière, and Jean de Meun is an image of the world, a view that focuses on and mirrors human *mores* in their variety and typicalness. In Jean de Meun's case, the principal type is the *fol amoureux*. But he is wary of moralizing such that an ethical system or code of conduct would explicitly identify what is right and wrong, good and bad. The reader must choose. The choices are not aesthetic, they are ethical.[3] Christine de Pizan puts the distinction nicely: "You say it's good, I say it's bad."[4]

This does not mean that certain lines of thought do not emerge from the *Rose* to give a more objective answer to Friedman's question about Jean's own ideas. Certainly one of the *Rose*'s authorities, Boethius, offers a model for the way the world turns and how we may deal with it. Jean reveals enough of the Boethian model for even the unlettered members of his audience to understand the ways of fortune and foolishness as well as the power of even fallen reason to distinguish between true and false goods. In this Jean anticipates Christine de Pizan, who also used the Boethian model for her own treatises, notably the *Avision Christine* and the *Chemin de long estude*.

Perhaps we can illustrate Jean's art more cogently for the Middle Ages by contrasting Jean's *modus agendi* as *moraliste* with Christine de Pizan's as *moralisatrice*. Christine's ethics are informed by her religious and social ideas. She is moreover an *écrivain engagé*: she teaches rules of conduct. The rules are translated into admonitions to various kinds of individuals to live according to a specific moral code.

> Bons et vaillans, or soient esveilliées
> Voz grans bontez, ou vesves sont taillées
>   D'avoir mains maulz de cuer haitié;
> Secourez les!
>
> (*Autres ballades* 1:vi)[5]

> [Good and worthy men, alert your good and worthy qualities! When you see widows made to suffer great harm lightheartedly—help them!]

Or:

> Sages et bons, gracieux et courtois,
> Doivent estre par droit tous chevaliers;
> Larges et frans, doulz, paisibles et cois;
> Pour acquerir honneur grans voiagiers,
> En fais d'armes entreprenans et fiers,
> Droit soustenir et deffendre l'Eglise,
> D'armes porter doit estre leur mestiers,
> Qui maintenir veult l'ordre a droite guise.
>
> (*Cent ballades* 1:lxiv)

> [All knights ought rightly to be prudent and good, kind and courteous, generous and noble, gentle, peaceful, and temperate; they should undertake great travels for honor's sake and be resourceful and fierce in feats of arms; they should support what is right and defend the Church. Their profession should be to bear arms if they wish to uphold the order rightly.]

For Christine, in part as a medieval woman, it is especially important to eschew even the suspicion of sin or wrongdoing. The sharp rebuke pronounced by the so-called Sebille de Monthault, dame de la Tour, an avatar of Reason, to the young wife in the *Livre du duc des vrais amants* as she is embarking on a clandestine liaison is founded on both religious and social morality.

> Ha! ma dame, pour Dieu soiez avisiée que telles folles opinions ne vous deçoivent! car, quant a la plaisance, soiez certaine qu'en amours a cent mille fois plus de dueil, de cuisançons et dongiers perilleux, par especial du cousté des dames, qu'il n'y a de plaisance. Car, avecques ce que Amours livre de soy mainte diverse amertume, la paour de perdre honneur et qu'il soit sceu leur demeure ou cuer continuelment qui chier acheter leur fait tel plaisance. Et quant a dire: ce ne seroit mie mal puis que fait de pechié n'y sera, hé las! ma dame, ne soit nul ne nulle si asseurée de soy qu'elle se rende certaine, quelque bon propos qu'elle ait, de garder toujours mesure en si faitte amour, et qu'il ne soit sceu comme j'ay cy devant dit; certes, c'est chose impossible. (*Duc des vrais amants*)[6]
>
> [Ah! my lady, for God's sake take care not to be taken in by such foolish ideas! As for pleasure, you can be sure that love offers a hundred thousand times more grief, torment, and perilous constraints, especially for women, than it does pleasure. For besides the fact that Love on her own causes much bitterness, the fear of being dishonored or found out is always on the mind—the pleasure it gives costs them dearly. As for claiming that it's not wrong because no sinful act occurs—alas! my lady, no man or woman should be so self-confident that she becomes convinced, however good her intentions, that she can stay in control of such love and keep it from being found out, as I said above, because it's impossible.]

This is strong, clear language. Christine's morality and experience ultimately lead her to the feminine isolation set forth allegorically in the *Cité des dames* and realistically enjoined in its pendant, the *Livre des trois vertus*, which also contains Sebille de Monthault's admonition.[7]

In the *Mutacion de fortune*, Christine de Pizan as narrator claims to become fictionally a man and, in the *Cité des dames*, a "virago," because she practices the virtues associated with the etymon of virtue, *vir*.[8] To her, the essence of such "virility" is virtue. Virtue informs her condemnation of Jean's *Rose*. Clean speech, honesty, respect for religious sanctity, women, and marriage: these are standards she upholds throughout her writing and which she uses to evaluate conduct.

Whatever critical or moral position one takes regarding the opposition between Jean de Meun and Christine de Pizan, that opposition is a model and first instance of a phenomenon of great importance and interest in French literature from the Middle Ages through at least the Enlightenment—extending from Faux Semblant through the early modern period to Rameau's nephew in Diderot's eighteenth-century dialogue.[9] It is the uneasy balance between the *moraliste* as observer and the *moralisateur* as judge. "Uneasy" because the disabused *moraliste* does not quite exclude the *moralisateur*'s moral judgment. Jean expresses affirmative moral positions just as do Molière and La Fontaine; Christine de Pizan is as capable as Rousseau of dealing with moral and social ambiguities openly and of satirizing foolishness with ironic humor. Yet, immoderation is possible on both sides. To exceed the limits produces outrage. Christine de Pizan would gladly burn the *Rose*; Jean de Meun's Jealous Husband, although true to life, exceeds for most the limits of sensible satire—as would an author who, for example, allowed a personification of Nazi racism to expatiate for almost a thousand lines on his hatred of Jews in a work without a critique of Nazism to balance his words. The example, although contemporary, is apposite.[10] Where then may one draw the line between such a work and one like Swift's *A Modest Proposal*? Perhaps one may draw it there where the victim is included in the audience. Has any woman reading Jean de Meun's *Rose* ever been seduced into practicing what the Vieille teaches?

To be sure, we must take into account mentalities, epochs, and audiences in evaluating the moral impact and taste of an author's language—even when the language is cousin to the deed. I can recall the uproarious laughter that greeted Woody Allen's farcical discussion of child abuse when *All You Ever Wanted to Know about Sex* came out in the late 1960s. In the early 1990s, the same humor makes audiences squirm or walk out of the theater. The pleasure or even joy at hearing and saying hitherto unacceptable words gives way to an awareness of the reality those words express. Something similar may occur in our successive readings of *coilles* and the realities that word covers in the *Rose*: the joke ceases to be funny. Still, it strikes me as intensely interesting and educational that the joke had to precede the truth, just as Jean's *Rose* had to precede his *Testament* and Christine de Pizan's outrage. It is educational, it forms one's moral judgment, to confront the *moraliste* and the *moralisateur* when they are at odds with one another. In doing so, we set up *contraires choses*. We come to know ourselves and our world better. On the level of moral reception Jean de Meun and Christine de Pizan are both relevant and provocative. They are cousins to the deed in a story about rose plucking. If the letter of that story is meant to please, as Jean says it should, the pleasure does not preclude its moral bite, "and the satire bites sharpest when we notice where we are fighting in it."[11]

The attack on Jean de Meun in the "Querelle" mirrors similar attacks against other *moralistes*: Rabelais, Molière, and La Fontaine. The issue is always the morality of the presentation. As Molière puts it in the *Critique de l'École des femmes*, the *moraliste* is essentially a writer of comedy—a most difficult and onerous task: "C'est une étrange enterprise que celle de faire rire les honnêtes gens."[12] People do not laugh when they see themselves ridiculed any more than when their moral standards are not met or the ridicule falls on deeds (like child abuse) too shocking for humor. It is probably impossible to distinguish neatly the *moraliste* from the *moralisateur* in specific instances of criticism. It certainly is impossible in the case of the "Querelle."

Jean de Meun made matters even more difficult by his very *modus agendi*. He did not allow the reader any distance from the images that appear in his *Miroër aus Amoreus*. The *fol amoureux* and other instances of folly like the Jealous Husband, Faux Semblant, and Genius draw a broad picture of human folly in an amorous and, more accurately, erotic, at times violent and obscene, context. For the *moraliste*, the success of the enterprise is ridiculing forcefully the folly of evil. The successful demonstration should arouse the desire to avoid the folly.

But the problem in Jean's *Rose* is that, as allegory, the lessons work on so many levels that the reader has scarcely any sure guidelines about the "golden mean" that Reason at least extols on occasion, a mean that would permit him or her to recover an ethical point of view like that offered in, say, Boethius or Alain de Lille, works Jean cites extensively, albeit often out of their original context. What of the sliding context itself? What difference does it make, for example, that Amant ceases to be generous and faithful only after the midpoint? This may suggest that his generosity and fidelity in intent prior to that transformation are laudable because closer to the *amitié* that Reason herself recommends.

In the *Critique de l'École des femmes*, Molière falls back on the judgment of the court. Fortunately for Molière, that court included a powerful arbiter favorably disposed to his art as *moraliste*. Jean too falls back on the judgment of his readers—those evoked in his major intervention on language, misogyny, and antifraternalism *avant la lettre* in the *Rose*. The norm he proposes is not the court's, but the mirror's. However, that mirror does not show the text; rather, it shows the reader. Is the image reflected in the *Rose*'s mirror faithful?

Perhaps the last word should belong to Christine de Pizan. "Tu dis qu'il est bon; je dis qu'il est mauvais." I suspect that that is just what Jean de Meun himself expected. For, if we generalize Pierre Col and Christine de Pizan to embrace all humanity, then all of us can find in the *Rose* a true, false, or ambiguous image of ourselves. Christine herself suggested the possibility of such double readings of the *Rose* at the outset of her *Cité des dames*. By antiphrasis, the reader may perceive the opposite meaning of a work like the *Rose* even if that meaning was not intended by the first author.[13] However it may be with Jean de Meun's intention, the antiphrasis for the *Rose* is found in Christine's *Cité*. Jean addresses "good women" in his auctorial intervention, asserting that he is not writing about them. Christine de Pizan for her part is writing, and thus building, her City of Ladies for those good women, excluding those whose morals make them unworthy of living there.[14] Thus, by antiphrasis Jean's allegory anticipates Christine's letter at the same time that her letter rejects women who are unworthy of entering her City. Like Jean, she urges such women to change their ways and join the ranks of the worthy women Jean excludes from the *Rose*'s allegory.

Notes
Bibliography
Index

Notes

INTRODUCTION

1. *Allegorical Imagery*, p. 251; cf. also p. 239. Let me state at the outset that I consider Tuve's book to contain the best and most sympathetic analysis of Jean's *Rose* to date.

2. Ibid., p. 239.

3. On "auctorial" as a term referring to either author or narrator, see my *Art of Medieval French Romance*, pp. 4–6. On *intentio*, *antancion*, and related terms used to describe "intention" in medieval works, see Hunt, "Introductions to the 'Artes,' " pp. 85–112; A. J. Minnis, *Medieval Theory of Authorship*; my *Art of Medieval French Romance*, pp. 37–38, 217–22; and Copeland, *Rhetoric, Hermeneutics, and Translation*, pp. 76–80, 164. See as well Grosse, *Das Buch im Roman*, pp. 13–34.

4. For a complete, annotated survey of these and other interpretations of the *Rose*, see Arden, *Roman de la rose: An Annotated Bibliography*.

5. Gravdal, *Ravishing Maidens*, p. 71.

6. Andreas Capellanus envisages these types and their loves in the *De amore*.

7. On this variant reading of Jean's *Rose*, see below, p. 25.

CHAPTER 1. SOURCES AND IMPLIED AUDIENCES

1. See *Le Débat*, pp. 60.42, 64.147, 162.14 (Gerson); 91.105–6, 92.116 (Pierre Col); 121.184, 139.786 (Christine de Pizan). On Jean's artistry: pp. 12.29, 13.53–58, 21.297–300, 50.52–58, 53.155–57 (Christine de Pizan); 32.3–5 (Jean de Montreuil, "Epître" 120); 89.12 (Pierre Col). For a balanced treatment of the "Querelle," see the introduction to *"La Querelle de la rose": Letters and Documents*; see also A. J. Minnis, "Theorizing the Rose," pp. 13–36; and Rossiaud, *La prostitution médiévale*, especially pp. 107–9, 165–66, 177–92, but also passim. Of the *Rose*'s critics in the "Querelle," Rossiaud offers a sympathetic appreciation of Gerson but is rather dismissive of Christine de Pizan (p. 187), perhaps because he did not take account of anything she wrote after the "Querelle."

2. *Medieval Imagination*, especially chap. 4. Succinctly put, my reading there

shows Amant moving from carnal desire toward a more humane love with noble features. Cf. Stakel, *False Roses*, pp. 24–31.

3. See *Le Débat*, pp. 28.12–30.4, 85.657–86.669 (Jean Gerson), 95.211–14 (Pierre Col).

4. By contrast, Christine de Pizan refuses to distinguish between the two authors: *Le Débat*, pp. 135.646–47, 141.840–42.

5. On *Rose* manuscripts, see Ernest Langlois, *Les manuscrits du* Roman de la rose; and Huot, *The* Romance of the Rose *and Its Medieval Readers* and, in general, the items listed in the index, s.v. "Manuscripts," in Arden, *Roman de la rose: An Annotated Bibliography*, p. 376.

6. See Jung, "Gui de Mori et Guillaume de Lorris"; David F. Hult, "Gui de Mori"; Badel, *Le* Roman de la rose *au XIVe siècle*, pp. 144–45, 362–76; Huot, *The* Romance of the rose *and Its Medieval Readers*, chaps. 3 and 6. On the *Roman de la poire*'s rewrite of Guillaume's part prior to Jean's continuation, see Huot, "From *Roman de la rose* to *Roman de la poire*."

7. Cf. Tuve, *Allegorical Imagery*, p. 259; and Hult, *Self-Fulfilling Prophecies*, pp. 93–94. See as well Brook, "Pruned Rose."

8. D. W. Robertson, Jr., advances this argument to account for Christine de Pizan's and Gerson's rejection of Jean's *Rose*; see *Preface to Chaucer*, pp. 361–65. The history of *Rose* reception is more complex and diverse than Robertson allows; for example, see Rossiaud, *La prostitution médiévale*, pp. 58–59, 102–10, 165–68.

9. Cf. Baumgartner, "De Lucrèce à Héloïse, p. 441; Uitti, "From *clerc* to *poète*," pp. 209–16; Bouché, "Ovide et Jean de Meun," p. 85; Brownlee, *Poetic Identity in Guillaume de Machaut*, especially pp. 12–20; Poirion, "Jacques Legrand," pp. 227–34. In *Le Roman de Troie*, "poete" is roughly equivalent to Latin "*vates*"; see Benoît de Sainte-Maure, *Le roman de Troie*, s.v. "Poëte–s."

10. On this poet, of whom only half a line is known for certain today, see Langlois, ed., *Le Roman de la rose*, v. 10508–18 n (3: 304); and Lecoy, ed., *Le Roman de la rose*, v. 10478–88 n (2: 278), as well as *Paulys Realencyclopädie der classischen Altertumswissenschaft*, 7:1345–50.

11. Cf. Hult, "Closed Quotations." Gui de Mori can be equally ambiguous; see Hult, *Self-Fulfilling Prophecies*, pp. 47–52; Brownlee, "Jean de Meun and the Limits of Romance," pp. 115–19. Jean is actually using a strategy developed by Guillaume de Lorris for the various voices in his part of the *Rose*; see Vitz, "The 'I' of the *Roman de la rose*," in her *Medieval Narrative and Modern Narratology*, pp. 38–63; Dahlberg, *Literature of Unlikeness*, pp. 113–15.

12. Ritamary Bradley, "Backgrounds of the Title *Speculum*." See also Eberle, "Lovers' Glass"; Frappier, "Variations sur le thème du miroir"; Kolb, "*Oiseuse*"; Alvar, "Oiseuse, Vénus, Luxure."

13. Knoespel, *Narcissus and the Invention of Personal History*. See as well Gier, "L'amour, les monologues."

14. *Le Débat*, pp. 83.596–85.656, 124.299–125.333, 139.785–99. Although she does not treat the *Rose* extensively, Roberta Krueger, in *Women Readers*, studies the variety of audience responses, especially of the women Jean postulates in his own audiences.

15. *Anticlaudianus*, p. 56. Cf. Ziolkowski, *Alan of Lille's Grammar of Sex*, pp. 95–103; Grünkorn, "Zum Verständnis von fiktionaler Rede," pp. 35–37; Simpson, "Information," pp. 115–40.

16. See especially Brownlee, "Reflections in the *Miroër aus Amoreus*"; Peter L. Allen, "*Ars amandi, ars legendi.*"

17. This reading is perhaps best represented by Louis, *Le roman de la rose*; and Payen, *La rose et l'utopie*. Both base their reading on a direct appreciation of the *Rose* rather than on historical criticism or modern scholarship (see Louis, pp. 7–9; Payen, p. 7). Such a reading of the letter almost imposes only a literal reading. Rossiaud, *La prostitution médiévale*, has shown the prevalence in the fourteenth and fifteenth centuries of this literal reading and has thereby contributed an important element to the history of *Rose* reception in the France of that period. His evidence shows that moral outrage begins in earnest in the sixteenth century, which is quite late.

18. In fact, as least one translation predates Jean's *Rose*, while another poor one is nearly contemporary with it. On these and other medieval translations of the *Consolation* into French, see Thomas and Roques, "Traductions françaises de la *Consolatio Philosophiae*"; *Altfranzösische Übersetzung der* consolatio philosophiae *des Boethius*; and (with additional bibliography) Cropp, "Le prologue de Jean de Meun"; and Cropp, "*Le livre de Boece de consolacion*," pp. 63–65. Even in translation Boethius was thought to be too difficult for lay readers, especially in the fourth and fifth books; see Atkinson and Cropp, "Trois traductions de la *Consolatio Philosophiae*," pp. 201–2.

19. On this subject and the following quote, see Douglas Kelly, *Art of Medieval French Romance*, pp. 227–28.

20. Cf. Gunn, *Mirror of Love*, pp. 57–58; Milan, "Golden Age and the Political Theory of Jean de Meun," especially p. 148. When access to or knowledge of a major source like Boethius was lacking, Jean provided the relevant information; see, for example, Ott, "Jean de Meun und Boethius," pp. 215–19.

21. *Reason and the Lover*, pp. 90–96; and his "Carthaginian Love," pp. 67–68. For a similar reading of Dangier, see Dahlberg, "First Person and Personification." These readings will appear tendentious and circular, or insightful and compelling, depending on the reader's choice of context. I would place R. Howard Bloch's reading of v. 6898–906 as "oral copulation" in the same category of special, seemingly far-fetched context, albeit in the fabliau register. See his *Etymologies and Genealogies*, p. 138. Hult elaborates on Bloch's suggested reading in "Language and Dismemberment," pp. 115–20. What might the allegory be for this letter?

22. This is Fleming's "supertext" that "appears only by inference or implication." (*Reason and the Lover*, p. 69) See as well his "Carthaginian Love." Cf. Rowe, "Reson in Jean's *Roman de la rose*," p. 123 n. 21, on Augustine's works as the *Rose* supertext: Fleming "privileges the Augustinian texts of which he rightly and deftly finds echoes. This permits him to determine what Jean thinks by reading Augustine rather than the *Roman*." The exaggeration is only partly unfair. The issue is: Does the *Rose* contain enough of Augustine's thought for Fleming or anyone else to recognize its substance without knowledge of the supertext? That

would be the case for all those ignorant of Latin or of any translations of Augustine's works. See as well Ott, "Neuere Untersuchungen über den Rosenroman," pp. 92–94. Analogous reservations are voiced by Peden, "Macrobius and Mediaeval Dream Literature," pp. 66–68.

23. See, for example, the glosses from as late as the sixteenth century published by Maxwell Luria, "Sixteenth-Century Gloss on the *Roman de la rose*." Cf. Quilligan, *Language of Allegory*, p. 22.

24. See, for example, the surveys of scholarship in Badel, *Le* Roman de la rose *au XIVe siècle*; Ott, *Der Rosenroman*; Heather M. Arden, *Romance of the Rose*.

25. *Redemption of Chivalry*.

26. Badel, *Le* Roman de la rose *au XIVe siècle*, pp. 81–82. It still has that reputation. See Wood, "La Vieille, Free Love, and Boethius," on the distinction between obvious, literal reading and learned recognition of a source.

27. §4.1. On what follows, see my *Arts of Poetry and Prose*, pp. 50–52, 64–68.

28. In *Ars poetica*, especially p. 6. On the title of Gervase's treatise which I am using, see Franz Josef Worstbrock's review of Gräbener ed., *Anzeiger für deutsches Altertum und deutsche Literatur*, p. 99 n.1.

29. See my *Art of Medieval French Romance*, chap. 4.

30. On "skill," see my *Medieval Imagination*, pp. xii, 199–201.

31. See my *Arts of Poetry and Prose*, pp. 57–64.

32. Faral, "*Le Roman de la rose* et la pensée française au XIIIe siècle," pp. 433–36, 445 (on rewriting Guillaume de Lorris); Freeman, "Problems in Romance Composition"; Dragonetti, "*La musique et les lettres*," pp. 378–79; Brownlee, "Orpheus' Song Re-Sung"; Peter L. Allen, *Ars amandi, ars legendi*," pp. 182–83; Steinle, "Anti-Narcissus." For good illustrations of this skill, but with different kinds of works, see Anderson, *Before the Knight's Tale*; Busby, "*Cristal et Clarie*."

33. Stakel, *False Roses*, p. 116. This corresponds to the poet's office as described in the Copenhagen commentary on the *Ovide moralisé*; see my *Art of Medieval French Romance*, pp. 256–57. For good illustrations, see Heitmann, "Typen der Deformierung antiker Mythen" (however, Heitmann does not discuss any examples from the *Rose*).

34. See Bermejo, "Notas sobre las modalidades retóricas," pp. 101–2. It has been suggested that Jean made modifications on Guillaume's torso as well; see Poirion, "From Rhyme to Reason," pp. 65–68.

35. See *Historia troyana Daretis Frigii*; *L'Ovide moralisé*, 1:1140–41; and my *Art of Medieval French Romance*, p. 77.

36. See Joseph Iscanus, *Werke und Briefe*, pp. 6–19.

37. *Le Roman de Troie*, v. 139–44. For Jean's rewriting of Guillaume in this context, see especially Ott, "Jean de Meun und Boethius," pp. 221–24. Julián Muela Ezquerra suggests parallels between Jean's war of the sexes and the Trojan War in "Técnicas retóricas y producción," p. 379.

38. V. 15212–13 in Langlois's edition.

39. V. 15212 in Poirion's edition. Cf. as well the variants to this line in Langlois's edition.

40. Oral readings of the *Rose* would compound the problem; on such readings, see Walters, "Reading the *Rose*," pp. 1–7. Cf. Ott, "Neuere Untersuchungen über den Rosenroman," p. 92. Neither Matheolus nor Juvenal had been translated into French at the time Jean composed the Jealous Husband's diatribe, yet the material borrowed from those two authors adequately expresses their misogyny. Jean de Meun includes women in his implied audience, addressing them notably in his intervention on misogyny. Note in this context Christine de Pizan's objection to certain misogynist writers who sought to keep their books away from women out of fear of correction, in "*Livre de la cité des dames* of Christine de Pisan," §27.

41. On translations of the *Consolation*, see note 18 above.

42. V. 33–39. Cf. the cleric's higher nobility because princes and kings "ne sevent de lestreüre" (*Rose* v. 18609) [are unlettered] and therefore may not even be able to read works written in their own language.

43. On "montage" as a term, see Jacqueline Cerquiglini, "Le clerc et l'écriture."

CHAPTER 2. THE LITERAL TEXTS: LANGUAGE AND LETTER

1. Froissart, *Prison amoureuse*, v. 2241–46. On multiple levels of exposition in Froissart, see my *Medieval Imagination*, pp. 160–69. Christine de Pizan seems to have read the *Rose* in much the same way; see *Le Débat*, p. 50.43–47. Pierre Col also recommends rereading; see *Le Débat*, pp. 110.738–41 and 112.805–807. Cf. Quilligan, *Language of Allegory*, p. 227; Jung, "Jean de Meun et l'allégorie," p. 25; and his "Jean de Meun et son lecteur," p. 243–44.

2. "Le dit," in *Grundriß der romanischen Literaturen des Mittelalters*, p. 94; see as well her "Polysémie, ambiguïté et équivoque," pp. 167–80. On *praelectio*, or "preliminary reading," see Copeland, *Rhetoric, Hermeneutics, and Translation*, pp. 19–22.

3. "*Bele* et noive" in Poirion's edition (emphasis mine). Cf. *Rose*, v. 1598–1600, 2063–64.

4. See in general Lausberg, *Handbuch der literarischen Rhetorik*, §§893–901; on *ironia*, see §§902–4.

5. See, for example, Tuve, *Allegorical Imagery*, p. 48 n. 22 and the references there.

6. See Judson Boyce Allen, *Friar as Critic*; Demats, *Fabula*. Historical readings are founded on euhemerism, or the reading of historical events into myths, whereas astrological readings identify scientific knowledge in myths.

7. For other, secondary sources, see Jean Batany, *Approches du* Roman de la rose, especially chaps. 4, 6, and 7; Friedman, "Jean de Meun and Ethelred of Rievaulx."

8. Gunn, *Mirror of Love*, pp. 76–94, 509–22; Poirion, *Le Roman de la rose*, pp. 103–6. See as well Armand Strubel, *Guillaume de Lorris, Jean de Meun*, Le Roman de la rose, pp. 6–8; Ott, "Jean de Meun und Boethius," pp. 203–5; and Lecoy's analysis of the plot in his edition. C. S. Lewis is less successful in distinguishing plot from what he calls digressions; for example, he locates Ami's Ovidian developments in the plot, but not the Vieille's, in *Allegory of Love*, pp. 138–39.

9. Gunn, *Mirror of Love*, p. 66: "the separate discourses—and therefore the whole line of argument—are themselves expansions or amplifications on the line of narrative"; cf. *Mirror of Love*, p. 165.

10. Dragonetti has argued that the *Rose* is really by only one author; see "Pygmalion ou les pièges de la fiction dans le *Roman de la rose*," in "*La musique et les lettres*," pp. 345–67; and Thut, "Narcisse versus Pygmalion." I do not find the argument convincing. However, even if it is correct, the fiction of two beginnings—the textual fact of two narrators posing as two authors—validates the reading of two beginnings; see Walters, "Author Portraits and Textual Demarcation." Other studies tend to confirm both the validity and the importance of dual authorship; see Brownlee, "The Problem of Faux Semblant," pp. 264–69 and 271 n. 17, on the mirror Guillaume-Jean in Guillaume de Saint-Amour's attacks on the new age of "Jean"; and Poirion, "From Rhyme to Reason"; Hult, *Self-Fulfilling Prophecies*; Zumthor, "Narrative and Anti-Narrative"; and his "De Guillaume de Lorris à Jean de Meung"; Hult, "Closed Quotations"; Brook, "Continuator's Monologue", pp. 8–14.

11. Poirion, *Le Roman de la rose*, pp. 106–7. Cf. Vanossi, *Dante e il* Roman de la rose, pp. 34–36; Nykrog, *L'amour et la rose*, pp. 9–10.

12. The kiss he later receives from her (GL 3459–61) is not rewritten as such by Jean de Meun, although he makes reference to it (JM 6717–21).

13. On these lines, see my " 'Li chastiaus.' "

14. Jung, "Gui de Mori et Guillaume de Lorris," p. 109.

15. Douglas Kelly, " 'Li chastiaus,' " pp. 72–77; Payen, "L'espace et le temps," pp. 253–54; Brownlee, "Reflections in the *Miroër aus Amoreus*." Cf. Benedetto, *Il* Roman de la rose *e la letteratura italiana*, pp. 21–22. On Jean's adaptation and correction of Guillaume's Narcissus exemplum, see Knoespel, *Narcissus and the Invention of Personal History*, pp. 93–104; on Genius's correction of Guillaume's Garden of Deduit, see Brownlee, "Jean de Meun and the Limits of Romance."

16. See Winthrop Wetherbee, "Literal and the Allegorical," pp. 275–79; Stakel, *False Roses*, pp. 27–28, 58–59. Cf. Emmerson and Herzman, "Apocalyptic Age of Hypocrisy." Ami prepares for the change; see Payen, *La rose et l'utopie*, p. 39. On actions as *signa* of the *homo interior*, see the important article by Friedman, "Occulta cordis."

17. Brownlee, "Problem of Faux Semblant." On the "genre Faux Semblant" and its relation to the two-part *Rose*, see Dembowski, "Le Faux Semblant." On *semblant* and *semblance* in medieval romance, see Solterer, "Le bel semblant."

18. "Le *Roman de la rose* et la notion de carrefour idéologique," p. 195, especially n. 8. Ami allows small gifts to buy favor (v. 8160–8214), but they may be limited to empty promise (v. 7404–20).

19. *Recueil général de jeux-partis français*, CXIII, v. 5–10; cf. also LIII; and Walters, "Reading the *Rose*," pp. 8–10. In the same article, Walters discusses the "contextual environment," or contents, of *Rose* manuscripts.

20. See Bouché, "Ovide et Jean de Meun," as well as Gérard Blangez's interesting analysis of Jean's art of composition, that is, of combining and adapting diverse kinds and levels of sources: "Comment composait Jean de Meun." On

Jean's use of other Ovidian material, see Cahoon, "Raping the Rose"; Peter L. Allen, *Art of Love*, especially chap. 4. On Ovid as filtered through the medieval commentary tradition, see A. J. Minnis, "Theorizing the Rose."

21. Douglas Kelly, *Medieval Imagination*, p. 40; cf. Strubel, *La rose, Renart et le graal*, pp. 230–33.

22. Douglas Kelly, "Topical Invention" pp. 242–45; and my *Art of Medieval French Romance*, pp. 264–72. The Latin terminology is adopted from Andreas Capellanus's *De amore*, Book II.

23. Tuve, *Allegorical Imagery*, p. 261. That this is not entirely true does not diminish the force of the observation for Amant and Rose. Reason projects love as friendship, and Pygmalion is a special case (see below, pp. 76–78). Héloise obviously loves Abelard; see Baumgartner, "De Lucrèce à Héloïse," pp. 438–39.

24. Ernest Langlois recognized quite early the great influence of Boethius in Jean's *Rose* but did not perceive the significance of that influence; see his *Origines et sources du* Roman de la rose, pp. 94–95, 128–29, 136–38, 185–86, 188. On Jean's use of Boethius's *Consolation*, see especially Ott, "Jean de Meun und Boethius"; and Fleming, *Reason and the Lover*, pp. 40–63 (with additional bibliography, p. 53 n. 88); Fleming, Roman de la rose: *A Study in Allegory and Iconography*, pp. 123–28; Cherniss, "Jean de Meun's Reson and Boethius"; Ott, *Der Rosenroman*, pp. 168–70; Rowe, "Reson in Jean's *Roman de la rose*," pp. 100–101; Lynch, *High Medieval Dream Vision*, pp. 120–26; Fleming, "Jean de Meun and the Ancient Poets," pp. 88–90.

25. See "Lovers' Glass," pp. 250–53.

26. Similarly, Jean refracts Alain de Lille's description of Nature herself in the *De planctu Naturae*, where she appears as a cosmic figure of universal power, so as to focus on the sublunar principle of procreation—an inversion of Alain's figure such that the sexual metaphor in Alain becomes the letter of Jean's re-interpretation of her role. On Jean's adaptation of Alain's writing, see Wetherbee, "Literal and the Allegorical," and his *Platonism and Poetry*, especially chaps. 5 and 7.2; Economou, *Goddess Natura in Medieval Literature*, chap 4.

27. Jean translates Boethius's "carmina" by "chançonnetez"; see Jean's "Boethius' *De consolatione*," Book I Meter i.1 in both French and Latin versions. (References to the *Consolation of Philosophy* are to Jean's translation unless otherwise indicated, followed by the corresponding passage in the Latin edition, *Philosophiae consolatio*. I am quoting from the translation both to render Boethius as Jean read him, and to bring out certain important differences between the translation and the standard edition, which is presumably closer to what Boethius wrote.) Jean refers to similar songs he says he composed in his youth in *Testament Maistre Jehan de Meun*, v. 5–6 (p. 121). On Guillaume's *Rose* as transformed lyric, see L. T. Topsfield, "*Roman de la rose* of Guillaume de Lorris"; Hult, *Self-Fulfilling Prophecies*, pp. 208–50; Huot, *From Song to Book*, pp. 2 and 83–90; Arden, *Romance of the Rose*, pp. 22–23; Kay, *Subjectivity in Troubadour Poetry*, pp. 171–83; Brook, "Love's External Foes." So far as I know, no one has extended the discussion of the *Rose*'s lyrical models to Jean's continuation.

28. Book V Prose v.32/7.27–28. Emphasis mine: Raison is obviously personified here, hence my use of the capital letter not found in the edition.

29. Ott, "Jean de Meun und Boethius," pp. 216–19.

30. Cf. Book I Prose i.29–32/9.28–30, Book IV Prose iv.149–50/42.132–33.

31. Emphasis mine. This addition to Boethius is not identified by Dedeck-Héry, the editor of Jean's translation. The argument that Amant cannot understand Reason will not stand if Reason represents his own reason; cf. Cherniss, "Jean," pp. 682–85. Amant's problem is that he refuses to follow Reason, or even listen to her in the end. He could understand if he wanted to.

32. *Anticlaudianus*, ed. Bossuat, 8:274–82; trans. Sheridan, pp. 199–200.

33. "Lovers' Glass," pp. 244–45.

34. By the term "complex," I mean the personified attributes grouped about the image of the man or the woman in the *Rose*; see my *Medieval Imagination* pp. 39, 84–95.

35. Cf. as well Book V Prose iv. On the sense of *corrompu*, see my *Art of Medieval French Romance*, pp. 125–29.

36. Svevo, *La coscienza di Zeno*, p. 66.

37. The translation reveals the real intent of the word "*giron*." It also shows that Jean does not shy away from expressive, explicit metaphors even in translating Boethius.

38. Nykrog, *L'amour et la rose*, pp. 72–74.

39. See now Ziolkowski, *Alan of Lille's Grammar of Sex*, chap. 1; and Leupin, "Écriture naturelle et écriture hermaphrodite." Cf. as well Poirion, "Alain de Lille et Jean de Meun"; Quilligan, "Words and Sex."

40. There is no exact modern English equivalent for the literal word. Cullions has gone out of usage. I should like to thank Professor Fred Cassidy for his assistance in checking through the files of the *American Regional Dictionary* for me on this matter.

41. The more accurate literal translation of *andoilles* is, of course, "sausage chitterlings," as in Dahlberg's translation. But that translation does not carry the obvious second meaning of "penises"; my less accurate literal translation is more accurate figuratively. Colette Rimlinger-Leconte does not discuss this or any other erotic metaphor in her "L'expression métaphorique chez Jean de Meung."

42. The expression may carry a moral, even Christian connotation in the thirteenth century; see Andrieux-Reix, *Ancien français*, pp. 112–18. Cf. Muscatine, "Courtly Literature and Vulgar Language"; Heffernan, "Bird-Snare Figure," pp. 180–82.

43. *Reliques* designate both male genitalia, as in Reason's metaphor, and female genitalia, as in Amant's at the end of the *Rose*; see Vanossi, *Dante e il* Roman de la rose, p. 25.

44. However, his authority is the Roman historian, Sallust; see v. 15148 n (2:297). See Taylor, "Chaucer's *Cosyn to the Dede*," pp. 320–24.

45. "De la signification selon Jean de Meun," p. 180.

46. Cf. Nykrog, *Les fabliaux*, pp. 215–26. Two manuscript traditions excerpted the distasteful language as early as the late thirteenth century; see Huot, "Authors, Scribes, Remanieurs," especially pp. 210–11, 216. John Fleming does not consider these contemporary or near contemporary examples in "Moral Reputation of the *Roman de la rose* before 1400."

47. Macrobius, *Commentarii in Somnium Scipionis*, 1.2.11; see Rowe, "Reson in Jean's *Roman de la rose*," p. 105. Curiously, Macrobius does treat the fable in the *Saturnalia* 1.8.6–12.

48. "Le discours linguistique de Jean de Meun," pp. 250–51. Jean is actually making a blatantly obscene adaptation of religious metaphors common in courtly literature, notably in Guillaume de Lorris, whose device Jean tactically adapts to his own purposes; see Ruhe, *Le dieu d'amours avec son paradis*, especially pp. 105–108, 128–32.

49. *Le Débat*, p. 123.281–82. Christine was not totally opposed to effective use of vulgarity; on her "fiens" (*Le Débat*, p. 126.366), see Joseph L. Baird and John R. Kane, *"La Querelle de la Rose": Letters and Documents*, p. 25. I would replace their translation "dung" with "shit."

50. On Material Style, see Franz Quadlbauer, *Die antike Theorie der genera dicendi* and my *Arts of Poetry and Prose*, pp. 71–78. Both Christine de Pizan, in *Le Débat*, pp. 116–18, 121–26, and Pierre Col, *Le Débat*, pp. 90–98, 99–102, underscore how tastes regulate Material Style.

51. *Parisiana Poetria*, 5.70–76; see Nykrog, *Les fabliaux*, chap. 9, and my *Arts of Poetry and Prose*, pp. 74–76.

52. Cf. as well 1:782–90. The Copenhagen commentary retains the word "genitaires"; see *Le commentaire de Copenhague de l' "Ovide moralisé*," pp. 22–23.

53. VIII Glose l. 11, in "Classical Mythology," p. 171. The Commentary on the verse *Échecs amoureux* uses the word "membres"; see BN ms. fr. 9197 fol. 39r°, 41v°, 44r°, and 129r°. The verse *Échecs amoureux* is illegible in the sole manuscript that contains the castration of Saturn; see *Die Liebesgarten-Allegorie der "Échecs amoureux*," which begins later—at p. 38 of the summary made by Ernst Sieper prior to the damage that occurred to the manuscript during the bombing of Dresden in World War II. For Sieper's summary of the castration, see his *Les échecs amoureux*, pp. 17–18. Perhaps the word was *membre*; see Galpin, "Les eschez amoureux," p. 285.

54. *Reason and the Lover*, p. 106; on this issue, see Poirion, "De la signification selon Jean de Meun," pp. 167–78.

55. Eric Hicks, in *La Vie et les Epistres*, leaves the question of Jean's authorship open; see pp. xxvi–xxxiii.

56. Ibid., "coillons": "genitalibus," p. 18.536 (French) and 522 (Latin); "coillons": "testiculis," p. 19.566 and 568 (French), and 552 and 554 (Latin); "vit," p. 19.568, a word Reason also uses unabashedly, translates "veretro," l. 554.

57. Ibid., p. 18.534–35; see also l. 551 and, in the Latin, ll. 519–20 and 537.

58. Ibid., pp. 18–19; see Poirion, "De la signification selon Jean de Meun," p. 170 n. 11.

59. Fleming, *Reason and the Lover*, p. 106 n. 7.

60. Cf. Regalado, " 'Des contraires choses,' " p. 76.

61. "Jean de Meun et l'allégorie," p. 34. Cf. Poirion, "De la signification selon Jean de Meun," p. 173. Fabliaux offer several examples of the obscene juxtaposition of *coilles* and *andoilles*; see *Nouveau recueil complet des fabliaux*,

53.91–92, 57.12–24. Cf. Bouché, "L'obscène et le sacré," p. 83: "verdeur de langage . . . soit dans la crudité, soit dans le choix de métaphores suggestives qui, loin de voiler l'obscénité du propos, l'aggravent." This occurs just after Reason lectured Amant on the proper use of metaphors; cf. "Obscène et le sacré," pp. 85–86. See as well Louis, *Le* Roman de la rose: *essai d'interprétation de l'allégorisme érotique*, on Reason's "argot du milieu" (p. 98), especially pp. 96–101, 118–21.

62. Rossiaud, *La prostitution médiévale*, pp. 51–52, 58–59.

63. *Le Testament*, stanza CXI. For a full linguistic analysis of this stanza, see Louis Thuasne's commentary in his edition of Villon's *Œuvres*, 2:303–305. No one seems to have commented on Reason's use of *andoilles* or the propriety of the word; no translations convey the double-entendre (except modern French translations, but by implication only). Examples of *andoille* as penis date from the late twelfth century. See *Tobler-Lommatzsch*, vol. 1, col. 384.25–26; Stefano, *Dictionnaire des locutions en moyen français*, p. 23; *Le Parnasse satyrique du quinzième siècle*, s.v. *andouille*, to which add vi.3–4 (p. 58).

64. Cf. Gerson's objection to the "excès de legiereté" in the *Rose*, in *Le Débat*, p. 74.384.

65. See Gravdal, *Ravishing Maidens*, chap. 3.

66. Cf. Poirion, "Les mots et les choses," p. 8.

67. *False Roses*, p. 1; see also Lynch, *High Medieval Dream Vision*, pp. 144–45.

68. Quilligan, "Allegory, Allegoresis, and the Deallegorization of Language," p. 185.

69. Heather M. Arden, *Roman de la rose: An Annotated Bibliography*, p. xix.

70. "*Ars amandi, ars legendi*" p. 191.

71. *Language of Allegory*, p. 24. See especially her fourth chapter, "The Reader"; Peter L. Allen, "*Ars amandi, ars legendi*," pp. 194–95; and A. J. Minnis, "Theorizing the Rose," p. 35.

CHAPTER 3. THE SCIENTIFIC AND PHILOSOPHICAL MODES OF TREATMENT

1. "Lovers' Glass"; see also Goldin, *Mirror of Narcissus*, pp. 52–68; Schmid, "Augenlust und Spiegelliebe," especially pp. 563–68.

2. Calin, *Muse for Heroes*, p. 133.

3. "Lovers' Glass," p. 248; see also Freeman, "Problems in Romance Composition," pp. 165–66; Stakel, *False Roses*, pp. 88–93; Callay, "Road to Salvation," pp. 507–8; Bruni, "Boncompagno da Signa," pp. 116–20. Unlike Nature's mirrors, the crystals in Narcisse's fountain in Guillaume mirror "sanz coverture" (v. 1555) and "sanz decevoir" (v. 1558) [without cover or deception]. However, he himself was taken in by what he saw "Cil miroërs m'a deceü" (v. 1607) [this mirror deceived me], since he did not recognize his own love as distinguished from Narcisse's; see Goldin, *Mirror of Narcissus*, pp. 54–58.

4. On the general features of the Aristotelian *accessus*, see Sandkühler, *Die*

frühen Dantekommentare; Judson Boyce Allen, *Ethical Poetic of the Later Middle Ages*; A. J. Minnis, *Medieval Theory of Authorship*.

5. See, for example, passages like *Le Débat*, pp. 15.106–7, 32.15–17 (Epître 120; cf. 36.16), 40.6–7, 42.15–16 (cf. 42.27), 50.57–58, 51.94, 51.103–52.104.

6. Quoted from Badel, *Le* Roman de la rose *au XIVe siècle*, p. 486; on Laurent de Premierfait's possible connection with the *Rose* "Querelle," see pp. 482–89. See also Lynch, *High Medieval Dream Vision*, p. 119 and 225 n. 18; Dronke, "Francesca and Héloïse," pp. 130–35; Richards, *Dante and the* Roman de la rose, pp. 73–77. Richards identifies passages that Dante may have adapted from the *Rose*; see pp. 85–105.

7. See Vanossi, *Dante e il* Roman de la rose, chap. 8, especially pp. 332–49.

8. Some manuscripts contain a brief epilogue that completes Guillaume's poem independently of Jean; see verse 4058 n (Langlois 2:330–33).

9. "Epistola XIII," §9 (pp. 612 and 614), in Dante Alighieri, *Opere minori*, vol 2. Cf. my "Assimilation et montage"; Cerquiglini, "Dit," in *Grundriß der romanischen Literaturen*, pp. 86–94; Zumthor, "Narrative and Anti-Narrative," pp. 199–200. Christine de Pizan uses the *modi* in the *Cité des dames*; see McLeod, "Poetics and Antimisogynist Polemics." On John Gower's use of the *modus divisivus*, see Copeland, *Rhetoric, Hermeneutics, and Translation*, pp. 207–20.

10. Sandkühler, *Die frühen Dantekommentare*, pp. 37–39.

11. *Determinatio* is a process whereby a word is explained by defining or otherwise identifying its attributes; see Douglas Kelly, *Arts of Poetry and Prose*, pp. 81–82.

12. Sandkühler, *Die frühen Dantekommentare*, pp. 87–88.

13. Friedman, "Jean de Meun and Ethelred of Rievaulx," p. 135. Cf. Schnell, *Causa amoris*, p. 51. Amant calls such friendship "ne soi quele amor sauvage" (v. 5347), which Dahlberg translates as "some bestial love." Traditionally a woman was called *sauvage* if she refused to love, a sense which may resonate as the rarity of such friendship.

14. On *fin* and my translation "noble," see my *Medieval Imagination*, pp. 20–22; Ferrante, "*Cortes' Amor* in Medieval Texts." It is a positive word and gives substance to the designation "fins amanz" in verse 4361—"frans amans" in Poirion's edition (v. 4391), which he translates as "vrais amants" (v. 4391 n).

15. *Opera Omnia: I. Opera ascetica*, pp. 279–350. Note that, although Eve was not a *vir*, she was a *secundus homo*. Jean's use of Aelred of Rievaulx in adapting Cicero's definition of friendship is discussed by Friedman, "Jean de Meun and Ethelred of Rievaulx," and Fleming, "Carthaginian Love." Helmut G. Walther points out that Thomas Aquinas does not believe in the equality of Adam and Eve in the Garden, using Adam's "sovereignty" over his wife to argue that "sovereignty" of any kind was part of God's plan for the world, even in Paradise. It follows that Thomas did not accept Aelred's view, or that he would not have done so. May one conclude that this is another reason for Jean's opposition to the mendicant orders? See Walther, "Utopische Gesellschaftskritik oder satirische Ironie?" pp. 94–95, 101–3.

16. On these stages or *gradus*, see *De spiritali amicitia* I.65–66.

17. Aelred's "natural friendship" is not the same as Jean's *amour naturelle*, which is love of offspring because of a desire to maintain the human species, a love which Jean says humans share with animals and which is, therefore, morally neutral (v. 5733–58). Neither Friedman nor Fleming nor anyone else, as far as I have been able to determine, discusses friendship between man and woman or quotes any passage that treats it in the *De spiritali amicitia*. But cf. Baumgartner, "De Lucrèce à Héloïse," pp. 439–40. Gervase Mathew discusses medieval evidence for ideal friendship between man and woman, including the semantic overlap of *amour* and *amitié*, but he fails to identify such friendship in Reason's analysis in the *Rose*; see "Ideals of Friendship."

18. Hubert Silvestre has argued that Jean de Meun himself is the author of those letters as well as of the *Historia calamitatum*; see his "L'idylle d'Abélard et Héloïse," pp. 180, 196–98. Silvestre bases his conception of the *Rose* on Louis Rossi and Jean-Charles Payen (see p. 197 n. 98). Eric Hicks has since shown that Jean could not have written the Latin *Historia*; see *La Vie et les Epistres*, pp. xxii–xxvi.

19. "L'idylle d'Abélard et Héloïse," pp. 197–98.

20. Ibid., p. 197.

21. See my *Medieval Imagination*, pp. 17–19. However, Christine's writings after the "Querelle" reject almost any kind of love, even a good love. On, for example, the *Duc des vrais amants* and the *Cent ballades d'amant et de dame*, see my "Amitié comme anti-amour."

22. Andreas Capellanus, *De amore*, p. 3.

23. Douglas Kelly, *Medieval Imagination*, pp. 85–92. The seminal study is Batany, "Paradigmes lexicaux et structures littéraires."

24. On what follows, see Tuve, *Allegorical Imagery*, p. 251.

25. See Andrieux-Reix, *Ancien français*, pp. 175–79.

26. Also named "Cortoisie" (v. 1765); on the semantic overlap in the *Rose* between the two words, see my *Medieval Imagination*, pp. 69, 275 n. 18, and, more generally, Andrieux-Reix, *Ancien français*, pp. 44–47, 176–78. On the relation between *franchise*, *amitié*, and *bel acueil*, see Mathew, "Ideals of Friendship," pp. 50–51.

27. Douglas Kelly, *Medieval Imagination*, pp. 85–86, 88.

28. On Jean's tournament, see Bouché, "Burlesque et renouvellement des formes."

29. Cf. the Vieille: "Qui s'amor en un seul leu livre / N'a pas son queur franc ne delivre, / Ainz l'a malement asservi" (v. 13131–33) [she who loves only one person does not have a noble, free heart, but has wrongly committed it to servitude].

30. See also verses 18843–45.

31. On the special case of Héloise, see verses 8749–50, 9411–12; and Baumgartner, "De Lucrèce à Héloïse," pp. 437–41.

32. Paré, *Les idées et les lettres au XIIIe siècle*, p. 32. (Paré's emphasis).

33. See Chrétien de Troyes, *Le Chevalier au lion*, v. 6624–25; and my "Le jeu de la vérité." For other examples of the expression, see Gerbert de Montreuil, *La continuation de Perceval*, v. 1774, 2186.

34. The fundamental discussion is still Lionel J. Friedman, "Gradus amoris."

35. See Sandkühler, *Die frühen Dantekommentare*, pp. 42–43, on this sense of division.

36. *False Roses*, chap. 2.

37. Latini distinguishes between these two levels, which both mean "sentiment exalté de sa propre valeur, accompagné de mépris pour celle d'autrui"; see P. A. Messelaar, *Le vocabulaire des idées*, p. 343. I have consulted Messelaar's monograph for what follows.

38. Messelaar defines *envie* as French "envie" (*Le vocabulaire des idées*, pp. 148–49), which in English can be either "envy" or "desire to possess another or what another has"—e.g., a rose.

39. Latini, *Li Livres dou tresor*, II.cxxxi.8 (p. 313).

40. See my "Courtly Love in Perspective." I now reject philosophical gradualism as an explanation for the scale of loves; the notion of Material Style is adequate as a rhetorical device for distinguishing conduct appropriate to different social, economic, and moral orders. See my *Arts of Poetry and Prose*, pp. 71–78 and *Art of Medieval French Romance*, pp. 52–56.

41. Whether or not Andreas satirizes or spoofs love is not relevant here. What is relevant is the actual use of the *scala amorum*. I assume that if he parodied or satirized different kinds of love, literature and society must have contained analogous loves to parody or satirize.

42. On *finesse* as a social skill analogous to Pascal's *esprit de finesse*, see my *Medieval Imagination*, pp. 20–22.

43. Cf. the principle of the mean, or "moien" (v. 5730), between excessive "contraries" (v. 5709).

44. Sandkühler, *Die frühen Dantekommentare*, pp. 38–39; cf. Judson Boyce Allen, *Ethical Poetic of the Later Middle Ages*, pp. 75–76.

45. Jung, "Jean de Meun et son lecteur," pp. 242–44; see in general Paré, *Les idées et les lettres au XIIIe siècle*, and Gisela Hilder, *Der scholastische Wortschatz bei Jean de Meun*.

46. As she was in Guillaume de Lorris's second adventure, the kiss.

47. *Ad C. Herennium De ratione dicendi*, I.iv.7. My references will be to its usual title, *Ad Herennium*.

48. See Solterer, *Master and Minerva*; Pratt, "Analogy or Logic; Authority or Experience?" pp. 57–66.

49. Sandkühler, *Die frühen Dantekommentare*, pp. 37–38. Jean uses examples far more than Guillaume; see Zumthor, "Narrative and Anti-Narrative," pp. 188, 200–202; Strubel, *La rose Renart et le graal*, pp. 222–24; Bermejo, "Notas sobre las modalidades retóricas."

50. Cf. *Rose* v. 18238–56; Judson Boyce Allen, *Ethical Poetic of the Later Middle Ages*, pp. 16–18; Douglas Kelly, *Art of Medieval French Romance*, pp. 227–28.

51. Robertson, *Preface to Chaucer*, pp. 99–103; Tuve, *Allegorical Imagery*, pp. 262–63 and n. 16; Fleming, Roman de la rose: *A Study in Allegory and Iconography*, pp. 228–37. By contrast, cf. Poirion, *Le Roman de la rose*, pp. 198–99. On satire in the *Rose*, see the intelligent observations of Hicks, "Sous les pavés, le sens."

52. On the consent of Pygmalion's beloved, see Bermejo, "Notas sobre las modalidades retóricas," p. 101. Cf. Hill, "Narcissus, Pygmalion, and the Castration of Saturn," pp. 408–13; Knoespel, *Narcissus and the Invention of Personal History*, pp. 101–3; Picone, "Dante e il mito di Narciso," pp. 389–93. On the sexual ambiguity of Paphus, see Thut, "Narcisse versus Pygmalion," p. 128; cf. Huot, "Medusa Interpolation," pp. 869–72; Muela Ezquerra, "Técnicas retóricas."

53. On the contrast between Pygmalion and Mirra, see Payen, *La rose et l'utopie*, pp. 235–36. Cf. *La Queste del saint graal*, pp. 138–39, where Lancelot tries this explanation and a hermit rejects it. The explanation of inherited sin was first suggested to Lancelot by Symeu, himself a sinner; see *Lancelot*, II.xxxvii.40. Inherited sin is found only in the Old Law.

54. See Muela Ezquerra, "Técnicas retóricas," p. 392; and Walters, "A Parisian Manuscript of the *Romance of the Rose*," p. 41; both delineate the positive evolution of Pygmalion's love.

55. Cf. also v. 4717–22: "Par la loi de ceste amistié / Dist Tulles en un suen ditié / Que bien devons fere requeste / A noz amis, s'el est honeste; / Et leur requeste refeson, / S'ele contient droit et raison." [Tully says in his work that such friendship obliges us to ask things of our friends, provided the request is honorable; and we should do as they ask us if it is just and reasonable.] It is just and reasonable to make love and have children in Reason's scheme of things. On the difference between the obscenity of Amant's relation to his statue and the conventional courtly ethos in the Pygmalion episode, see Vasquez, *El episodio de Pigmalión*, pp. 37–45, 64–77. Vasquez believes that the Pygmalion episode was written before the *Rose*, then inserted into it. This would not alter the significance of the differences in both content and style between the Pygmalion and Amant fables.

56. Marc M. Pelen, *Latin Poetic Irony*, pp. 154–55 n. 65. On this erotic image of the rose as well as weather imagery in general like that evoked in Nature's complaint, see the interpretation of the *Pervigilium Veneris* by Peter King, "Flos Veneris." On Rose's possible pregnancy, see Hill, "Narcissus, Pygmalion, and the Castration of Saturn," pp. 414–17; Wetherbee, "Literal and the Allegorical," pp. 268 n. 22 and 286; Huot, "Medusa Interpolation."

57. On women who do not want to become pregnant, cf. Reason, v. 4521–26.

58. On unreproductive sexuality, see v. 19513–52; on sodomy in particular, v. 19599–656; incest, v. 21157–80; virginity, v. 19553–98; and castration, v. 20007–52.

59. See Daniel Poirion, "Narcisse et Pygmalion," p. 159. Rainer Kauke, "Jupiter et Saturne chez Jean de Meun," p. 259, thinks Venus is irrelevant in the *Rose*.

60. This recalls Reason's *amitié*. Cf. v. 4561–62 and above, pp. 57–61.

61. This is how I interpret: "Mes il l' [his mother] ot ainceis conneüe, / Sa seror ravoit il eüe" (v. 6177–78) [He knew his mother and had his sister]. Nero is therefore in the same class as Mirra. *Ainceis* refers to an act prior to Nero's dismemberment of his mother. Since Nero is clearly the antithesis of Socrates, Seneca's forced suicide mirrors Socrates's own death (v. 6148–55).

62. My examples exclude reference to those features of the stories not pertinent to the erotic conflict, that is, the comparison of Chacus with Peur (v. 15543–56) and of Hercules's assault on Chacus's castle with Amant's "herculean" effort to break Rose's hymen (v. 21591–97).

63. On *nagier* as the sex act, see v. 14271–74; the image is evoked by the Vieille apropos of shared orgasm.

64. Analogous to Nero's fratricide and matricide (v. 13227–32).

65. On love suicides, see Lefay-Toury, *La tentation du suicide*, especially chap. 1: "L'héritage antique." Penelope is an exception. But Ulysses had been unfaithful to her (v. 14376–78). The Jealous Husband believes that there are no more Penelopes (v. 8622).

66. Poirion (v. 13924 n) notes that his manuscript reads *cuers* ("hearts") for *cons*; Dahlberg does not translate this French proper noun.

67. The Jealous Husband also wants his wife to be a *serve*; see v. 8435–36, 8517–23, 9439–43. Reason will be Amant's *serve* if he will let her (v. 5812). The allegory distinguishes between these literal *serves*.

68. Pelen, *Latin Poetic Irony*, pp. 116–19.

69. On these terms, see Andreas's *De amore*, Book II, chaps. 1–4.

70. The Monk shares with Jean the examples of Nero, Hercules, Samson, and Croesus. On these senses of tragedy, see my *Arts of Poetry and Prose*, pp. 75–76. In general, see Henry Ansgar Kelly, *Ideas and Forms of Tragedy.*

71. For background on urban mores, see Rossiaud, *La prostitution médiévale*, chaps. 2 (Ami) and 3 (the Vieille).

72. See Batany, *Approches du* Roman de la rose, pp. 56–57. The same holds for Andreas Capellanus; see my "Courtly Love in Perspective," pp. 124–28.

73. An example of the adaptation of the same matter in different ways is the incipient romance variously begun by the same author, Bauduins Butors; see "Four Rough Drafts."

74. On the catalogue as structuring device, see McLeod, *Virtues and Venom*; on examples in Jean's *Rose*, see also Regalado, "Des contraires choses."

75. Knoespel, *Narcissus and the Invention of Personal History*, pp. 103–4. On time in the *Rose*, see Payen, "L'espace et le temps."

76. Vulcan is presumably a background figure in the Adonis exemplum, but he is not mentioned.

77. Adonis links with the divinities and makes them virtually contemporary with Amant and Rose.

78. *Latin Poetic Irony*, pp. 117–19. The juxtaposition is analogous to that between the rape of Lucrece and the castration of Abelard; see Baumgartner, "De Lucrèce à Héloïse."

79. See Jager, "Reading the *Roman* Inside Out."

CHAPTER 4. THE POETIC AND RHETORICAL MODES OF TREATMENT

1. Vatican lat. ms. 2877, f. 6v°; text quoted from Judson Boyce Allen, *Ethical Poetic of the Later Middle Ages*, p. 209.

2. Gallo, "*Poetria nova* of Geoffrey of Vinsauf," pp. 73–80; cf. my *Art of Medieval French Romance*, pp. 63–66, 264–72; Simpson, "Information."

3. What appears *inutilis* may, of course, become *utilis* on an allegorical level. On the *digressio inutilis*, see Woods, "Poetic Digression." The fourth kind of digression, description, is discussed under the *modus descriptivus*.

4. Horace, *Ad Pisones*, in *Opera*, v. 333–34. Although Horace is not the only author to express this commonplace idea in antiquity, his statement is typical for poets. On the rhetorical tradition of *docere*, *delectare*, and *movere*, see Lausberg, *Handbuch der literarischen Rhetorik*, §§257, 325–34.

5. Horace, *Ad Pisones*, in *Opera*, v. 119–35, 240–41. On what follows, see Copeland, *Rhetoric, Hermeneutics, and Translation*, especially pp. 166–78.

6. See my "Theory of Composition," pp. 127–30. On creation as an inappropriate notion in medieval art, see Langer, *Divine and Poetic Freedom*, pp. 84–86; and my *Art of Medieval French Romance*, pp. 38–41.

7. 2.3.132; cf. 133–37, in Faral, *Les arts poétiques du XII*[e] *et du XIII*[e] *siècle*.

8. For Horace commentaries, see Munk Olsen, *L'étude des auteurs classiques latins*, 1:422–23, 3.2:62, to which add Friis-Jensen, "*Ars Poetica* in Twelfth-Century France."

9. *Scholia in Horatium*, 4:464–65.

10. See my *Arts of Poetry and Prose*, pp. 47–52.

11. Cf. Matthew of Vendôme, *Ars versificatoria*, in *Opera*, 4.1–49.

12. For two different approaches to the *Rose*'s use of Vergil, see Fleming, "Jean de Meun and the Ancient Poets," especially pp. 90–99; and Stephen G. Nichols, "Ekphrasis, Iconoclasm, and Desire."

13. In the commentary tradition *scaena* came to mean not only stage, but also a recitation or script; see Friis-Jensen, "*Arts Poetica* in Twelfth-Century France," p. 353.

14. Also see my *Medieval Imagination*, pp. 86–87. Cf. Schmid, "Augenlust und Spiegelliebe," p. 567, on the passage from *rage* at the fountain to the effect of Cupid's arrows on Amant's heart.

15. On *fabula* and its meanings, see Priscian, *Praeexercitamina*, 3.430–31; and in general Lausberg, *Handbuch der literarischen Rhetorik*, §§413–14, 1107–10; Dronke, *Fabula*; Demats, *Fabula*.

16. Douglas Kelly, *Medieval Imagination*, pp. 29–30.

17. Medieval *mentir* can mean 'to err,' as here, as well as 'to lie.' Other examples in the *Rose* of the former sense, in which deliberate prevarication is not a possible meaning, are found in v. 5271, 7995, 8866, and 12272. Cf. *Le petit Robert* s.v. *mentir*: "2° (*Choses*) Exprimer une chose fausse. . . . "

18. In *Poems of Cupid*.

19. See Rupert T. Pickens, "*Somnium* and Interpretation"; Zink, *La subjectivité littéraire*, pp. 243–45. On the problematic authority of Macrobius's classification in the Middle Ages and of other dream theories which may have influenced Jean de Meun, see Peden, "Macrobius and Mediaeval Dream Literature."

20. See Ott, "Pauvreté et richesse," pp. 234–35.

21. The suggestion is made by Charles Dahlberg, "Love and the *Roman de la*

rose," p. 568; and Fleming, Roman de la rose: *A Study in Allegory and Iconography*, p. 101. Tuve points out that no one thought of the identification before Clément Marot in the sixteenth century (*Allegorical Imagery*, p. 233).

22. *Allegory of Love*, pp. 136, 147–48.

23. See my *Medieval Imagination*, pp. 172–73.

24. See my "Topical Invention"; *Arts of Poetry and Prose*, pp. 71–78; *Art of Medieval French Romance*, pp. 48–61, 210–22. On the relation between description and definition, see Jung, "Jean de Meun et l'allégorie," pp. 30–31.

25. Vitz, *Medieval Narrative and Modern Narratology*, p. 85.

26. Cf. Ott, "Pauvreté et richesse," p. 238.

27. Perhaps the *roi des ribauts* supervised evening games like those illustrated in Jacques Bretel's *Tournoi de Chauvency*, pp. lxxi–lxxii. In general see Rossi, "Notula sul Re dei ribaldi"; Rossiaud, *La prostitution médiévale*, pp. 58, 70, 76–78, 232 n. 6, 252 n. 7, 254 n. 18, 255 n. 21, 265 n. 4, and 285 n. 61. See as well Du Cange, *Glossarium mediae et infimae latinitatis*, 7:183–85; Godefroy, *Dictionnaire de l'ancienne langue française*, 7:183–84; *Tobler-Lommatzsch*, 8:1257.21–46 (in the sense of "penis," ll. 47–51). As Faux Semblant's mirror, Genius performs an analogous role as *mestre des leus* (*Rose*, v. 16256); see Callay, "Road to Salvation," pp. 501–2, 508–9.

28. On *franchise*, see above, pp. 62–65.

29. In Ovid's *Metamorphoses*, Pygmalion eschews love out of disgust for prostitutes, who offended Venus and eventually turned to stone. By contrast, Pygmalion's prayer to Venus turns a stone statue into a marriageable woman.

30. Stakel, *False Roses*, pp. 23–24.

31. But see Vitz, "Inside/Outside."

32. *Medieval Imagination*, pp. 93–95.

33. Louis, *Le* Roman de la rose: *essai d'interprétation de l'allégorisme érotique*, pp. 11–14; cf. Lewis, *Allegory of Love*, pp. 118–25, especially, "Any protracted wooing involves a conflict not only between the man and the woman but between the woman and herself; it is this second conflict which occupies the most interesting scenes in the *Romance*" (p. 118). See as well Paris, "Fin du treizième siècle," pp. 7 and 9.

34. On Ami as "self-love," cf. Fleming, Roman de la rose: *A Study in Allegory and Iconography*, pp. 166–67; Emmerson and Herzman, "Apocalyptic Age of Hypocrisy," pp. 629–30. Ami, in this equation, is the opposite of Reason, who tells Amant what he should not like about himself. Still, the two personifications are talking about the same characteristics.

35. Cf. Knoespel, *Narcissus and the Invention of Personal History*, pp. 94–96.

36. Louis, *Le Roman de la rose*, p. 13; Douglas Kelly, *Medieval Imagination*, pp. 91–92.

37. Douglas Kelly, *Medieval Imagination*, pp. 84–92.

38. Tuve, *Allegorical Imagery*, pp. 21–22.

39. Dinshaw, *Chaucer's Sexual Poetics*, p. 9.

40. And in medieval literature in general, especially in the Latin tradition; see Ziolkowski, *Alan of Lille's Grammar of Sex*, passim.

41. Contrast C. S. Lewis's woefully inadequate response to this kind of "absurdity" (*Allegory of Love*, p. 140) with Benedetto's perceptive analysis of Bel Acueil (*Il* Roman de la rose *e la letteratura italiana*, p. 11).

42. Fowler, *Dictionary of Modern English Usage*, s.v. *syllepsis*.

43. Grevisse, *Le bon usage*, §466.3.

44. For example, the feminine noun *la majesté* referring to the sovereign in direct address. The *Petit Robert*, s.v. *majesté*, gives: "Sa Majesté le roi viendra-t-il?" introducing *le roi* to govern the masculine pronoun, much as Guillaume de Lorris and Jean insert *le dieu* before the feminine noun *Amour*, permitting a masculine God of Love. Grevisse contrasts this phenomenon in the specific case of *majesté* with those cases in which the masculine noun in apposition is left out: "Sa Majesté est contente," "Sa Majesté viendra-t-elle?" where "sa Majesté" is a king. But cf. "Sa Majesté est le protecteur des faibles," a syllepsis analogous to "C'est la sentinelle qui le premier s'inquiète," cited above; for these examples, see Grevisse, *Le Bon usage*, p. 1129; see also §§303–4, 378 *bis*, 466 rem. 5, and 496.

45. The manuscripts are not in agreement as to when the syllepsis first occurs. In Langlois's edition, it occurs with the first appearance of Male Bouche, contrary to Lecoy's. (Poirion's and Strubel's editions also show syllepsis from the first appearance of Male Bouche, except that Strubel, v. 3034, reads "ele"—probably an error because it makes the line hypermetric.) Sarah Kay refers to another example of syllepsis, Verité, the *ami* [*sic*!] of Richesse in the manuscript used for Poirion's edition of the *Rose* (*Subjectivity* p. 250 n. 10). This appears to be a variant not found in the other manuscripts.

46. David Hult first noted the syllepsis in the Lecoy edition of Guillaume. He attributes it to the identification of Male Bouche as a masculine *losengier*, or "slanderer," (v. 3551) rather than as a feminine *jangleor*, or "gossip" (v. 2819); see his *Self-Fulfilling Prophecies*, p. 244 n. 80. What follows complements and enlarges upon this explanation for Jean's part of the *Rose*. "*La* jangleor," v. 2819, is the last time Male Bouche is marked by the feminine in Lecoy's edition. Curiously, Vanossi also uses masculine pronouns in his Italian summary of the *Rose*: "Faus Semblant riuscirà a convincer*lo*. . . *lo* strangola, *gli* taglia la lingua. . ." (emphasis mine; *Dante e il* Roman de la rose, p. 35). On the other hand, Payen, after quoting v. 12065—"*il* fist forgier"—continues on Male Bouche with "*celle-ci*, en bonne commère. . ." (emphasis mine; *La Rose et l'utopie*, p. 101). André Lanly uses the masculine in his modern French translation of the *Rose* (Paris: Champion, 1971), 1:181 n. 2819. Strubel's translation follows the Old French with the masculine for v. 2833–34, the feminine for v. 3034.

47. Lewis, *Allegory of Love*, p. 123.

48. As occurs in some manuscripts; see Huot, *The* Romance of the Rose *and Its Medieval Readers*, pp. 190–91.

49. Just as the *Rose*'s implied unlettered audience cannot know what Vergil, Cicero, Horace, Boethius, or Alain de Lille wrote except insofar as Jean quotes or paraphrases them, similarly it can know what misogynist authorities like Theophrastus and Juvenal wrote only as he reports them. Jean thought that these authors had not yet been translated into French. By rewriting their words, Jean as-

sumes the mantle of their authority. We may therefore confine our discussion to their words as Jean reports them.

50. See Muela Ezquerra, "Técnicas retóricas," pp. 376–84.

51. Latzke, "Der Fürstinnenpreis." Cf. Alistair Minnis, "Aspects of Medieval French and English Traditions," pp. 332–33.

52. There is a translation problem here. Classical Latin *homo* is almost universally a word for human beings of both genders. Only two exceptions are identified in the *Thesaurus linguae latinae*, vol. 6.3, s.v. *homo*: "man" in an army (col. 2889.43–67). The general sense is lost in the Middle Ages, when *homme* came to signify, as today, "male man" more often than "human being." Consider the following passage in Nicolas Oresme's preface to his translation of Aristotle, *Le livre de ethiques*: "L'en ne pourroit translater proprement tout latin en françois. Si comme entre innumbrables examples puet apparoir de ceste tres commune proposicion: *homo est animal*; car *homo* signifie homme et femme et nul mot de françois ne signifie equipeillement. . . . Et pour ce, ceste proposicion est vraye: *mulier est homo*, et ceste est fausse: 'femme est homme' " [one could not properly translate every Latin word into French. As this very common expression chosen from among countless examples will show: *Homo est animal.* For *homo* means man and woman, yet no French word signifies both equally. . . . Hence the following proposition is true: *mulier est homo*—a woman is a man, a human being, and this one is false: "a woman is a male man"]. Cited from Nicole Oresme, *Le livre de ethiques d'Aristote*, p. 100. I should like to thank my friend and colleague Ullrich Langer for calling this passage to my attention.

53. On Aelred's homosexuality, see Boswell, *Christianity, Social Tolerance, and Homosexuality*, pp. 221–26; McGuire, *Friendship and Community*, chap. 7. Neither Friedman nor Fleming refers to this background to Aelred's analysis of friendship. For bibliographies on homosexuality in the twelfth and thirteenth centuries, see Silvestre, "L'idylle d'Abélard et Héloïse," p. 176 n. 34; Harley, "Narcissus, Hermaphroditus, and Attis"; Kuster and Cormier, "Old Views and New Trends."

54. See Poirion, "Alain de Lille and Jean de Meun," pp. 136–37, 146–47; Harley, "Narcissus, Hermaphroditus, and Attis." As they note, castrates, hermaphrodites, and homosexuals were all of a kind for medieval people.

55. Gunn, *Mirror of Love*, p. 131.

56. The male counterpart to the "vaillanz dames" addressed in Jean's intervention on *meurs femenins*. On sex acts castigated or ridiculed as unnatural from the thirteenth into the sixteenth century, see Rossiaud, *La prostitution médiévale*, chap. 7.

57. The criminal's wife also tells the truth (v. 16333). So do Phanie and Héloise.

58. "Image et imagination dans les inventions des poètes: miroir et réceptivité dans les Dits allégoriques"; cf. Ziolkowski, *Alan of Lille's Grammar of Sex*, pp. 58–60. The "femininity" of the mystic, allied to the soul (*anima*), is a commonplace feature of the relation between man and God; see Vitz, "Inside/Outside," pp. 87–89, which also accounts, perhaps, for Amant's "passivity" in the *Rose* (pp. 67 and 91).

59. See R. Howard Bloch, *Medieval Misogyny.*

60. A thirteenth-century example of such cooperation is found in the Ship of Solomon episode in the *Queste del saint graal*; see my "L'invention dans les romans en prose," pp. 120–21.

61. "Crins" (v. 13255), "cheveus" (v. 13264), "oreilles" (v. 13267), "sa couleur" (v. 13275), "col et gorge" (v. 13283), "espaules" (v. 13289), "mains" (v. 13293), "mameles" (v. 13299), "la chambre Venus" (v. 13306), "piez" (v. 13311), "jambe" (v. 13312), then focusing on the face: "aleine" (v. 13315), "bouche" (v. 13319), "fossetes" (v. 13323), "joes" (v. 13325), "levres" (v. 13327), "denz" (v. 13333) [locks, hair, ears, complexion, neck and bosom, shoulders, hands, nipples, "Venus's chamber," feet, legs—breath, mouth, dimples, cheeks, lips, teeth].

62. Innocent III, *De miseria humane conditionis*, quoted from Economou, "Two Venuses and Courtly Love," p. 18.

63. The following lines correspond to descriptions of *meurs femenins* that are the same as or analogous to the given vice that Nature finds in men. *Orgueilleus*: v. 9915–20; *murtriers*: v. 16346–58; *lierres*: v. 13721–22; *fel*: v. 18102–3; *couvoiteus*: v. 8252; *avers*: v. 14403–8, v. 16314–16; *trichierres*: v. 13034, 13559–60, 16346–49; *desesperez*: v. 5804–8, 9761–76; *gloz*: v. 8252–53; *haïneus*: v. 9387–90, 16293–303; *despisanz*: v. 16527–38; *mescreanz*: v. 9023–24; *mantirres*: v. 18097–98, 18106–11; *parjurs*: v. 16317–58; *fausaires*: v. 8247–50; *fos*: v. 8621–28, 9011, 12771; *vantierres*: v. 12734–59 (related to *orgueilleus*); *inconstanz*: v. 9873–86 (related to *trichierres*); *foloiables*: v. 9933–38, 14459 (related to *fol*); *desagraables*: v. 16293–94, 18269–73, 19188–91; *traïstres*: v. 9383–90, 16565–73 (related to *trichierres*); *faus ypocrites*: v. 9370–71 (related to *trichierres*). I have not found specific passages identifying women as *anvieus*, *mesdisanz*, *pareceus*, *sodomites*, or *ydolatres*, except that sodomites are termed "effeminate."

64. Guillaume de Lorris uses the same technique to contrast the images on the wall of Deduit's Garden and those that dance on the inside; see my *Medieval Imagination*, pp. 58–84.

65. This etymology for *mollis* makes the expression *fortis mulier* an oxymoron. Cf. Newman, "Flaws in the Golden Bowl." On "mollesse en l'âge puéril" as masturbation, see Rossiaud, *La prostitution médiévale*, p. 100.

66. Among the numerous glosses on this passage, see especially *Patrologia latina*, 134:340–41, 181:867–68, and, in the *Supplementum*, 1:421, 1437, and 4:2200.

67. See as well the examples in Du Cange 5:447–48, s.v. *1 molles*. Note as well that Jupiter, by castrating his father, introduced the age of "ease," that is, of *mollities*.

68. Quoted from Bezzola, *Les origines et la formation de la littérature courtoise*, p. 463 n. 2.

69. *Novum Glossarium mediae latinitatis*, vols. M–N, s.v. 1. *mollis*, cols. 734–35, and s.v. *mollities*, cols. 735–36, from which many of my examples are drawn.

70. Jane Chance Nitzsche, *Genius Figure in Antiquity and the Middle Ages*, pp. 123–24.

71. *Summa Parisiensis on the Decretum Gratiani*, p. 247; cf. p. 248: "Qui per animi virtutem vir est, sive sit vir sive sit mulier. . . . Mulieri vero, hoc est quæ per mentis mollitiem mulier dicitur" [Whoever is a man by moral virtue, whether that person be man or woman. . . . For a woman in fact, that is, one who is called a woman because of moral weakness].

72. See, for example, Hildegard of Bingen, *Scivias*, 2:806, s.v. *mollities*.

73. Payen, *La Rose et l'utopie*, pp. 17–18. Cf. again Faux Semblant's assumption of both male and female guises.

74. Baumgartner, "De Lucrèce à Héloïse," p. 442.

75. Pope, *From Latin to Modern French*, §§377–78. Langlois found by a study of rhymes in both parts of the *Rose* that neither Guillaume nor Jean intended preconsonantal "*s*" to be pronounced; see his edition, 1:98 (*ale*, *alis*, and *alles*). In v. 19619–20 Jean plays on the double meaning of *male*: sodomites "conferment leur regles males / Par excepcions anormales" [keep their bad/masculine rules by abnormal exceptions] and in v. 19636–38: "puissent il perdre / Et l'aumosniere et les estalles / Don il ont signe d'estre malles!" [may they lose the purse and testicles which are the sign of their masculinity/evil]. See also 1:272–75 in Langlois's edition. It is perhaps noteworthy that the only feminine adjective left to Male Bouche also means "male." *Masle* in the late thirteenth century would surely have been pronounced like modern *mâle*. I do not think Jean is merely indulging in typical French word play. The joke has deeper, more serious implications for his *modus descriptivus*. As we have seen, the femininity of evil as "male" problematizes both the general import of woman's garrulousness and the very attribute of gender as distinguished from sex in the *Rose*. Note, for the moment, the confusion of female volubility, Male Bouche's gossiping, and Amant's own loquacity.

76. See Michel Zink's suggestive article, "Bel-Accueil le travesti"; and Harley, "Narcissus, Hermaphroditus, and Attis." How troubling or even apparent the sexual ambiguities may have been to medieval audiences is moot. The medieval notion of rewriting, as we have seen, supposes reinterpretation of sources, and this must be taken into account in using the sources to interpret the rewritten version. The evidence seems to support the action of unconscious homoerotic images rather than conscious ones. On the other hand, Jean does play with them on occasion; see Ott, "Jean de Meun und Boethius," pp. 204–5.

77. See Faral, *Les arts poétiques du XIIe et du XIIIe siècle*, pp. 74–75; Brinkmann, *Zu Wesen und Form mittelalterlicher Dichtung*, pp. 49–50; Woods, "Poetic Digression."

78. See Strubel, *La Rose, Renart et le graal*, pp. 211–12.

79. Besides Woods's article, "Poetic Digression," see my derivative, "Rhetoric of Adventure in Medieval Romance."

80. The Vieille's description of Amant for Bel Acueil shows how successfully he has hidden his self; see p. 129.

81. Douglas Kelly, *Medieval Imagination*, p. 87; on what follows, cf. Drag-

onetti, "*La musique et les lettres*," pp. 94–95; Nouvet, "Les inter-dictions courtoises," pp. 239–43; Uitti, "Understanding Guillaume de Lorris"; Vitz, "Inside/Outside," p. 88.

82. See my *Medieval Imagination*, pp. 109–10.

83. Cf. Rose's restraint with the Vieille. Is this Abstinence Contrainte?

84. See Guillaume de Lorris, for example, v. 1297–98; and, in general, v. 635 n in Langlois's edition of the *Rose* (2:301–2) as well as my *Medieval Imagination*, pp. 76–77. For Fleming's reading of such paradise gardens, see his Roman de la rose: *A Study in Allegory and Iconography*, pp. 55–73.

85. See Heinrich, *Über den Stil*; Gunn, *Mirror of Love*; Scheidegger, "La peinture à l'or du *Roman de la rose*."

86. Like good lovers in Genius's exhortation, v. 19666–68, and Pygmalion, v. 21023–25.

87. And what about their families (if they had any)? What did their children live on? Their expenses recall Ami's profligacy on the road of Trop Doner. Rutebeuf gives a far grayer picture of the *ribauts de Grève*, one which is no doubt closer to their reality. See his *Dit des ribaux de Grève*, in *Œuvres complètes*, 1:531; see also Langlois v. 5053 n (2:341); and Regalado, *Poetic Patterns in Rutebeuf*, pp. 12, 308–9. The Parisian Grève was a major gathering place for prostitutes, as were taverns like those the *ribauts* spent their money in; see Rossiaud, *La prostitution médiévale*, p. 67. On the other hand, there is evidence for persons who decide to become *ribaldi* out of humility; but they clean stables, for example, rather than pursue pleasure (Du Cange 7:183, cols. 2–3).

CHAPTER 5. ALLEGORIES, MORAL ISSUES, AND AUDIENCES

1. Sandkühler, *Die frühen Dantekommentare*, p. 39.

2. Brownlee, "Problem of Faux Semblant," p. 262. For its continuation in Nature and Genius, see Lynch, *High Medieval Dream Vision*, pp. 132–38. On the Faux Semblant section as "an explicit gloss on the quest for the Rose," see Emmerson and Herzman, "Apocalyptic Age of Hypocrisy," p. 627.

3. On this passage, see Quilligan, *Language of Allegory*, pp. 242–45.

4. Works of vanity might include not only Chrétien's *Cligés* but also his *Conte du graal* (Douglas Kelly, *Art of Medieval French Romance*, pp. 316–17). It would not be astonishing if, toward the end of his life, Jean looked upon his first work as frivolous or full of vanity, as did some of his critics even before the "Querelle."

5. See *Testament Maistre Jehan de Meun*, pp. 69, 82–83, 96.

6. The idea is also "written" in the *Testament* attributed to Jean de Meun (v. 501–784, 861–900; cf. pp. 31, 33–34).

7. The companionship of Abstinence Contrainte provides the link with Amant's sexual appetites, anticipating the plurality of *cons* evoked at the end of the *Rose*. Stakel's problem with Abstinence because she abstains from *food* (*False Roses*, pp. 48–49) evaporates in the allegory: gluttony and lust are commensurable.

8. See Burnley, "*Fine amor*"; and Wack, *Lovesickness in the Middle Ages*. A

generally perceived cure for lovesickness was frequentation of the municipality's official house of prostitution; see Rossiaud, *La prostitution médiévale.*

9. See, for example, Bezzola, *Les origines et la formation de la littérature courtoise*, pp. 461–85.

10. Douglas Kelly, "Romance and the Vanity of Chrétien de Troyes." For a thorough discussion of these matters, see Schnell, *Causa amoris.*

11. On the supposed change in mentality, see Robertson, *Preface to Chaucer*, pp. 361–65.

12. Badel, *Le* Roman de la rose *au XIVe siècle*; Huot, *The* Romance of the Rose *and Its Medieval Readers*; cf. even Fleming, Roman de la rose: *A Study in Allegory and Iconography*, p. 67 n. 20.

13. See Kennedy, *Lancelot and the Grail.*

14. For a background analysis of the logic and rhetoric of the "Querelle," see Joseph L. Baird and John R. Kane, "*La Querelle de la Rose*: In Defense of the Opponents"; as well as Hicks's introduction to his edition of the *Débat*; and Ott, *Der Rosenroman*, pp. 32–40. However, I think Baird goes too far in making lightness of tone, even bantering obscenity, or eroticism, the basis for reading the "Querelle" as more game than earnest, in his "Pierre Col and the *Querelle de la Rose.*"

15. She does so herself in the *Epître au dieu d'amour* and the *Dit de la Rose.*

16. See above chapter 1, n. 3.

17. Gui de Mori also envisages a "pure love"; see Huot, *The* Romance of the Rose *and Its Medieval Readers*, Appendix A1 (pp. 338–39), and A2 v. 116–131 (pp. 342–43), and v. 119 n (p. 344). Christine's view changed several years later; in the *Duc des vrais amants* an honorable, almost platonic love fails. See Krueger, *Women Readers*, chap. 8.

18. Is this another "woman's word"? See references to *fraise*, "strawberry," as male genitals in *Le Roman d'Eneas*, v. 8576. Such persons are "godel" (v. 8585); see Salverda de Grave, "Anc. franç. *godel.*"

19. Villon is referring to himself and Grosse Margot.

20. Payen, "Le *Roman de la rose* et la notion de carrefour idéologique," p. 193.

21. Sylvia Keck uses a frame like Stakel's (*False Roses*, chap. 2), but does not integrate it into the plot; see her "Faux Semblant," p. 264.

22. Benedetto, *Il* Roman de la rose *e la letteratura italiana*, pp. 44–46; Friedman, " 'Jean de Meung,' Antifeminism, and 'Bourgeois Realism,' " p. 16; Stone, "Hierarchies and Meaning," pp. 9–10; and his "Old and New Thoughts on Guillaume de Lorris," pp. 165–68; Ott, "Jean de Meun und Boethius," pp. 210–14; Badel, "Raison 'fille de Dieu,' " 1:43. Cf. Pierre Col in *Le Débat*, p. 95.211–14: "Des qu'il [Jean de Meun] commensa a escripture, il entre en raison; et Dieu sceit combien il se tient: a painne se peut il oster (aussy ne s'i estoit gaires tenu le premier aucteur)." [As soon as Jean de Meun began to write, he took reason as his subject. God knows how attracted he was to it; he could hardly pull himself away—and, indeed, the first author paid almost no attention to it.]

23. I recall again "reson toute forsenable, / . . . forcenerie resnable" (v. 4269–70), as Reason herself describes love.

24. For the main points, see Pelen, *Latin Poetic Irony*, pp. 117–19, 129, and 150 n. 23; Stakel, *False Roses*, pp. 75–78; and Rowe, "Reson in Jean's *Roman de la rose*."

25. Pelen, *Latin Poetic Irony*, p. 118. But cf. Jesus's own words on eunuchs who castrate themselves to gain heaven, in Matthew 19:12.

26. Stakel, *False Roses*, p. 75.

27. For example, "Il set plus que Reson ne fet. / Mes ainceis qu'il eüst finee / Sa reson. . . . " (v. 9976–78) [he knows more than Reason does. But before he had finished speaking . . .].

28. Lewis, *Allegory of Love*, pp. 66–71; Douglas Kelly, *Medieval Imagination*, p. 36. Cf. Smith, *Prudentius' "Psychomachia,"* pp. 282–96.

29. Cf. v. 5727–32.

30. On the semantic range of *raison* in Jean de Meun, see Badel, "Raison 'fille de Dieu,' " pp. 42–50.

31. Cf. v. 18840–47, and Wetherbee, "Theme of Imagination in Medieval Poetry," pp. 47–48.

32. Cf. v. 6915–22, 7043–50.

33. Benedetto, *Il* Roman de la rose *e la letteratura italiana*, pp. 50–52; Callay, "Road to Salvation"; Rossman, *Perspectives of Irony*, pp. 147–50.

34. Dahlberg, *Literature of Unlikeness*, p. 122. On Jean's substitution of the traditional stellar and sexual Genius with Genius as the personification of indiscriminate concupiscence alongside a Nature whose only function is sexual, see Baker, "Priesthood of Genius," pp. 284–86; Polak, "Plato, Nature and Jean de Meun," pp. 92–98; Wetherbee, "Theme of Imagination in Medieval Poetry," pp. 47–48.

35. *Latin Poetic Irony*, p. 118.

36. Ibid.

37. Cf. pp. 44.46–47 (Jean de Montreuil). But perhaps Col's *Rose* manuscript belonged to a family that reconciles Raison's and Genius's views; see Huot, *The* Romance of the Rose *and Its Medieval Readers*, pp. 170–79. One notes here that even heterosexual carnality is as unnatural as homosexuality and castration. The defenders of Jean de Meun in the "Querelle" are closer to Wetherbee's reading of the *Rose* ("Literal and the Allegorical," pp. 287–91) than to Robertson's and Fleming's, who deny the occurrence of pregnancy.

38. Note the retention of the masculine gender in this allegorically heterosexual contact, which, on the literal level, is essentially sodomitical and therefore as barren as the love *maladie* of which it is a species.

39. Zink, *La subjectivité litteraire*, p. 134. Cf. Paré, *Les idées et les lettres au XIIIe siècle*, pp. 19–22.

40. See Paré, *Les idées et les lettres au XIIIe siècle*, pp. 28–29.

41. On this distinction between intended allegory and imposed allegory, see Tuve, *Allegorical Imagery*, chap. 4.

42. Some later readers did add marginal comments; see Huot, *The* Romance of the Rose *and Its Medieval Readers*, chap. 2. There is no way to know whether any such marginalia go back to the authors.

43. Several scholars have remarked on this feature of the *Rose*'s glossing; see

Dragonetti, "*La musique et les lettres*," p. 369 n. 3; Jung, "Jean de Meun et l'allégorie"; Regalado, " 'Des Contraires choses,' " pp. 69–71; Dornbush, *Pygmalion's Figure*, p. 60; Brownlee, "Reflections in the *Miroër aus amoreus*," p. 63; Peter L. Allen, "*Ars amandi, ars legendi*," pp. 198–99; Vitz, "Inside/Outside," p. 77. Additional examples are found in the earliest French translation of Boethius's *Consolation*; see Thomas and Roques, "Traductions françaises de la *Consolatio Philosophiae*," pp. 424–28. Benedetto thinks Jean intended to write a gloss or commentary, but that the allegorical meaning of the poem is obvious without it (*Il* Roman de la rose *e la letteratura italiana* pp. 79–80); there are numerous illustrations of this in Benedetto's analysis of the *Rose*. On rewriting as glossing, see as well Hult's interesting observations on Macrobius in "Vers la société de l'écriture," pp. 167–68.

44. Jung, "Gui de Mori et Guillaume de Lorris."

45. Demats, *Fabula*, pp. 61–63. This did not preclude subsequent commentary and glossing like that for the *Échecs amoureux*; see *Le Commentaire de Copenhague de* l'Ovide moralisé.

46. Cf. above Guillaume and Jean on *espondre* (v. 2073, 10573, 15117), pp. 16–17; 145–46.

47. "Interpreter's Dilemma," p. 177. Bruckner uses André Jolles's definitions of "Case" and "Nouvelle." I am not concerned with the validity of Jolles's term "Nouvelle," which is akin to the traditional fable with a moral, but only with the kind of "form" to which his term refers. On the applicability of Jolles's terminology to medieval literature, see Jauss, "Alterity and Modernity." Cf. also Edwards, "Poetic Invention" and Grünkorn, "Zum Verständnis von fiktionaler Rede."

48. Several other *jeux-partis* illustrate these issues. See CLX and pp. 35, 166 n. 19.

49. The situation in CLX is analogous to the passage from *amor carnalis* and *amor mundialis* to good human love as *amicitia* in Aelred of Rievaulx.

50. *False Roses*, pp. 58–59, 61–63.

51. See Tuve, *Allegorical Imagery*, p. 248. Stakel, *False Roses*, p. 10, notes that *faux* in Old French includes the notion of deceit.

52. Dahlberg, "Love and the *Roman de la rose*," p. 583; Pelen, *Latin Poetic Irony*, pp. 146–47.

53. On irony in the *Rose*, see Rossman, *Perspectives of Irony*, especially chaps. 1 and 5.

54. Douglas Kelly, *Medieval Imagination*, p. 87.

55. Cf. an analogous image in Villon's *Le Lais Villon et les poèmes variés*, *Lais*, v. 273–320; and David Kuhn's interpretation of these lines in *La poétique de François Villon*, pp. 122–30.

56. Lecoy notes that the word can signify "loca pudenda" (*Rose* 3:244 s.v.). Cf. the analogy between the image and that which Dragonetti identifies in Geoffrey of Vinsauf's *Poetria nova*, where the metaphor "pilgrimages" takes one far from its "proper places," in "Une métaphore du sens propre dans le *Roman de la rose*," in *La Musique et les lettres*," pp. 381–82; and Callay, "Road to Salvation," p. 501.

57. Peur saves the rose in the "tournament."

58. Cf. v. 18327–34.

59. See *Rose*, ed. Strubel p. 1063 n.

CONCLUSION: JEAN DE MEUN AS *MORALISTE*

1. Nykrog, *L'amour et la rose*, p. 79, suggests this idea, but elaborates it differently from the way I do. On what follows, see the entries in Oscar Bloch and Walther von Wartburg, *Dictionnaire étymologique de la langue française*; and Alain Rey, *Dictionnaire historique de la langue française*; as well as Jürgen von Stackelberg, *Französische Moralistik*, especially chap. 1, "Zum Begriff Moralistik."

2. " 'Jean de Meung,' Antifeminism, and 'Bourgeois Realism,' " p. 14; cf. Calin, *Muse for Heroes*, pp. 128–29.

3. Quilligan, *Language of Allegory*, p. 241. See as well Nichols, "Rhetoric of Sincerity," pp. 127–29.

4. *Le Débat*, p. 145.973.

5. *Autres ballades* and *Cent ballades* (following quotation) are quoted from Christine de Pizan, *Œuvres poétiques*.

6. From *Œuvres*, 3:166–67. See also Krueger, *Women Readers*, chap. 8.

7. Christine de Pizan, *Le livre des trois vertus*, pp. 110–20; for the passage quoted, see p. 115.146–58.

8. "*Livre de la Cité des dames* of Christine de Pisan," p. 775, in reference to Dido as a *femme forte* because of the prudence she manifests in escaping her brother Pygmalion and founding Carthage; see also pp. 765–75. For Christine, "virago" is a Latin noun.

9. Cf. Diderot's words on this eighteenth-century *ribaut*: "Je n'estime pas ces originaux-là. D'autres en font leurs connaissances familières, même leurs amis. Ils m'arrêtent une fois l'an, quand je les rencontre, parce que leur caractère tranche avec celui des autres, et qu'ils rompent cette fastidieuse uniformité que notre éducation, nos conventions de société, nos bienséances d'usage, ont introduite. S'il en paraît un dans une compagnie, c'est un grain de levain qui fermente et qui restitue à chacun une portion de son individualité naturelle. Il secoue, il agite, il fait approuver ou blâmer; il fait sortir la vérité; il fait connaître les gens de bien; il démasque les coquins; c'est alors que l'homme de bon sens écoute, et démêle son monde." In *Le neveu de Rameau*, pp. 25–26.

10. Cf. A. J. Minnis, "Theorizing the Rose," p. 22. On *exaggeratio* as overstatement, see my *Art of Medieval French Romance*, p. 50.

11. Tuve, *Allegorical Imagery*, p. 251.

12. From Molière, *Théâtre*, 2:129.

13. "*Livre de la Cité des dames* of Christine de Pisan," §4a.

14. Ibid., §7: "Une cité . . . en laquelle n'abitera fors toutes dames de renommee et femmes dignes de loz: car a celles ou vertu ne sera trouvee, les murs de nostre cité seront forclos" [a city in which will live only famous ladies and women worthy of praise; for those lacking virtue will be shut out of our city], just as the gates of paradise will be closed to all those who take Genius's sermon literally.

Bibliography

PRIMARY WORKS

Editions and Translations of the *Roman de la rose*

Quotations and other references to the *Roman de la rose* are from Félix Lecoy's edition for the Classiques français du moyen âge. I have also consulted the following editions by Langlois, Poirion, and Strubel and compared their readings with Lecoy's. Important differences are discussed where it is appropriate. Translations are mine except when otherwise specified. But I have compared my translations of quotations from the *Rose* with those of Charles Dahlberg, *The Romance of the Rose*, and those in Strubel's facing translation. All foreign languages are translated except modern French. The epigraph, including punctuation, is taken from Emily Dickinson, *The Poems*, §258.

Dahlberg, Charles, trans. *The Romance of the Rose*, by Guillaume de Lorris and Jean de Meun. Princeton: Princeton University Press, 1971.

Langlois, Ernest, ed. *Le Roman de la rose*, by Guillaume de Lorris and Jean de Meun. 5 vols. Société des Anciens Textes français. Paris: Firmin-Didot, Champion, 1914–24.

Lecoy, Félix, ed. *Le Roman de la rose*, by Guillaume de Lorris and Jean de Meun. 3 vols. Classiques français du moyen âge, 92, 95, 98. Paris: Champion, 1965–70.

Méon, Dominique Martin, ed. *Le Roman de la rose*, by Guillaume de Lorris and Jean de Meun. 4 vols. Paris: Didot l'Aîné, 1814.

Poirion, Daniel, ed. *Le Roman de la rose*, by Guillaume de Lorris and Jean de Meun. Paris: Garnier-Flammarion, 1974.

Strubel, Armand, ed. and trans. *Le Roman de la rose*, by Guillaume de Lorris and Jean de Meun. Lettres Gothiques. Paris: Librairie Générale Française-Livre de poche, 1992.

Other Primary Sources

Adam of Bremen. *Gesta Hammaburgensis ecclesiae pontificum ex recensione Lappenbergii*. Ed. G. Waitz. 2nd ed. In usum scholarum ex Monumentis Germaniae historicis recusa. Hannover: Hahn, 1876.

Ad C. Herennium De ratione dicendi (Rhetorica ad Herennium). Ed. and trans. Harry Caplan. Loeb Classical Library. Cambridge: Harvard University Press; London: Heinemann, 1954.

Aelred of Rievaulx. *Opera omnia: I. Opera ascetica.* Ed. A. Hoste and C. H. Talbot. Corpus Christianorum: continuatio mediaeualis, 1. Turnhout: Brepols, 1971.

Alain de Lille. *Anticlaudianus.* Ed. R. Bossaut. Textes philosophiques du moyen âge 1. Paris: Vrin, 1955.

Alain de Lille. *Anticlaudianus or The Good and Perfect Man.* Trans. James J. Sheridan. Toronto: Pontifical Institute of Medieval Studies, 1973.

Altfranzösische Übersetzung der "Consolatio philosophiae" des Boethius (Handschrift Troyes Nr. 898): Edition und Kommentar. Ed. Rolf Schroth. Europäische Hochschulschriften, ser. 13: Französische Sprache und Literatur, 36. Bern: H. Lang; Frankfurt am Main: P. Lang, 1976.

Andreas Capellanus. *De amore libri tres.* Ed. E. Trojel. Copenhagen: Gadiana, 1892.

Benoît de Sainte-Maure. *Le Roman de Troie.* Ed. Léopold Constans. 6 vols. Société des Anciens Textes français. Paris: Firmin-Didot, 1904–12.

Biblia sacra iuxta vulgatam Clementinam nova editio. 4th ed. Madrid: Biblioteca de Autores Cristianos, 1965.

Boethius. *Philosophiae consolatio.* Ed. Ludovicus Bieler. Corpus Christianorum: series latina, 44. Turnhout: Brepols, 1984.

Bretel, Jacques. *Le tournoi de Chauvency.* Ed. Maurice Delbouille. Bibliothèque de la Faculté de Philosophie et Lettres de l'Université de Liége, 49. Liége: Vaillant-Carmanne; Paris: Droz, 1932.

Butors, Bauduins. "The Four Rough Drafts of Bauduins Butors." Ed. Lewis Thorpe. *Nottingham Mediaeval Studies* 12 (1968): 3–20, 13 (1969): 49–64, 14 (1970): 41–63.

Chaucer, Geoffrey. *The Riverside Chaucer.* 3rd ed. Ed. Larry D. Benson. Boston: Houghton Mifflin, 1987.

Chrétien de Troyes. *Le chevalier au lion (Yvain).* Ed. Mario Roques. Classiques français du moyen âge, 89. Paris: Champion, 1982.

Chrétien de Troyes. *Le chevalier de la charrette (Lancelot).* Ed. Alfred Foulet and Karl D. Uitti. Classiques Garnier. Paris: Bordas, 1989.

Christine de Pizan. "Classical Mythology in the Works of Christine de Pisan, with an Edition of *L'Epistre Othea* from the Manuscript Harley 4431." Ph.D. diss., Wayne State University, 1977.

Christine de Pizan. "The *Livre de la Cité des dames* of Christine de Pisan: A Critical Edition." Ed. Maureen Cheney Curnow. Ph.D. diss., Vanderbilt, 1975.

Christine de Pizan. *Le livre des trois vertus.* Ed. Charity Cannon Willard and Eric Hicks. Bibliothèque du XVe siècle, 50. Paris: Champion, 1989.

Christine de Pizan. *Œuvres poétiques.* Ed. Maurice Roy. 3 vols. Société des Anciens Textes français. Paris: Firmin-Didot, 1886–96.

Christine de Pizan. *Poems of Cupid, God of Love: Christine de Pizan's "Epistre au dieu d'Amours" and "Dit de la Rose"—Thomas Hoccleve's "The Letter of Cupid" with George Sewell's "The Proclamation of Cupid".* Ed. and trans.

Thelma S. Fenster and Mary Carpenter Erler. Leiden, New York, Copenhagen and Cologne: Brill, 1990.

*Le Commentaire de Copenhague de l'*Ovide moralisé *avec l'edition du Septième Livre*. Ed. Jeannette Theodora Marie van t'Sant. Amsterdam: H. J. Paris, 1929.

Dante Alighieri. *Opere minori*. Ed. Arsenio Frugani and Giorgio Brugnoli, Vol. 2. In *La letteratura italiana: storia e testi*. Milan and Naples: Ricciardi, 1973.

Le Débat sur le Roman de la rose. Ed. Eric Hicks. Bibliothèque du XVe siècle, 43. Paris: Champion, 1977.

Dickinson, Emily. *The Poems*. Ed. Thomas H. Johnson. 3 vols. Cambridge and London: Harvard University Press, 1951, 1955, 1979.

Diderot, Denis. *Le Neveu de Rameau*. Ed. Jean-Pol Caput. Nouveaux Classiques Larousse. Paris: Larousse, 1972.

Les Échecs amoureux. Die Liebesgarten-Allegorie der Échecs amoureux: *kritische Ausgabe und Kommentar*. Ed. Christine Kraft. Europäische Hochschulschriften, ser. 13: Französische Sprache und Literatur, 48. Frankfurt am Main, Bern, and Las Vegas: P. Lang, 1977.

Les Échecs amoureux Commentary. B. N. ms. fr. 9197.

Exposé sur le Cantique des cantiques. Ed. J.-M. Déchanet. Trans. M. Dumontier. Sources chrétiennes, 82. Paris: du Cerf, 1962.

Froissart, Jean. *Méliador*. Ed. Auguste Longnon. 3 vols. Société des Anciens Textes français. Paris: Firmin-Didot, 1895–99.

Froissart, Jean. *La prison amoureuse*. Ed. Anthime Fourrier. Bibliothèque française et romane, B13. Paris: Klinksieck, 1974.

Gerbert de Montreuil. *La continuation de Perceval*. Ed. Mary Williams and Marguerite Oswald. 3 vols. Classiques français du moyen âge, 28, 50, 101. Paris: Champion, 1922–73.

Gervase of Melkley. *Ars poetica* [= *versificaria*]. Ed. Hans-Jürgen Gräbener. Forschungen zur romanischen Philologie, 17. Münster: Aschendorff, 1965.

Hildegard of Bingen. *Scivias*. Ed. Adelgundis Führkötter and Angela Carlevaris. 2 vols. Corpus Christianorum: continuatio mediaeualis, 43. Turnhout: Brepols, 1978.

Historia troyana Daretis Frigii. Ed. Jürgen Stohlmann. Beihefte zum "Mittellateinischen Jahrbuch," 1. Wuppertal, Ratingen, and Düsseldorf: Henn, 1968.

Horace. *Ad Pisones*, in *Opera*. Ed. Edward C. Wickham and H. W. Garrod. 2nd ed. Oxford: Clarendon Press, 1901.

Hrabanus Maurus. *De clericorum institutione*. In Vol. 107 of *Patrologia latina*, 294–420, edited by J.-P. Migne. Paris: [n.p.], 1851.

Hrabanus Maurus. "Epistolae." Ed. Ernest Dümmler. In *Epistolae Karolini Aevi*. Vol. 3 of *Epistolarum Tomus V* of the *Monumenta Germaniae historica*. Berlin: Weidmann, 1899.

Hrotsvitha of Gandersheim. *Opera*. Ed. H. Homeyer. Munich, Paderborn, and Vienna: Schöningh, 1970.

Isidore of Seville. *Etymologiarum sive originum libri XX*. Ed. W. M. Lindsay. 2 vols. Oxford: Clarendon Press, 1911.

Jean de Meun. "Boethius' *De consolatione* by Jean de Meun." Ed. V. L. Dedeck-Héry. *Mediaeval Studies* 14 (1952): 165–275.

Jean de Meun. *Le Testament Maistre Jehan de Meun: un caso letterario*. Ed. Silvia Buzzetti Gallarati. Serie monografica: scrittura e scrittori, 4. Turin: dell'Orso, 1989.

Jean Le Fevre. *Le respit de la mort*. Ed. Geneviève Hasenohr-Esnos. Société des Anciens Textes français. Paris: Picard, 1969.

John of Garland. *Parisiana Poetria*. Ed. Traugott Lawler. Yale Studies in English, 182. New Haven and London: Yale University Press, 1974.

Joseph Iscanus. *Werke und Briefe*. Ed. Ludwig Gompf. Mittellateinische Studien und Texte, 4. Leiden and Cologne: Brill, 1970.

Lancelot. Ed. Alexandre Micha. Vol. 1. Textes littéraires français, 149. Geneva: Droz, 1978.

Latini, Brunetto. *Li Livres dou tresor*. Ed. Francis J. Carmody. University of California Publications in Modern Philology, 22. Berkeley and Los Angeles: University of California Press, 1948.

Macrobius. *Commentarii in Somnium Scipionis*. Ed. Jacobus Willis. Leipzig: Teubner, 1963.

Macrobius. *Saturnalia*. Ed. Jacobus Willis. Leipzig: Teubner, 1963.

Matthew of Vendôme. *Ars versificatoria*. In vol. 3, *Opera*. Ed. Franco Munari. Storia e Letteratura, 171. Rome: Storia e Letteratura, 1988.

Molière. *Théâtre*. 5 vols. Paris: Hachette, 1949.

Mölk, Ulrich, ed. *Französische Literarästhetik des 12. und 13. Jahrhunderts: Prologe-Excurse-Epiloge*. Sammlung romanischer Übungstexte, 54. Tübingen: Niemeyer, 1969.

Nouveau recueil complet des fabliaux (NRCF). Ed. Willem Noomen and Nico van den Boogard. 7 vols. to date. Assen and Maastricht: Van Gorcum, 1983–.

Oede de la Couroierie. "Die Gedichte Jehan's de Renti und Oede's de la Couroierie." Ed. Johannes Spanke. *Zeitschrift für französische Sprache und Literatur* 32 (1908): 157–218.

Oresme, Nicole. *Le Livre de ethiques d'Aristote*. Ed. Albert Douglas Menut. New York: Stechert, 1940.

L'Ovide moralisé. Ed. C. de Boer. Verhandelingen der koninklijke Akademie van Wetenschappen te Amsterdam: Afdeeling Letterkunde, n.s., 15, 21, 30.3, 37, 43. Amsterdam: Müller, 1915–38.

Le Parnasse satyrique du quinzième siècle. Ed. Marcel Schwob. Paris: Welter, 1905.

Patrologiae cursus completus: series latina—Supplementum. Ed. Adalbertus Hamman. 5 vols. Paris: Garnier, 1958–74.

Priscian. *Praeexercitamina*. In vol. 3, *Grammatici latini*. Ed. Heinrich Keil. Leipzig: Teubner, 1859.

"*La Querelle de la rose*": *Letters and Documents*. Trans. Joseph L. Baird and John R. Kane. North Carolina Studies in the Romance Languages and Literatures, 199. Chapel Hill: University of North Carolina Department of Romance Languages and Literatures, 1978.

La Queste del saint graal. Ed. Albert Pauphilet. Classiques français du moyen âge, 33. Paris: Champion, 1980.

Recueil général des jeux-partis français. Ed. Arthur Långfors, with A. Jeanroy and L. Brandin. 2 vols. Société des Anciens Textes français. Paris: Champion, 1926.

Le Roman d'Eneas. Ed. J.-J. Salverda de Grave. 2 vols. Classiques français du moyen âge, 44 and 62. Paris: Champion, 1925–29.

Le Roman de Renart: première branche. Ed. Mario Roques. Classiques français du moyen âge, 78. Paris: Champion, 1948.

Rutebeuf. *Œuvres complètes.* Ed. Edmond Faral amd Julia Bastin. 2 vols. Paris: Picard, 1969.

Scholia in Horatium א ב *in codicibus parisinis latinis 17897 et 8223 obvia, quae ab Heirico Autissiodorensi profecta esse videntur.* Ed. H. J. Botschuyver. Amsterdam: [n.p.], 1942.

Summa Parisiensis on the Decretum Gratiani. Ed. Terence P. McLaughlin. Toronto: Pontifical Institute of Mediaeval Studies, 1952.

Svevo, Italo. *La coscienza di Zeno.* Ed. Gabriella Contini. Oscar Narrativa, 730. Milan: Mondadori, 1985.

Svevo, Italo. *Novelle.* Ed. Gabriella Contini. Oscar Narrativa, 791. Milan: Mondadori, 1986.

Thibaut de Champagne. *Les chansons.* Ed. A. Wallensköld. Société des Anciens Textes français. Paris: Champion, 1925.

La Vie et les epistres: Pierres Abaelart et Heloys sa fame. Traduction du XIIIe siècle attribuée à Jean de Meun, avec une nouvelle édition des textes latins d'après le ms. Troyes Bibl. mun. 802. Ed. Eric Hicks. Vol. 1. Nouvelle Bibliothèque du moyen âge, 16. Paris: Champion, 1991.

Villon, François. *Le Lais Villon et les poèmes variés.* Ed. Jean Rychner and Albert Henry. Textes littéraires français, 239. Geneva: Droz, 1977.

Villon, François. *Œuvres.* Ed. Louis Thuasne. 3 vols. Paris: Picard, 1923.

Villon, François. *Le Testament.* Ed. Jean Rychner and Albert Henry. Textes littéraires français, 207. Geneva: Droz, 1974.

DICTIONARIES

Bloch, Oscar, and Walther von Wartburg. *Dictionnaire étymologique de la langue française.* 5th ed., rev. and enl. Paris: Presses Universitaires de France, 1968.

Du Cange. *Glossarium mediae et infimae latinitatis.* 10 vols. 1883–87. Reprint, Graz: Akademische Druck- und Verlagsanstalt, 1954.

Fowler, H. W. *A Dictionary of Modern English Usage.* 2nd ed., rev. by Sir Ernest Gowers. New York and Oxford: Oxford University Press, 1965.

Godefroy, Frédéric. *Dictionnaire de l'ancienne langue française.* 10 vols. Paris: Vieweg, 1881–88, Bouillon, 1889–1902.

Novum glossarium mediae latinitatis ab anno DCCC usque ad annum MCC. Ed. Franz Blatt and Jacques Monfrin. Copenhagen: Munksgaard, 1957–89.

Le petit Robert: dictionnaire alphabétique et analogique de la langue française. Ed. Paul Robert, A. Rey, and J. Rey-Debove. Rev. ed. Paris: Le Robert, 1981.

Rey, Alain. *Dictionnaire historique de la langue française.* 2 vols. Paris: Dictionnaires Le Robert; Montreal: Dicorobert, 1992.

Stefano, Giuseppe di. *Dictionnaire des locutions en moyen français.* Bibliothèque du moyen âge, 1. Montreal: CERES, 1991.

Thesaurus linguae latinae. Leipzig: Teubner, 1900–.

Tobler-Lommatzsch: Altfranzösisches Wörterbuch. Berlin: Weidmann, 1925–36, Steiner, 1952–.

Webster's New International Dictionary of the English Language. 2nd ed. Unabridged. Springfield, Mass.: Merriam, 1959.

SECONDARY SOURCES

Allen, Judson Boyce. *The Ethical Poetic of the Later Middle Ages: A Decorum of Convenient Distinction.* Toronto, Buffalo, and London: Toronto University Press, 1982.

Allen, Judson Boyce. *The Friar as Critic: Literary Attitudes in the Later Middle Ages.* Nashville: Vanderbilt University Press, 1971.

Allen, Peter L. "*Ars amandi, ars legendi*: Love Poetry and Literary Theory in Ovid, Andreas Capellanus, and Jean de Meun." *Exemplaria* 1 (1989): 181–205.

Allen, Peter L. *The Art of Love: Amatory Fiction from Ovid to the* Romance of the Rose. Middle Ages Series. Philadelphia: University of Pennsylvania Press, 1992.

Alvar, Carlos. "Oiseuse, Vénus, Luxure: trois dames et un miroir." *Romania* 106 (1985): 108–17.

Anderson, David. *Before the Knight's Tale: Imitation of Classical Epic in Boccaccio's "Teseida".* Middle Ages Series. Philadelphia: University of Pennsylvania Press, 1988.

Andrieux-Reix, Nelly. *Ancien français: fiches de vocabulaire.* Paris: Presses Universitaires de France, 1987.

Arden, Heather M. *The Romance of the Rose.* Twayne's World Authors Series (French Literature), 791. Boston: Twayne, 1987.

Arden, Heather M. *The Roman de la rose: An Annotated Bibliography.* Garland Medieval Bibliographies, 8 = Garland Reference Library of the Humanities, 1358. New York and London: Garland, 1993.

Atkinson, J. Keith, and Glynnis M. Cropp. "Trois traductions de la *Consolatio Philosophiae* de Boèce." *Romania* 106 (1985): 198–232.

Badel, Pierre-Yves. "Raison 'fille de Dieu' et le rationalisme de Jean de Meun." In *Mélanges de langue et de littérature française offerts à Jean Frappier par ses collègues, ses élèves et ses amis.* 2 vols. Publications romanes et françaises, 112. Geneva: Droz, 1970. Pp. 41–52.

Badel, Pierre-Yves. *Le* Roman de la rose *au XIVe siècle: étude de la réception de l'œuvre.* Publications romanes et françaises, 153. Geneva: Droz, 1980.

Baird, Joseph L. "Pierre Col and the *Querelle de la Rose.*" *Philological Quarterly* 60 (1982): 273–86.

Bibliography

Baird, Joseph L., and John R. Kane. "*La Querelle de la Rose*: In Defense of the Opponents." *French Review* 48 (1974): 298–307.

Baker, Denise N. "The Priesthood of Genius: A Study of the Medieval Tradition." *Speculum* 51 (1976): 277–91.

Batany, Jean. *Approches du* Roman de la rose: *ensemble de l'œuvre et vers 8227 à 12456*. Bordas Études, 363. Paris, Brussels, and Montréal: Bordas, 1973.

Batany, Jean. "Paradigmes lexicaux et structures littéraires au moyen âge." *Revue d'histoire littéraire de la France* 70 (1970): 819–35.

Baumgartner, Emmanuèle. "De Lucrèce à Héloïse: remarques sur deux *exemples* du *Roman de la rose* de Jean de Meun." *Romania* 95 (1974): 433–42.

Benedetto, Luigi Foscolo. *Il* Roman de la rose *e la letteratura italiana*. Beihefte zur Zeitschrift für romanische Philologie, 21. Halle: Niemeyer, 1910.

Bermejo, Esperanza. "Notas sobre las modalidades retóricas de inserción de anécdotas en el *Roman de la Rose* de Jean de Meun." In *La lengua y la literatura en tiempos de Alfonso X*. Actas del Congreso Internacional, Murcia, 5–10 marzo 1984. Ed. Fernando Carmona and Francisco J. Flores. Departamento de Literaturas Románicas, Facultad de Letras, Universidad de Murcia. Murcia: Sucesores de Nogués, 1985. Pp. 91–108.

Bezzola, Reto R. *Les origines et la formation de la littérature courtoise en Occident (500–1200). Deuxième partie: La société féodale et la transformation de la littérature de cour. Tome II: Les grandes maisons féodales après la chute des Carolingiens et leur influence sur les lettres jusqu'au XIIe siècle*. Bibliothèque de l'École des Hautes Études: Sciences historiques et philologiques, 313. Paris: Champion, 1960.

Blangez, Gérard. "Comment composait Jean de Meun (à partir d'une étude du *discours d'Ami*)." In *Etudes de langue et de littérature française offertes à André Lanly*. Nancy: Publications Nancy II, 1980. Pp. 31–36.

Bloch, R. Howard. *Etymologies and Genealogies: A Literary Anthropology of the French Middle Ages*. Chicago and London: University of Chicago Press, 1983.

Bloch, R. Howard. *Medieval Misogyny and the Invention of Western Romantic Love*. Chicago and London: University of Chicago Press, 1991.

Boswell, John. *Christianity, Social Tolerance, and Homosexuality: Gay People in Western Europe from the Beginning of the Christian Era to the Fourteenth Century*. Chicago and London: University of Chicago Press, 1980.

Bouché, Thérèse. "Burlesque et renouvellement des formes: l'attaque du château dans le *Roman de la rose* de Jean de Meun." In *Hommage à Jean-Charles Payen: Farai chansoneta novele—essais sur la liberté créatrice au moyen âge*. Caen: Centre de Publications de l'Université de Caen, 1989. Pp. 87–98.

Bouché, Thérèse. "L'obscène et le sacré ou l'utilisation paradoxale du rire dans le *Roman de la rose* de Jean de Meun." In *Le rire au moyen âge dans la littérature et dans les arts*. Actes du Colloque International des 17, 18 et 19 novembre 1988. Ed. Thérèse Bouché and Hélène Charpentier. Bordeaux: Presses Universitaires de Bordeaux, 1990. Pp. 83–95.

Bouché, Thérèse. "Ovide et Jean de Meun." *Moyen âge* 83 (1977): 71–87.

Bradley, Ritamary. "Backgrounds of the Title *Speculum* in Medieval Literature." *Speculum* 29 (1954): 100–115.

Brinkmann, Hennig. *Zu Wesen und Form mittelalterlicher Dichtung*. Darmstadt: Wissenschaftliche Buchgesellschaft, 1979.

Brook, Leslie Charles. "The Continuator's Monologue: Godefroy de Lagny and Jean de Meun." *French Studies* 45 (1991): 1–16.

Brook, Leslie Charles. "Love's External Foes: From the Lyric to the *Roman de la rose*." In *L'imaginaire courtois et son double*. Congrès Triennal de la Société Internationale de Littérature Courtoise (ICLS), Fisciano (Salerno), 24–28 juillet 1989. Ed. Giovanna Angeli and Luciano Formisano. Pubblicazioni dell'Università degli Studi di Salerno: Sezione Atti, Convegni, Miscellanee, 35. Naples: Edizioni Scientifiche Italiane, 1992. Pp. 255–69.

Brook, Leslie C. "The Pruned Rose: The Text of B.N. MS fr. 25524." *Romanische Forschungen* 105 (1993): 94–101.

Brownlee, Kevin. "Jean de Meun and the Limits of Romance: Genius as Rewriter of Guillaume de Lorris." In *Romance: Generic Transformation from Chrétien de Troyes to Cervantes*, ed. Kevin Brownlee and Marina Scordilis Brownlee. Hanover, N.H. and London: University Presses of New England for Dartmouth College, 1985. Pp. 114–34.

Brownlee, Kevin. "Orpheus' Song Re-Sung: Jean de Meun's Reworking of *Metamorphoses*, X." *Romance Philology* 36 (1982): 201–9.

Brownlee, Kevin. *Poetic Identity in Guillaume de Machaut*. Madison and London: University of Wisconsin Press, 1984.

Brownlee, Kevin. "The Problem of Faux Semblant: Language, History, and Truth in the *Roman de la rose*." In *The New Medievalism*, ed. Marina S. Brownlee, Kevin Brownlee, and Stephen G. Nichols. Baltimore and London: The Johns Hopkins University Press, 1991. Pp. 253–71.

Brownlee, Kevin. "Reflections in the *Miroër aus Amoreus*: The Inscribed Reader in Jean de Meun's *Roman de la rose*." In *Mimesis: From Mirror to Method, Augustine to Descartes*, ed. John D. Lyons and Stephen G. Nichols, Jr. Hanover, N.H. and London: University Presses of New England for Dartmouth College, 1982. Pp. 60–70, 257–58.

Bruckner, Matilda Tomaryn. "An Interpreter's Dilemma: Why Are There So Many Interpretations of Chrétien's *Chevalier de la charrette*?" *Romance Philology* 40 (1986): 159–80.

Bruni, Francesco. "Boncompagno da Signa, Guido delle Colonne, Jean de Meung: metamorfosi dei classici nel Duecento." *Medioevo romanzo* 12 (1987): 103–28.

Burnley, J. D. "*Fine amor*: Its Meaning and Context." *Review of English Studies* 31 (1980): 29–48.

Busby, Keith. "*Cristal et Clarie*: A Novel Romance?" In *Convention and Innovation in Literature*, ed. Theo D'haen, Rainer Grübel, and Helmut Lethen. Utrecht Publications in General and Comparative Literature, 24. Amsterdam and Philadelphia: Benjamins, 1989. Pp. 77–103.

Cahoon, Leslie. "Raping the Rose: Jean de Meun's Reading of Ovid's *Amores*." *Classical and Modern Literature* 6 (1986): 261–85.

Calin, William. *A Muse for Heroes: Nine Centuries of the Epic in France.* Toronto, Buffalo, and London: University of Toronto Press, 1983.

Callay, Brigitte L. "The Road to Salvation in the *Roman de la rose.*" In *Pascua Mediaevalia: Studies voor Prof. Dr. J. M. De Smet*, ed. R. Lievens, E. Van Mingroot, and W. Verbeke. Mediaevalia Lovaniensia, 1.10. Leuven: Universitaire Pers Leuven, 1983. Pp. 499–509.

Cerquiglini, Jacqueline. "Le clerc et l'écriture: le *voir dit* de Guillaume de Machaut et la définition du *dit.*" In *Literatur in der Gesellschaft des Spätmittelalters*, ed. Hans Ulrich Gumbrecht. Begleitreihe zum Grundriß der romanischen Literaturen des Mittelalters, 1. Heidelberg: Winter, 1980. Pp. 151–68.

Cerquiglini, Jacqueline. "Polysémie, ambiguïté et équivoque dans la théorie et la pratique poétiques du moyen âge français." In *L'ambiguïté: cing études historiques*, ed. Irène Rosier. Lille: Presses Universitaires de Lille, 1988. Pp. 167–80.

Cherniss, Michael D. "Jean de Meun's Reson and Boethius." *Romance Notes* 16 (1975): 678–85.

Copeland, Rita. *Rhetoric, Hermeneutics, and Translation in the Middle Ages: Academic Traditions and Vernacular Texts.* Cambridge Studies in Medieval Literature, 11. Cambridge: Cambridge University Press, 1991.

Cropp, Glynnis M. "*Le livre de Boece de consolacion*: From Translation to Glossed Text." In *The Medieval Boethius: Studies in the Vernacular Translations of* De consolatione Philosophiae, ed. A. J. Minnis. Cambridge: D. S. Brewer, 1987. Pp. 63–88.

Cropp, Glynnis M. "Le prologue de Jean de Meun et *Le livre de Boece de Consolacion.*" *Romania* 103 (1982): 278–98.

Dahlberg, Charles. "First Person and Personification in the *Roman de la rose*: Amant and Dangier." *Mediaevalia* 3 (1977): 37–58.

Dahlberg, Charles. *The Literature of Unlikeness.* Hanover, N.H. and London: University Press of New England, 1988.

Dahlberg, Charles. "Love and the *Roman de la rose.*" *Speculum* 44 (1969): 568–84.

Demats, Paule. *Fabula: trois études de mythographie antique et médiévale.* Publications romanes et françaises, 122. Geneva: Droz, 1973.

Dembowski, Peter F. "Le Faux Semblant et la problématique des masques et déguisements." In *Masques et déguisements dans la littérature médiévale*, ed. Marie-Louise Ollier. Études médiévales. Montreal: Presses de l'Université de Montréal; Paris: Vrin, 1988. Pp. 43–53.

Dinshaw, Carolyn. *Chaucer's Sexual Poetics.* Madison and London: University of Wisconsin Press, 1989

Dornbush, Jean M. *Pygmalion's Figure: Reading Old French Romance.* Edward C. Armstrong Monographs on Medieval Literature, 5. Lexington, Ky.: French Forum, 1990.

Dragonetti, Roger. *"La musique et les lettres": études de littérature médiévale.* Publications romanes et françaises, 171. Geneva: Droz, 1986.

Dronke, Peter. *Fabula: Explorations into the Uses of Myth in Medieval Platonism.* Mittellateinische Studien und Texte, 9. Leiden and Cologne: Brill, 1974.

Dronke, Peter. "Francesca and Héloïse." *Comparative Literature* 27 (1975): 113–35.

Eberle, Patricia J. "The Lovers' Glass: Nature's Discourse on Optics and the Optical Design of the *Romance of the Rose*." *University of Toronto Quarterly* 46 (1977): 241–62.

Economou, George D. *The Goddess Natura in Medieval Literature*. Cambridge: Harvard University Press, 1972.

Economou, George D. "The Two Venuses and Courtly Love." In *In Pursuit of Perfection: Courtly Love in Medieval Literature*, ed. Joan M. Ferrante and George D. Economou. Port Washington, N.Y., and London: Kennikat, 1975. Pp. 17–50.

Edwards, Robert R. "Poetic Invention and the Medieval *Causae*." *Mediaeval Studies* 55 (1993): 183–217.

Emmerson, Richard Kenneth, and Ronald B. Herzman. "The Apocalyptic Age of Hypocrisy: Faus Semblant and Amant in the *Roman de la rose*." *Speculum* 62 (1987): 612–34.

Faral, Edmond. *Les arts poétiques du XIIe et du XIIIe siècle: recherches et documents sur la technique littéraire du moyen âge*. Bibliothèque de l'École des Hautes Études, 238. Paris: Champion, 1924.

Faral, Edmond. "*Le Roman de la rose* et la pensée française au XIIIe siècle." *Revue des deux mondes*, 7th ser., 35 (1926): 430–57.

Ferrante, Joan M. "*Cortes'Amor* in Medieval Texts." *Speculum* 55 (1980): 686–95.

Fleming, John V. "Carthaginian Love: Text and Supertext in the *Roman de la rose*." *Assays* 1 (1981): 51–72.

Fleming, John V. "Jean de Meun and the Ancient Poets." In *Rethinking the* Romance of the Rose*: Text, Image, Reception*, ed. Kevin Brownlee and Sylvia Huot. Middle Ages Series. Philadelphia: University of Pennsylvania Press, 1992. Pp. 81–100.

Fleming, John V. "The Moral Reputation of the *Roman de la rose* before 1400." *Romance Philology* 18 (1965): 430–35.

Fleming, John V. *Reason and the Lover*. Princeton: Princeton University Press, 1984.

Fleming, John V. *The* Roman de la rose*: A Study in Allegory and Iconography*. Princeton: Princeton University Press, 1969.

Frappier, Jean. "Variations sur le thème du miroir, de Bernard de Ventadour à Maurice Scève." *Cahiers de l'Association Internationale des Etudes Françaises* 11 (1959): 134–58.

Freeman, Michelle A. "Problems in Romance Composition: Ovid, Chrétien de Troyes, and the *Romance of the Rose*." *Romance Philology* 30 (1976): 158–168.

Friedman, Lionel J. "Gradus amoris." *Romance Philology* 19 (1965): 167–77.

Friedman, Lionel J. "Jean de Meun and Ethelred of Rievaulx." *L'esprit créateur* 2 (1962): 135–41.

Friedman, Lionel J. " 'Jean de Meung,' Antifeminism, and 'Bourgeois Realism.' " *Modern Philology* 57 (1959): 13–23.

Friedman, Lionel J. "Occulta cordis." *Romance Philology* 11 (1957): 103–19.

Friis-Jensen, Karsten. "The *Ars poetica* in Twelfth-Century France: The Horace of Matthew of Vendôme, Geoffrey of Vinsauf, and John of Garland." *Cahiers de l'Institut du Moyen-Age Grec et Latin, Université de Copenhague* 60 (1990): 319–88.

Gallo, Ernest. "The *Poetria nova* of Geoffrey of Vinsauf." In *Medieval Eloquence: Studies in the Theory and Practice of Medieval Rhetoric*, ed. James J. Murphy. Berkeley, Los Angeles, London: University of California Press, 1978. Pp. 68–84.

Galpin, Stanley L. "Les eschez amoureux: A Complete Synopsis, with Unpublished Extracts." *Romanic Review* 11 (1920): 283–307.

Gier, Albert. "L'amour, les monologues: le *Lai de Narcisse*." In *Conjunctures: Medieval Studies in Honor of Douglas Kelly*, ed. Keith Busby and Norris J. Lacy. Faux Titre, 83. Amsterdam and Atlanta: Rodopi, 1994. Pp. 129–37.

Goldin, Frederick. *The Mirror of Narcissus in the Courtly Love Lyric*. Ithaca and London: Cornell University Press, 1967.

Gravdal, Kathryn. *Ravishing Maidens: Writing Rape in Medieval French Literature and Law*. New Cultural Studies Series. Philadelphia: University of Pennsylvania Press, 1991.

Grevisse, Maurice. *Le bon usage: grammaire française avec des remarques sur la langue française d'aujourd'hui*. 7th ed. Gembloux: Duculot; Paris: Geuthner, 1961.

Grosse, Max. *Das Buch im Roman: Studien zu Buchverweis und Autoritätszitat in altfranzösischen Texten*. Munich: Fink, 1994.

Grundriß der romanischen Literaturen des Mittelalters. Vol. 8.1, *La littérature française aux XIV*[e] *et XV*[e] *siècles*. Ed. Daniel Poirion. Heidelberg: Winter, 1988.

Grünkorn, Gertrud. "Zum Verständnis von fiktionaler Rede im Hochmittelalter: Das Verhältnis von lateinischer Kommentartradition und höfischem Roman." In *Fiktionalität im Artusroman*. Dritte Tagung der Deutschen Sektion der Internationalen Artusgesellschaft in Berlin vom 13.–15. Februar 1992. Ed. Volker Mertens and Friedrich Wolfzettel, with Matthias Meyer and Hans–Jochen Schiewer. Tübingen: Niemeyer, 1993. Pp. 29–44.

Gunn, Alan M. F. *The Mirror of Love: A Reinterpretation of* The Romance of the Rose. Lubbock: Texas Tech Press, 1952.

Harley, Marta Powell. "Narcissus, Hermaphroditus, and Attis: Ovidian Lovers at the Fontaine d'Amors in Guillaume de Lorris." *PMLA* 101 (1986): 324–37.

Heffernan, Carol F. "The Bird-Snare Figure and the Love Quest of *The Romance of the Rose*." In *The Spirit of the Court*. Selected Proceedings of the Fourth Congress of the International Courtly Literature Society (Toronto 1983). Ed. Glyn S. Burgess and Robert A. Taylor. Cambridge: D. S. Brewer, 1985. Pp. 179–84.

Heinrich, Fritz. *Über den Stil von Guillaume de Lorris und Jean de Meung*. Ausgaben und Abhandlungen aus dem Gebiete der romanischen Philologie, 29. Marburg: Elwert, 1885.

Heitmann, Klaus. "Typen der Deformierung antiker Mythen im Mittelalter am Beispiel der Orpheussage." *Romanistisches Jahrbuch* 14 (1963): 45–77.

Hicks, Eric. "Sous les pavés, le sens: le dire et le décorum allégoriques dans *Le roman de la rose* de Jean de Meun." *Études de lettres* 2–3 (1987): 113–32.

Hilder, Gisela. *Der scholastische Wortschatz bei Jean de Meun: die Artes liberales*. Beihefte zur Zeitschrift für romanische Philologie, 129. Tübingen: Niemeyer. 1972.

Hill, Thomas D. "Narcissus, Pygmalion, and the Castration of Saturn: Two Mythographical Themes in the *Roman de la Rose*." *Studies in Philology* 71 (1974): 404–26.

Hult, David F. "Closed Quotations: The Speaking Voice in the *Roman de la Rose*." *Yale French Studies* 67 (1984): 248–69.

Hult, David F. "Gui de Mori: lecteur médiéval." *Incidences*, n.s., 5.1 (1981): 53–70.

Hult, David F. "Language and Dismemberment: Abelard, Origin, and the *Romance of the Rose*." In *Rethinking the* Romance of the Rose*: Text, Image, Reception*, ed. Kevin Brownlee and Sylvia Huot. Middle Ages Series. Philadelphia: University of Pennsylvania Press, 1992. Pp. 101–30.

Hult, David F. *Self-Fulfilling Prophecies: Readership and Authority in the First* Roman de la rose. Cambridge: Cambridge University Press, 1986.

Hult, David F. "Vers la société de l'écriture: *Le roman de la rose*." *Poétique* 50 (1982): 155–72.

Hunt, R. W. "The Introductions to the 'Artes' in the Twelfth Century." In *Studia mediaevalia in honorem admodum reverendi patris Raymundi Josephi Martin*. Bruges: De Tempel, 1948. Pp. 85–112.

Huot, Sylvia. "Authors, Scribes, Remanieurs: A Note on the Textual History of the *Romance of the Rose*." In *Rethinking the* Romance of the Rose*: Text, Image, Reception*, ed. Kevin Brownlee and Sylvia Huot. Middle Ages Series. Philadelphia: University of Pennsylvania Press, 1992. Pp. 203–33.

Huot, Sylvia. "From *Roman de la rose* to *Roman de la poire*: The Ovidian Tradition and the Poetics of Courtly Literature." *Medievalia et Humanistica*, n.s., 13 (1985): 95–111.

Huot, Sylvia. *From Song to Book: The Poetics of Writing in Old French Lyric and Lyrical Narrative Poetry*. Ithaca and London: Cornell University Press, 1987.

Huot, Sylvia. "The Medusa Interpolation in the *Romance of the Rose*: Mythographic Program and Ovidian Intertext." *Speculum* 62 (1987): 865–77.

Huot, Sylvia. *The* Romance of the Rose *and Its Medieval Readers: Interpretation, Reception, Manuscript Transmission*. Cambridge Studies in Medieval Literature, 16. Cambridge: Cambridge University Press, 1993.

Ineichen, Gustav. "Le discours linguistique de Jean de Meun." *Romanistische Zeitschrift für Literaturgeschichte/Cahiers d'histoire des littératures romanes* 2 (1978): 245–51.

Jager, Eric. "Reading the *Roman* Inside Out: The Dream of Croesus as a *caveat lector*." *Medium Aevum* 57 (1988): 67–74.

Jauss, Hans Robert. "The Alterity and Modernity of Medieval Literature." *New Literary History* 10 (1979): 181–229.

Jung, Marc-René. "Gui de Mori et Guillaume de Lorris." *Vox romanica* 27 (1968): 106–37.

Jung, Marc-René. "Jean de Meun et l'allégorie." *Cahiers de l'Association Internationale des Études Françaises* 28 (1976): 21–36.

Jung, Marc-René. "Jean de Meun et son lecteur." *Romanistische Zeitschrift für Literaturgeschichte/Cahiers d'histoire des littératures romanes* 2 (1978): 241–44.

Kauke, Rainer. "Jupiter et Saturne chez Jean de Meun." *Romanistische Zeitschrift für Literaturgeschichte/Cahiers d'histoire des littératures romanes* 2 (1978): 258–63.

Kay, Sarah. *Subjectivity in Troubadour Poetry*. Cambridge Studies in French, 31. Cambridge: Cambridge University Press, 1990.

Keck, Sylvia. "Faux Semblant—guerrier du dieu d'amour." *Romanistische Zeitschrift für Literaturgeschichte/Cahiers d'histoire des littératures romanes* 2 (1978): 263–65.

Kelly, Douglas. "Amitié comme anti-amour: au-delà du *fin amour* de Jean de Meun à Christine de Pizan." In *Anteros*, ed. Ullrich Langer and Jan Miernowski. Caen: Paradigme, 1994. Pp. 75–98.

Kelly, Douglas. *The Art of Medieval French Romance*. Madison and London: University of Wisconsin Press, 1992.

Kelly, Douglas. *The Arts of Poetry and Prose*. Typologie des sources du moyen âge occidental, 59 (A-V.A.2*). Turnhout: Brepols, 1991.

Kelly, Douglas. "Assimilation et montage dans l'amplification descriptive: la démarche du poète dans le Dit du XIVe siècle." In *Mittelalterbilder aus neuer Perspektive: Diskussionsanstöße zu amour courtois, Subjektivität in der Dichtung und Strategien des Erzählens*. Kolloquium Würzburg 1984. Ed. Ernstpeter Ruhe and Rudolf Behrens. Beiträge zur romanischen Philologie des Mittelalters, 14. Munich: Fink, 1985. Pp. 289–301.

Kelly, Douglas, " 'Li chastiaus . . . Qu'Amors prist puis par ses esforz': The Conclusion of Guillaume de Lorris' *Rose*." In *A Medieval French Miscellany*. Papers of the 1970 Kansas Conference on Medieval French Literature. Ed. Norris J. Lacy. University of Kansas Humanistic Studies, 42. Lawrence: University of Kansas Publications, 1972. Pp. 61–78.

Kelly, Douglas. "Courtly Love in Perspective: The Hierarchy of Love in Andreas Capellanus." *Traditio* 24 (1968): 119–47.

Kelly, Douglas. "Image et imagination dans les inventions des poètes: miroir et réceptivité dans les Dits allégoriques." In *L'image au moyen âge*. Actes du Colloque Amiens 19–23 avril 1986. Wodan: recherches en littérature médiévale, 15. Göppingen: Kümmerle, 1992. Pp. 137–49.

Kelly, Douglas. "L'invention dans les romans en prose." In *The Craft of Fiction: Essays in Medieval Poetics*, ed. Leigh A. Arrathoon. Rochester, Mich.: Solaris, 1984. Pp. 119–42.

Kelly, Douglas. "Le jeu de la vérité." In *Chrétien de Troyes: Le Chevalier au lion. Approches d'un chef-d'œuvre*, ed. Jean Dufournet. Unichamp, 20. Paris: Champion, 1988. Pp. 105–17.

Kelly, Douglas. *Medieval Imagination: Rhetoric and the Poetry of Courtly Love*. Madison and London: University of Wisconsin Press, 1978.

Kelly, Douglas. "The Rhetoric of Adventure in Medieval Romance." In *Chrétien de Troyes and the Troubadours: Essays in Memory of the late Leslie Topsfield*. Ed. Peter S. Noble and Linda M. Paterson. Cambridge: Saint Catharine's College, 1984. Pp. 172–85.

Kelly, Douglas. "Romance and the Vanity of Chrétien de Troyes." In *Romance: Generic Transformation from Chrétien de Troyes to Cervantes*, ed. Kevin Brownlee and Marina Scordilis Brownlee. Hanover and London: University Press of New England for Dartmouth College, 1985. Pp. 74–90.

Kelly, Douglas. "Theory of Composition in Medieval Narrative Poetry and Geoffrey of Vinsauf's *Poetria nova*." *Mediaeval Studies* 31 (1969): 117–48.

Kelly, Douglas. "Topical Invention in Medieval French Literature." In *Medieval Eloquence: Studies in the Theory and Practice of Medieval Rhetoric*, ed. James J. Murphy. Berkeley and Los Angeles: University of California Press, 1978. Pp. 231–51.

Kelly, Henry Ansgar. *Ideas and Forms of Tragedy from Aristotle to the Middle Ages*. Cambridge Studies in Medieval Literature, 18. Cambridge: Cambridge University Press, 1993.

Kennedy, Elspeth. *Lancelot and the Grail: A Study of the Prose "Lancelot"*. Oxford: Clarendon Press, 1986.

King, Peter. "Flos Veneris." in *Essays Presented to G. I. Lieftinck*. Vol. 2, *Texts and Manuscripts*, ed. J. P. Gumbert and M. J. M. De Haan. Litterae textuales. Amsterdam: van Gendt, 1972. Pp. 61–72.

Knoespel, Kenneth J. *Narcissus and the Invention of Personal History*. Garland Publications in Comparative Literature. New York and London: Garland, 1985.

Kolb, Herbert. "*Oiseuse*: die Dame mit dem Spiegel." *Germanisch-romanische Monatsschrift*, n.s., 15 (1965): 139–49.

Krueger, Robert L. *Women Readers and the Ideology of Gender in Old French Verse Romance*. Cambridge Studies in French, 43. Cambridge: Cambridge University Press, 1993.

Kuhn, David. *La poétique de François Villon*. Paris: Colin, 1967.

Kuster, Harry J., and Raymond J. Cormier. "Old Views and New Trends: Observations on the Problem of Homosexuality in the Middle Ages." *Studi medievali*, 3d ser., 25 (1984): 587–610.

Langer, Ullrich. *Divine and Poetic Freedom in the Renaissance: Nominalist Theology and Literature in France and Italy*. Princeton: Princeton University Press, 1990.

Langlois, Ernest. *Les manuscrits du* Roman de la rose*: description et classement*. Travaux et Mémoires de l'Université de Lille, n.s., 1: Droit et Lettres, 7. Lille: Tallandier; Paris: Champion, 1910.

Langlois, Ernest. *Origines et sources du Roman de la rose*. Bibliothèque des Études Françaises d'Athènes et de Rome, 58. Paris: Thorin, 1891.

Latzke, Therese. "Der Fürstinnenpreis." *Mittellateinisches Jahrbuch* 14 (1979): 22–65.

Lausberg, Heinrich. *Handbuch der literarischen Rhetorik: eine Grundlegung der Literaturwissenschaft*. 2 vols. Munich: Hueber, 1960.

Lefay-Toury, Marie-Noëlle. *La tentation du suicide dans le roman français du XIIe siècle*. Essais sur le moyen-âge, 4. Paris: Champion, 1979.

Leupin, Alexandre. "Écriture naturelle et écriture hermaphrodite: le *De planctu Naturae* d'Alain de Lille, un art poétique du XIIe siècle." *Digraphe* 9 (1979): 119–30.

Lewis, C. S. *The Allegory of Love: A Study in Medieval Tradition*. New York: Oxford University Press, 1958.

Louis, René. *Le* Roman de la rose*: essai d'interprétation de l'allégorisme érotique*. Nouvelle Bibliothèque du moyen âge, 1. Paris: Champion, 1974.

Luria, Maxwell. "A Sixteenth-Century Gloss on the *Roman de la rose*." *Mediaeval Studies* 44 (1982): 333–70.

Lynch, Kathryn L. *The High Medieval Dream Vision: Poetry, Philosophy, and Literary Form*. Stanford: Stanford University Press, 1988.

McGuire, Brian Patrick. *Friendship and Community: The Monastic Experience 350–1250*. Cistercian Studies Series, 95. Kalamazoo: Cistercian Publications, 1988.

McLeod, Glenda. "Poetics and Antimisogynist Polemics in Christine de Pizan's *Le livre de la Cité des dames*." In *Reinterpreting Christine de Pizan*, ed. Earl Jeffrey Richards, with Joan Williamson, Nadia Margolis, and Christine Reno. Athens and London: University of Georgia Press, 1992. Pp. 37–47.

McLeod, Glenda. *Virtues and Venom: Catalogs of Women from Antiquity to the Renaissance*. Ann Arbor: University of Michigan Press, 1991.

Matarasso, Pauline. *The Redemption of Chivalry: A Study of the* Queste del saint graal. Histoire des idées et critique littéraire, 180. Geneva: Droz, 1979.

Mathew, Gervase. "Ideals of Friendship." In *Patterns of Love and Courtesy: Essays in Memory of C. S. Lewis*. Ed. John Lawlor. London: Arnold, 1966. Pp. 45–53.

Méla, Charles. " 'Poetria nova' et 'homo novus.' " *Littérature* 74 (1989): 4–26.

Messelaar, P. A. *Le vocabulaire des idées dans le "Tresor" de Brunet Latin*. Assen: Van Gorcum, 1963.

Milan, Paul B. "The Golden Age and the Political Theory of Jean de Meun: A Myth in *Rose* Scholarship." *Symposium* 23 (1969): 137–49.

Minnis, Alistair J. "Aspects of the Medieval French and English Traditions of the *De Consolatione Philosophiae*." In *Boethius: His Life, Thought and Influence*, ed. Margaret Gibson. Oxford: Blackwell, 1981. Pp. 312–61.

Minnis, Alistair J. *Medieval Theory of Authorship: Scholastic Literary Attitudes in the Later Middle Ages*. London: Scolar Press, 1984.

Minnis, Alistair J. "Theorizing the Rose: Commentary Tradition in the *Querelle de la Rose*." In *Poetics: Theory and Practice in Medieval English Literature*. The J. A. W. Bennett Memorial Lectures, Seventh Series, Perugia, 1990. Ed. Piero Boitani and Anna Torti. Cambridge: D. S. Brewer, 1991. Pp. 13–36.

Muela Ezquerra, Julián "Técnicas retóricas y producción del sentido en el episodio de Pigmalión del Roman de la Rose." In *La lengua y la literatura en tiempos de Alfonso X*. Actas del Congreso Internacional, Murcia, 5–10 marzo 1984. Ed. Fernando Carmona and Francisco J. Flores. Departamento de Literaturas Románicas, Facultad de Letras, Universidad de Murcia. Murcia: Sucesores de Nogués, 1985. Pp. 373–92.

Munk Olsen, Birger. *L'étude des auteurs classiques latins aux XIe et XIIe siècles.* 3 vols. Paris: Editions du Centre National de la Recherche Scientifique, 1982–89.

Muscatine, Charles. "Courtly Literature and Vulgar Language." In *Court and Poet.* Selected Proceedings of the Third Congress of the International Courtly Literature Society (Liverpool 1980). Ed. Glyn S. Burgess. ARCA: Classical and Medieval Texts, Papers and Monographs, 5. Liverpool: Cairns, 1981. Pp. 1–19.

Newman, Barbara. "Flaws in the Golden Bowl: Gender and Spiritual Formation in the Twelfth Century." *Traditio* 45 (1989–90): 111–46.

Nichols, Stephen G. "Ekphrasis, Iconoclasm, and Desire." In *Rethinking the* Romance of the Rose*: Text, Image, Reception*, ed. Kevin Brownlee and Sylvia Huot. Middle Ages Series. Philadelphia: University of Pennsylvania Press, 1992. Pp. 133–66.

Nichols, Stephen. "The Rhetoric of Sincerity in the *Roman de la rose.*" In *Romance Studies in Memory of Edward Billings Ham.* Ed. Urban T. Holmes. California State College Publications, 2. Hayward: California State College, 1967. Pp. 115–29.

Nitzsche, Jane Chance. *The Genius Figure in Antiquity and the Middle Ages.* New York and London: Columbia University Press, 1975.

Nouvet, Claire. "Les inter-dictions courtoises: le jeu des deux bouches." *Romanic Review* 76 (1985): 233–50.

Nykrog, Per. *L'amour et la rose: le grand dessein de Jean de Meun.* Harvard Studies in Romance Languages and Literatures 41. Cambridge: Department of Romance Languages and Literatures of Harvard University; Lexington, Ky.: French Forum, 1986.

Nykrog, Per. *Les fabliaux.* Publications romanes et françaises, 123. Geneva: Droz, 1973.

Ott, Karl-August. "Jean de Meun und Boethius: über Aufbau und Quellen des Rosenromans." In *Philologische Studien: Gedenkschrift für Richard Kienast*, ed. Ute Schwab and Elfriede Stutz. Germanische Bibliothek: ser. 3. Untersuchungen und Einzeldarstellungen. Heidelberg: Winter, 1978. Pp. 193–227.

Ott, Karl-August. "Neuere Untersuchungen über den Rosenroman: zum gegenwärtigen Stand der Forschung." *Zeitschrift für romanische Philologie* 104 (1988): 80–95.

Ott, Karl-August. "Pauvreté et richesse chez Guillaume de Lorris." *Romanistische Zeitschrift für Literaturgeschichte/Cahiers d'histoire des littératures romanes* 2 (1978): 224–39.

Ott, Karl-August. *Der Rosenroman.* Erträge der Forschung, 145. Darmstadt: Wissenschaftliche Buchgesellschaft, 1980.

Paré, Gérard. *Les idées et les lettres au XIIIe siècle: le* Roman de la rose. Université de Montréal: Bibliothèque de philosophie, 1. Montreal: Centre de Psychologie et de Pédagogie, 1947.

Paris, Paulin. "Fin du treizième siècle. Trouvères: le Roman de la rose." *Histoire littéraire de la France* 23 (1856): 1–61.

Paulys Realencyclopädie der classischen Altertumswissenschaft. Vol. 7. Stuttgart: Metzler, 1900.

Payen, Jean-Charles. "L'espace et le temps dans le *Roman de la rose.*" *Romanistische Zeitschrift für Literaturgeschichte/Cahiers d'histoire des littératures romanes* 2 (1978): 253–58. Reprint, *Etudes André Lanly.* Nancy: Publications Nancy II, 1980. Pp. 287–99.

Payen, Jean-Charles. "Le *Roman de la rose* et la notion de carrefour idéologique." *Romanistische Zeitschrift für Literaturgeschichte/Cahiers d'histoire des littératures romanes* 1 (1977): 193–203.

Payen, Jean-Charles. *La rose et l'utopie: révolution sexuelle et communisme nostalgique chez Jean de Meung.* Classiques du peuple "Critique." Paris: Éditions Sociales, 1976.

Peden, Alison M. "Macrobius and Mediaeval Dream Literature." *Medium Aevum* 54 (1985): 59–73.

Pelen, Marc M. *Latin Poetic Irony in the* Roman de la rose. Vinaver Studies in French, 4. Liverpool: Cairns, 1987.

Pickens, Rupert T. "*Somnium* and Interpretation in Guillaume de Lorris." *Symposium* 28 (1974): 175–86.

Picone, Michelangelo. "Dante e il mito di Narciso dal *Roman de la rose* alla *Commedia.*" *Romanische Forschungen* 89 (1977): 382–97.

Poirion, Daniel. "Alain de Lille et Jean de Meun." In *Alain de Lille, Gautier de Châtillon, Jakemart Giélée et leur temps.* Actes du Colloque de Lille octobre 1978, ed. H. Roussel and F. Suard. In *Bien dire et bien aprandre* 2 (1980): 135–51.

Poirion, Daniel. "De la signification selon Jean de Meun." In *Archéologie du signe*, ed. Lucie Brind'Amour and Eugene Vance. Papers in Mediaeval Studies/ Recueil d'études médiévales, 3. Toronto: Pontifical Institute of Mediaeval Studies, 1983. Pp. 165–85.

Poirion, Daniel. "From Rhyme to Reason: Remarks on the Text of the *Romance of the Rose.*" In *Rethinking the* Romance of the Rose: *Text, Image, Reception*, ed. Kevin Brownlee and Sylvia Huot. Middle Ages Series. Philadelphia: University of Pennsylvania Press, 1992. Pp. 65–77.

Poirion, Daniel. "Jacques Legrand: une poétique de la fiction." In *Théories et pratiques de l'écriture au moyen âge.* Actes du Colloque Palais du Luxembourg-Sénat, 5 et 6 mars 1987. Ed. Emmanuèle Baumgartner and Christiane Marchello-Nizia. Littérales, 4. Paris: Centre de Recherches du Département de Français de Paris X-Nanterre; Saint Cloud: Centre Espace-Temps-Histoire de l'E.N.S. Fontenay/Saint-Cloud, 1988. Pp. 227–34.

Poirion, Daniel. "Les mots et les choses selon Jean de Meun." *L'information littéraire* 26 (1974): 7–11.

Poirion, Daniel. "Narcisse et Pygmalion dans *Le roman de la rose.*" In *Essays in Honor of Louis Francis Solano*, ed. Raymond J. Cormier and Urban T. Holmes. University of North Carolina Studies in the Romance Languages and

Literatures, 92. Chapel Hill: University of North Carolina Press, 1970. Pp. 153–65.

Poirion, Daniel. *Le roman de la rose*. Connaissance des lettres, 64. Paris: Hatier, 1973.

Polak, Lucie. "Plato, Nature and Jean de Meun." *Reading Medieval Studies* 3 (1977): 80–103.

Pope, M. K. *From Latin to Modern French with Especial Consideration of Anglo-Norman: Phonology and Morphology*. Rev. ed. French Series, 6. Manchester: Manchester University Press, 1952.

Pratt, Karen. "Analogy or Logic; Authority or Experience? Rhetorical Strategies for and against Women." In *Literary Aspects of Courtly Culture*. Selected Papers from the Seventh Triennial Congress of the International Courtly Literature Society, University of Massachusetts, Amherst, USA, 27 July-1 August 1992. Ed. Donald Maddox and Sara Sturm-Maddox. Cambridge: D. S. Brewer, 1994. Pp. 57–66.

Quadlbauer, Franz. *Die antike Theorie der genera dicendi im lateinischen Mittelalter*. Österreichische Akademie der Wissenschaften: philosophisch-historische Klasse, Sitzungsberichte, 241.2. Graz, Vienna, and Cologne: Böhlaus, 1962.

Quilligan, Maureen. "Allegory, Allegoresis, and the Deallegorization of Language: the *Roman de la rose*, the *De planctu Naturae*, and the *Parlement of Foules*." In *Allegory, Myth, and Symbol*, ed. Morton W. Bloomfield. Harvard English Studies, 9. Cambridge and London: Harvard University Press, 1981. Pp. 163–86.

Quilligan, Maureen. *The Language of Allegory: Defining the Genre*. Ithaca and London: Cornell University Press, 1979.

Quilligan, Maureen. "Words and Sex: The Language of Allegory in the *De planctu Naturae*, the *Roman de la rose*, and Book III of *The Faerie Queene*." *Allegorica* 2.1 (1977): 195–216.

Regalado, Nancy Freeman. " 'Des contraires choses': la fonction poétique de la citation et des *exempla* dans le *Roman de la rose* de Jean de Meun." *Littérature* 41 (1981): 62–81.

Regalado, Nancy Freeman. *Poetic Patterns in Rutebeuf: A Study in Noncourtly Poetic Modes of the Thirteenth Century*. New Haven and London: Yale University Press, 1970.

Richards, Earl Jeffrey. *Dante and the* Roman de la rose*: An Investigation into the Vernacular Narrative Context of the* Commedia. Beihefte zur Zeitschrift für romanische Philologie, 184. Tübingen: Niemeyer, 1981.

Rimlinger-Leconte, Colette. "L'expression métaphorique chez Jean de Meung: étude du discours de Raison dans le *Roman de la rose*." In *Études de langue et de littérature française offertes à André Lanly*. Nancy: Publication Nancy II, 1980. Pp. 301–11.

Robertson, D. W., Jr. *A Preface to Chaucer: Studies in Medieval Perspectives*. Princeton: Princeton University Press, 1962.

Rossi, Luciano. "Notula sul Re dei ribaldi." *Cultura neolatina* 33 (1973): 217–21.

Rossiaud, Jacques. *La prostitution médiévale*. Paris: Flammarion, 1988.

Rossman, Vladimir R. *Perspectives of Irony in Medieval French Literature*. De proprietatibus litterarum: series maior, 35. The Hague and Paris: Mouton, 1975.

Rowe, Donald W. "Reson in Jean's *Roman de la rose*: Modes of Characterization and Dimensions of Meaning." *Mediaevalia* 10 (1984): 97–126.

Ruhe, Doris. *Le dieu d'amours avec son paradis: Untersuchungen zur Mythenbildung um Amor in Spätantike und Mittelalter*. Beiträge zur romanischen Philologie des Mittelalters, 6. Munich: Fink, 1974.

Salverda de Grave, J.-J. "Anc. franç. *godel*." *Neophilologus* 8 (1923): 220–21.

Sandkühler, Bruno. *Die frühen Dantekommentare und ihr Verhältnis zur mittelalterlichen Kommentartradition*. Münchner romanistische Arbeiten, 19. Munich: Hueber, 1967.

Scheidegger, Jean R. "La peinture à l'or du *Roman de la rose*." In *L'or au moyen âge (monnaie-métal-objets-symbole)*. Senefiance, 12. Aix-en-Provence: CUER MA, 1983. Pp. 395–414.

Schmid, Elisabeth. "Augenlust und Spiegelliebe: der mittelalterliche Narciß." *Deutsche Vierteljahrsschrift für Literaturwissenschaft und Geistesgeschichte* 59 (1985): 551–71.

Schnell, Rüdiger. *Causa amoris: Liebeskonzeption und Liebesdarstellung in der mittelalterlichen Literatur*. Bibliotheca Germanica, 27. Bern and Munich: Francke, 1985.

Sieper, Ernst. *Les Échecs amoureux: eine altfranzösische Nachahmung des Rosenromans und ihre englische Übertragung*. Litterarische Forschungen, 9. Weimar: Felber, 1898.

Silvestre, Hubert. "L'idylle d'Abélard et Héloïse: la part du roman." *Académie Royale de Belgique: Bulletin de la Classe des Lettres et des Sciences Morales et Politiques*, 5th ser., 71 (1985): 157–200.

Simpson, James. "The Information of Alan of Lille's 'Anticlaudianus': A Preposterous Interpretation." *Traditio* 47 (1992): 113–60.

Smith, Macklin. *Prudentius'* Psychomachia*: A Reexamination*. Princeton: Princeton University Press, 1976.

Solterer, Helen. "Le bel semblant: faus semblant, semblants romanesques." *Médiévales* 6 (1984): 26–36.

Solterer, Helen. *The Master and Minerva: Disputing Women in French Medieval Culture*. Berkeley and Los Angeles: University of California Press, 1995.

Stackelberg, Jürgen von. *Französische Moralistik im europäischen Kontext*. Erträge der Forschung, 172. Darmstadt: Wissenschaftliche Buchgesellschaft, 1982.

Stakel, Susan. *False Roses: Structures of Duality and Deceit in Jean de Meun's* Roman de la rose. Stanford French and Italian Studies, 69. Saratoga, Ca.: ANMA Libri, 1991.

Steinle, Eric M. "Anti-Narcissus: Guillaume de Lorris as Reader of Ovid." *Classical and Modern Literature* 6 (1986): 251–59.

Stone, Donald, Jr. "Hierarchies and Meaning in the *Roman de la rose*." *French Forum* 6 (1981): 5–12.

Stone, Donald, Jr. "Old and New Thoughts on Guillaume de Lorris." *Australian Journal of French Studies* 2 (1965): 157–70.

Strubel, Armand. *Guillaume de Lorris, Jean de Meun,* Le Roman de la rose. Études littéraires, 4. Paris: Presses Universitaires de France, 1984.

Strubel, Armand. *La rose, Renart et le graal: la littérature allégorique en France au XIIIe siècle.* Nouvelle Bibliothèque du Moyen Age, 11. Paris: Champion, 1989.

Taylor, P. B. "Chaucer's *Cosyn to the Dede.*" *Speculum* 57 (1982): 315–27.

Thomas, Antoine, and Mario Roques. "Traductions françaises de la *Consolatio Philosophiae* de Boèce." *Histoire littéraire de la France* 37 (1938): 419–88, 543–47.

Thut, Martin. "Narcisse versus Pygmalion: une lecture du *Roman de la rose.*" *Vox romanica* 41 (1982): 104–32.

Topsfield, L. T. "The *Roman de la rose* of Guillaume de Lorris and the Love Lyric of the Early Troubadours." *Reading Medieval Studies* 1 (1975): 30–54.

Tuve, Rosemond. *Allegorical Imagery: Some Mediaeval Books and Their Posterity.* Princeton: Princeton University Press, 1966.

Uitti, Karl D. "From *clerc* to *poète*: The Relevance of the *Romance of the Rose* to Machaut's World." In *Machaut's World: Science and Art in the Fourteenth Century*, ed. Madeleine Pelner Cosman and Bruce Chandler. Annals of the New York Academy of Sciences, 314. New York: New York Academy of Sciences, 1978. Pp. 209–16.

Uitti, Karl D. "Understanding Guillaume de Lorris: The Truth of the Couple in Guillaume's *Romance of the Rose.*" In *Contemporary Readings of Medieval Literature*, ed. Guy Mermier. Michigan Romance Studies, 8. Ann Arbor: University of Michigan Department of Romance Languages, 1989. Pp. 51–70.

Vanossi, Luigi. *Dante e il* Roman de la rose*: saggio sul* Fiore. Biblioteca dell'"Archivum Romanicum": ser. I. Storia-letteratura-paleografia, 144. Florence: Olschki, 1979.

Vasquez, Luis Cortes. *El episodio de Pigmalión del* Roman de la rose*: ética y estética de Jean de Meun.* Acta Salmanticensia: filosofía y letras, 122. Salamanca: Ediciónes Universidad de Salamanca, 1980.

Vitz, Evelyn Birge. *Medieval Narrative and Modern Narratology: Subjects and Objects of Desire.* New York and London: New York University Press, 1989.

Wack, Mary Frances. *Lovesickness in the Middle Ages: The* Viaticum *and Its Commentaries.* Middle Ages Series. Philadelphia: University of Pennsylvania Press, 1990.

Walters, Lori. "Author Portraits and Textual Demarcation in Manuscripts of the *Romance of the Rose.*" Appendix to *Rethinking the* Romance of the Rose*: Text, Image, Reception*, ed. Kevin Brownlee and Sylvia Huot. Middle Ages Series. Philadelphia: University of Pennsylvania Press, 1992. Pp. 359–73.

Walters, Lori. "A Parisian Manuscript of the *Romance of the Rose.*" *Princeton University Library Chronicle* 51 (1989): 31–55.

Walters, Lori. "Reading the *Rose*: Literacy and the Presentation of the *Roman de la rose* in Medieval Manuscripts." *Romanic Review* 85 (1994): 1–26.

Walther, Helmut G. "Utopische Gesellschaftskritik oder satirische Ironie? Jean de

Meun und die Lehre des Aquinaten über die Entstehung menschlicher Herrschaft." In *Soziale Ordnungen im Selbstverständnis des Mittelalters*, ed. Albert Zimmermann and Gudrun Vuillemin-Diem. Miscellanea Mediaevalia, 12.1. Berlin and New York: de Gruyter, 1979. Pp. 84–105.

Wetherbee, Winthrop. "The Literal and the Allegorical: Jean de Meun and the 'de Planctu Naturae'." *Mediaeval Studies* 33 (1971): 264–91.

Wetherbee, Winthrop P. *Platonism and Poetry in the Twelfth Century: The Literary Influence of the School of Chartres*. Princeton: Princeton University Press, 1972.

Wetherbee, Winthrop P. "The Theme of Imagination in Medieval Poetry and the Allegorical Figure 'Genius.' " *Medievalia et Humanistica*, n.s., 7 (1976): 45–64.

Wood, Chauncey. "La Vieille, Free Love, and Boethius in the *Roman de la rose*." *Revue de littérature comparée* 51 (1977): 336–42.

Woods, Marjorie Curry. "Poetic Digression and the Interpretation of Medieval Literary Texts." In *Acta Conventus Neo-Latini Sanctandreani*. Medieval and Renaissance Texts and Studies, 38. Binghamton: Center for Medieval and Early Renaissance Studies, 1986. Pp. 617–26.

Worstbrock, Franz Josef. Review of Hans-Jürgen Gräbener, ed. *Gervase von Melkley: Ars poetica*. *Anzeiger für deutsches Altertum und deutsche Literatur* 78 (1967): 99–107.

Zink, Michel. "Bel-Accueil le travesti: du *Roman de la rose* de Guillaume de Lorris et Jean de Meun à *Lucidor* de Hugo von Hofmannsthal." *Littérature* 47 (1982): 31–40.

Zink, Michel. *La subjectivité littéraire: autour du siècle de Louis IX*. Écriture. Paris: Presses Universitaires de France, 1985.

Ziolkowski, Jan. *Alan of Lille's Grammar of Sex: The Meaning of Grammar to a Twelfth-Century Intellectual*. Speculum Anniversary Monographs, 10. Cambridge, Mass.: Medieval Academy of America, 1985.

Zumthor, Paul. "De Guillaume de Lorris à Jean de Meung." In *Études de langue et de littérature du moyen âge offertes à Félix Lecoy par ses collègues, ses élèves et ses amis*. Paris: Champion, 1973. Pp. 609–20.

Zumthor, Paul. "Narrative and Anti-Narrative: *Le roman de la rose*." In *Approaches to Medieval Romance*, ed. Peter Haidu. Yale French Studies, 51. New Haven: Yale University Press, 1974. Pp. 185–204.

Index

The Index does not include Jean de Meun: *Roman de la Rose*, or *Roman de la rose* as separate entries.

Index

Index